Democratization and the Protection of Human Rights in Africa

Democratization and the Protection of Human Rights in Africa

Problems and Prospects

BRENDALYN P. AMBROSE

PRAEGER

Westport, Connecticut
London

Library of Congress Cataloging-in-Publication Data

Ambrose, Brendalyn P.
    Democratization and the protection of human rights in Africa :
problems and prospects / Brendalyn P. Ambrose.
        p.   cm.
    Includes bibliographical references (p.   ) and index.
    ISBN 0–275–95143–X (hardcover : acid-free paper)
        1. Democracy—Africa.   2. Africa—Politics and government—1960–
    3. Human rights—Africa.   4. Civil rights—Africa.   I. Title.
    JQ1879.A15A42   1995
    323'.096—dc20   95–3335

British Library Cataloguing in Publication Data is available.

Library of Congress Catalog Card Number: 95–3335
ISBN: 0–275–95143–X

First published in 1995

Praeger Publishers, 88 Post Road West, Westport, CT 06881
An imprint of Greenwood Publishing Group, Inc.

Printed in the United States of America

The paper used in this book complies with the
Permanent Paper Standard issued by the National
Information Standards Organization (Z39.48–1984).

10   9   8   7   6   5   4   3   2   1

Copyright Acknowledgments

The author and publisher are grateful for permission to reproduce portions of
the following copyrighted material:

Issa Shivji, *The Concept of Human Rights in Africa* (London: CODESRIA,
1989).

Kathleen Mahoney and Paul Mahoney, eds., *Human Rights in the Twenty-
First Century* (Utrecht, The Netherlands: Kluwer Academic Publishers, 1993).
Reprinted by permission of Kluwer Academic Publishers.

Kenneth Kaunda, "No Sleep for Africa," *Africa Forum* 2, no. 1 (1992): 15–16.

Every reasonable effort has been made to trace the owners of copyright
materials in this book, but in some instances this has proven impossible. The
author and publisher will be glad to receive information leading to more
complete acknowledgments in subsequent printings of the book, and in the
meantime extend their apologies for any omissions.

*This book is dedicated to all the suffering people
in Africa and to my beloved twin daughters,
Adele and Jenelle, who represent my driving force
as I do humanity's business.*

The democratic movement in Africa must be a humanistic one that lends renewed meaning to the integrity of the human person and the need for tolerance and accommodation.

Richard Joseph, "Africa: The Rebirth of Political Freedom"

Therefore all things whatsoever ye would that men should do to you, do ye even so to them.

Matthew 7:12

Contents

Preface

Whether by accident or design I happened to arrive on the continent of Africa at a time when it was bubbling with political excitement as the wind of democracy was sweeping from one corner to the next. From Cape Coast to Cairo, events were unfolding at breakneck speed.

In South Africa, a timetable was in place to start negotiations leading to a nonracial regime in that country, thus bringing an end to apartheid. In other parts of the continent, the clamor for democracy and respect for human rights was loudest. And this time, with the nudge coming from international aid donors, the sit-tight leaders in Africa were forced to listen and to act. Fundamentalism was on the rise in Algeria and Egypt. General Mengistu Haile Mariam had just fled Ethiopia, and General Samuel Doe had met his demise in Liberia, leaving that country in a serious crisis. Somalians were facing starvation, and the refugee crisis on the continent was further aggravated by crop failure and drought in southern Africa.

Following the success of the National Conference in Benin Republic, which saw the first military government in Africa to be voted out of power democratically, the people in Togo and Zaire were determined to democratize through a new process based largely on dialogue and introspection. They called a national conference, but this was met with resistance from their leaders. Throughout 1992 and up to 1993, democratization in Zaire and Togo was stalled by sit-tight leaders, determined to remain at the helm of affairs at all cost. In Nigeria, events were also on a roller coaster ride; a wave of uncertainty swept the country as the hand-over date for transition to the Third Republic was constantly shifted by the military leader, General Ibrahim Babangida. This left both Nigerians and the international community in doubt as to whether Babangida intended to give up his hold on the country.

This text captures most of these events as they occurred. For the most part, it gives analyses of events as they unfolded from 1991, especially throughout 1992 and 1993. Many of the political developments during this time stunned the international community as the expected changes did not occur. On this basis, the writer undertakes three things in this work: Firstly, I argue that while Africa does need democracy, liberal democracy is not the best option for Africa. Africans should be allowed to decide on a democracy that suits Africa's reality. Poverty presently grips over 265 million people, and the continent is constantly plagued by ethnic tension. In addition, the continent's external debt stands at more than $270 billion. Unlike what is prescribed for Africa, liberal democracy was successfully attained in western countries because those countries had already attained a level of economic development. In addition, there is confusion as Africans attempt to install a western system within existing traditional structures and cultural practices. Consequently, the current democratization exercise will not result in the social, political, and economic transformation that Africa needs.

Secondly, I argue that there is need to adopt a different strategy toward the protection of human rights in Africa. The notion of universal human rights appears to be more rhetoric than reality. Instead of African human rights NGOs (nongovernmental organizations) emphasizing civil and political rights, and organizing conferences which mainly the intellectual elites attend, there is need to assist at the grassroots level to overcome ignorance and want and achieve the level of empowerment whereby the oppressed can hold leaders accountable and become defenders of their own rights. Thirdly, I address the overwhelming economic and social problems facing Africa by calling for a collaborative effort among Africans themselves, Africans in the diaspora, and non-Africans in the international community to become more proactive in order to ensure the survival of the African continent and its peoples.

The book was written to give those interested in improving the human condition in Africa some insight into the political evolution on the continent at present. I trust that readers will find the book intellectually stimulating, while at the same time enjoyable to read. While I readily accept any criticism readers might have, I accept no credit. Any praise belongs to Almighty God.

Brendalyn Ambrose

Acknowledgments

The first person to whom I mentioned that I was writing a book of this nature was Dr. Alphonse Macdonald, Country Director of the United Nations Population Fund in Nigeria, and he encouraged my idea. Others to whom I am grateful include Professor Eme Awa, renowned Nigerian political scientist, former Dean, Faculty of Social Sciences, University of Nigeria, Nsukka, and former Chair of the National Electoral Commission (NEC), for some of his initial comments. I am also grateful to Dr. Babafemi Badejo of the Department of Political Science at the University of Lagos for his comments on portions of the first draft. I am also grateful to Dr. Samuel Woldu of the University of Ibadan, Nigeria, for proofreading the text and for his comments. I am grateful to Madame Michèle Jacquart, a lawyer specializing in international law and lecturer in civil law at the University of Ottawa, for her comments on the entire draft. I am also deeply grateful to Ntet Mitond, who heads a small NGO in Canada, and to Dr. Ahmed Mohiddin, a specialist in international affairs. Thanks to Eva Murray and all others who gave me moral support. I am also grateful to Sue Buckwell, Librarian at the British Council, Nigeria, for loaning me books and for her hospitality. I am grateful to Marie-Claude Orekoya of the United Nations Industrial Development Organization (UNIDO), Nigeria, for her hospitality. I thank Africa Leadership Forum for inviting me to participate in their Farm House Dialogues, particularly the series on "Democracy." My profoundest gratitude goes to Canadian University Services Overseas (CUSO). I am also grateful to Anne Marie Colas-Klemz for her wholehearted support, and to Joy and Nick Gadd. Although I undertook the writing of this book thousands of miles away from my immediate family, I owe gratitude to my mother, Rebecca. My brother, Samuel, had implicit faith in me, and his encouragement was a source of strength as I sought to bring this work to its fruition.

Introduction

As Africans reflect on the past and ponder their future, democracy and respect for human rights have come to be seen as the sole means of redemption for a people who have been forced to live with the tyranny of dictators and despots since independence. All over the continent, from Cape Coast to Cairo, Africans have experienced the woes of gross abuses inflicted by military dictators and self-styled life presidents. Under the leadership of these regimes, Africans have witnessed massive corruption, human rights abuses, and economic deprivations that have caused more than 265 million[1] people to live in absolute poverty. Africans are overwhelmingly convinced that the root cause of their dilemma is the absence of good governance and accountability by their leaders. Therefore, Africans expect democracy to replace guns with butter, poverty with plenty, and want to a life of hope and dignity.

The quest for democracy and social justice in Africa is not a recent phenomenon. As Claude Ake states, "the origins and aspirations of the democracy movement in Africa, as well as its form and content have no connection with events in Eastern Europe . . . the democracy movement in Africa predates them."[2] He reiterates that Africans have long been clamoring for social justice, arguing that they have been struggling determinedly for democracy for over a hundred years, but their struggles were not accorded international legitimacy. Instead, the democratic struggles in Africa were seen as anarchic tendencies, extremist interest articulation, ethnic conflicts, lawless political competition, or systemic crisis and breakdowns.[3] Recent events in Eastern Europe and the demise of the Soviet Union have given impetus to the clamor of the majority of Africans for democracy as a last hope for survival. In recent times, the international community has begun to call for multiparty leadership in Africa, with respect for human rights as its anchor.

From the disappointing performance of African governments at the beginning of the democratization movement, there has been little occasion for real hope. Instead, there is increasing fear as to whether the process of democratization will ever go beyond the voting stage—an exercise which has seen many long-ruling leaders succeeding themselves through the ballot box. I intend to contribute here to the cause of social justice in Africa by sharing from personal experiences as an African in the diaspora working in human rights in Africa. I do not intend to be portrayed as an expert on African affairs. My intention is to give analysis of the intrigues and difficulties involved on the rocky path toward democracy and to offer some solutions. There is much work to be done in the area of human rights protection. There is a paucity of materials on human rights education and literature on human rights. The weakness of the African Commission on Human and Peoples' Rights is a major area of frustration for victims of human rights violations. These problems are compounded by illiteracy and material lack.

When I arrived in Africa in 1991, I made a commitment to learn as much as I could about the continent by immersing myself into the local community and reading any literature I could find on the subject of human rights and democracy. (I worked mainly in Nigeria and the surrounding countries of Ghana, Togo, and Benin. At international conferences I had the opportunity to discuss and consult with people from all over the continent.) The first thing that caught my attention was reading that only a few months earlier, the Babangida administration in Nigeria had executed sixty-nine suspected coup plotters despite pleas from local human rights groups and Amnesty International. I spoke with people about public executions and asked whether they had ever witnessed one. Some had, and added that it was a gruesome experience.

The idea of human beings exterminating each other in such a heinous manner was very disturbing. I decided to start a quiet campaign against public executions, starting with people around me. Many who admitted that they had witnessed an execution said they were sickened by it, and they would never go to see another. A few days later, while I was driving with a friend who is a medical doctor, I began to talk about how inhuman it was for people to accept public executions. His response was far from what I expected: "Killing is done in different forms. When a government kills a person by putting a bullet in his head, it is not much different from when a government adopts bad policies that result in people living in such squalor and misery that they die a wretched death." He concluded by saying that death by execution may sound cruel but it is swift and less dehumanizing than wallowing in a wretched state until death finally rescues such a person. This got me thinking.

As I worked among the people, I witnessed the misery of the poor under the Structural Adjustment Program (SAP). It became clear that human rights protection, like many of the ills plaguing Africa, is caught in a web of class domination and selfish greed. Oftentimes those in the forefront of social justice are harassed by the police and the corrupt bureaucracy when they attempt to aid victims of human rights abuse. Also, many who purport to be defenders of human rights are the elites who at times have questionable agendas. For these reasons, I submit that the present attempt at democratization and protection of human rights in Africa will continue to be frustrated unless the struggle is waged by the oppressed people themselves. They must be organized at the grassroots level and be able to express their collective concerns effectively. I will show the limitations of the liberal notion of democracy, which Africans are struggling to adopt. African society is presently in confusion as it attempts to install a foreign ideology while still tied to feudal values and plagued by ethnic problems arising from colonially-imposed borders. And at the same time, poverty and ignorance pose even greater obstacles. While Africans grapple with these realities, they must also struggle to adapt to modernity, because there is little point in trying to turn back the hands of the clock.

The colonial structures which still exist pose another obstacle to the establishment of liberal democracy. The ruling class has made a mockery of the notion of democracy in terms of freedom, equality, and justice. Consequently, the democratization exercise has been no more than voting while largely ignoring the real issues facing most Africans. It appears that this is acceptable to the West. They have insisted on governance through the voting exercise and given little attention to other matters far more pressing to Africans. Western powers voice enormous concern about respect for human rights, freedom, equality, and so on, but they place little or no importance on the right to literacy training and basic needs (i.e., economic rights) which are essential prerequisites to the establishment of the western notion of democracy. Obviously, this raises questions about sincerity to the cause. Zehra Arat notes:

A closer examination of the relationship between Western democracies and developing countries would not yield an image of a "liberating West." First democracy at home did not lead these countries to seek democratization abroad. Their foreign policies were based on their national economic or political interests rather than on some globally applied principles of humanism or democratic ideology.[4]

In his well-documented work, *Pour L'Afrique J'Accuse,* René Dumont contends that the actions of the World Bank and the International Monetary Fund (IMF) were destructive to the economic means of survival of the African peasant and amounted only to further western domination of Africa. Dumont stresses that "the right to life is the first right of man."[5] In this statement he was underscoring the right to food as "the staff of life." How can one defend life while adopting policies that destroy one's capacity to feed oneself? Dumont argues that actions taken in the West hinder development and are designed to maintain western hegemony over the continent. He points to the destruction of the environment, the erosion of the African culture, and the pauperization of the African villager. In his view, some of the so-called international experts "have absolutely no understanding of the difference between 'our' development and that of Africans."[6]

The insistence of the West on the establishment of liberal democracy in Africa while ignoring the extent of deprivation on the continent gives validity to Dumont's contention. The West is asking Africans to build a house for which no foundation has been laid. If the West is serious about democratization in Africa, they should assist those forces that are struggling to bring about democratic governance from the grassroots level. In addition, civil and political rights must be juxtaposed with economic rights because hunger and malnutrition kill more than guns do. Arat makes a similar argument in this statement. "Contrary to liberal theory, civil and political rights cannot prevail if socioeconomic rights are ignored, and the stability of political democracy (liberal democracy) depends on the extent of balance between the two groups of human rights."[7] This is the type of arrangement that will lead to the development that Africa so badly needs, and will be the sole liberating mechanism for the majority of suffering Africans. It will be a long, arduous journey. Democracies take centuries to build, and Africa cannot cross five centuries in fifty years.

The picture for human rights protection is equally bleak and, like democratization, nothing much can be accomplished with Africa in its present state. Human rights claims are made by individuals against the state; thus the state is expected to adopt measures to ensure protection and equal rights for all citizens. In Africa, as Rhoda Howard pointed out, "The state does not behave in a neutral administrative fashion for the good of all; rather the state reflects the interests of those societal groups that make up and control it."[8] This dominant group has access to the country's wealth and uses it for its own selfish pursuits at the expense of the poor. For example, in Nigeria one percent of the population is said to control 75 percent of the country's wealth.[9] At the end of 1992, one Nigerian summed up the inequality in Nigerian society this way:

In the midst of mass poverty, few Nigerians cruised around in posh cars some carrying a price tag of over N2 million. Their exotic mansions dotted the skyline of the major cities. There were also mind-boggling donations made by the government to favoured associates, individuals and organizations. The fervent prayer by majority Nigerians in the new year, is that the standard of living for the generality of people must improve.[10]

While such is the life of the rich in Nigeria, the average Nigerian earns less than $600 a year. Many dwell in slums or sleep under bridges, and one in ten children die before the age of five because of inadequate medical care.[11]

The situation is not much different in Zaire, where President Mobutu Sese Seko is alleged to be three times richer than the entire country with a personal fortune estimated to be between six to eight billion dollars. His annual expenses are said to cost the Zairean treasury more than the expenditures on schools, hospitals, roads, and all other services combined.[12] Mobutu is accused of paying his cronies up to $100,000 per month, while some workers do not even make $50 per month. At the same time, there are reports that patients die in large numbers in a hospital named after Mobutu's mother because there are no bandages.[13]

Under apartheid in South Africa, there was gross inequality between the minority whites and the lives of the majority blacks. Blacks attended schools that were poorly equipped and sanitized, were taught an inferior curriculum, and lived in slums called homelands, while whites enjoyed magnificent lifestyles. A Commonwealth team which visited South Africa said: "The living standards of South Africa's white cities and towns must rank the highest anywhere; those of the black townships which surrounded them defy description in terms of 'living standards.' "[14] They admitted that apartheid is "awesome in its cruelty," and noted that apartheid has compartmentalized the South African society in an astounding manner. This is about to change as the transition to a nonracial form of governance takes effect.

The United Nations (UN) reports that forty percent of all children under five in Africa suffer from malnutrition so severe that it causes mental or physical damage. Meanwhile, cargo planes are often busy transporting fine wines, gourmet delicacies, and designer clothes for the exotic lifestyle of many African leaders. It is within this context that I will examine the concept of equality as one of the tenets of democracy and also as a human right. How much equality does the poor man have in Africa? What is the impact of inequality on the sustenance of democracy? I also seek answers to such questions as how the lack of basic needs (i.e., food, primary health care, and basic education) affect the ongoing democratization process. Is the realization of economic rights possible given the extent of deprivation on the continent?

The right to food needs little elaboration. Without food, one cannot live, so there would be no need to discuss democracy and human rights since no such interaction can take place with those who have starved to death. For political discourse, however, if one examines the consequences of lack of food one recognizes that a hungry person is happy to sell his vote to the highest bidder. In this case it is very likely that the wrong person will be elected. (This was demonstrated in the conduct of Nigeria's botched presidential primaries in October 1992—a topic discussed in Chapter 6.) On illiteracy, the problems arising from a lack of basic education are manyfold. An illiterate person cannot effectively exercise political freedom. A person who can neither read nor write has no interest in freedom of the press. He does not know what party to vote for or why, so he is often directed by the educated elite. In addition, efforts to improve health care are difficult to accomplish with illiterates, who may be unable to grasp concepts such as birth control or AIDS prevention, or how to treat simple ailments such as diarrhea.

This book takes a departure from the everyday rhetoric on democracy and human rights in Africa. While much of the current literature theorizes about liberal democracy from a number of different viewpoints, little or no attention is given to democratization from the grassroots level. A major pitfall of the democratization exercise in Africa is due to the fact that western scholars and Africans alike have overlooked the fact that the political structure for liberal democracy exists only in the urban areas. The villagers are totally ignored. To justify this statement, it is necessary to refer to a recent occurrence. When General Babangida cancelled the June 12 elections in 1993, many Nigerians who reside in Lagos began to flee to the villages. I telephoned a friend of mine and could not reach him. I tried about one week later and succeeded in reaching him. When I mentioned that I had tried earlier but was unsuccessful, he replied, "I went to my village." I then asked eagerly, "Are the people concerned and anxious about what is going on in the country?" His reply was, "No, they are not. The people in the village did not even know why those who live in Lagos were coming back to the village." This is evidence that they are oblivious to the political transformation taking place in their country.

In this book I argue that those Africans on the periphery must be part of the process. It is also important to recognize that there are people on the periphery in urban centers. Those are the ones who search the garbage for food, sleep under bridges, and whose ailments go untreated. Their plight is often worse than the village dwellers. I therefore emphasize that the poor and destitute on the periphery of economic and political activity must have equal access to the country's resources and to the political system. As things now stand, political aspirants manipulate the poor to gain their votes. They corrupt the village chiefs and other "respectable" personalities who wield influence among the poor, to tell the people where and how to cast their vote. No effort is made to educate the people and involve them in the dialogue. This is also where human rights organizations have fallen short. They often organize colloquia and conferences in urban hotels and invite international delegates, but they do not invite the farmers or market women to hear what they are talking about. The challenge ahead is to sensitize the grassroots population about their rights as well as how a democratic structure should work for them. This should be the primary preoccupation of human rights NGOs in Africa.

This book begins with an examination of governance in Africa during the precolonial, colonial, and postcolonial eras. It seeks to answer such questions as: How has governance in traditional Africa influenced the behavior of today's leaders? To what extent did people participate in the affairs of government then? Was there equality? Did people enjoy political and economic rights? How has African society changed over the years? Apartheid as another form of governance in Africa is examined. A picture is given of the grim realities of living under such a system of governance. Information is provided to show why Nelson Mandela has emerged as a significant figure in the dismantling of apartheid and the democratization of South Africa. The problems which have dogged the democratization process in South Africa are analyzed, and some projections made as to the post-transition scenario.

The concepts that have recently become familiar in development parlance—democracy and human rights—are examined. I would argue that democracy must be a marriage of the political and economic and, more importantly, people must be empowered to hold their leaders accountable. Therefore, I define democracy as a system of governance which allows people to freely elect their leaders and hold them accountable, and which provides opportunity for the greater number of people to use their human potential to survive in dignity. The liberal concept of democracy is carefully examined as to its feasibility in meeting the needs of majority Africans. The relation between democracy and human rights is also discussed. An overview is given of the various models of democratic transition in Africa. The current debate among African experts as they search for a model of governance suited to Africa is analyzed. Some of the pitfalls to the democratization process are examined in line with the concepts of democracy as postulated by such philosophers as Rousseau, Locke, and Mill. In addition, the contributions of contemporary African scholars, such as Osita Eze, Issa Shivji, Eme Awa, Claude Ake, and Adebayo Adedeji, to the debate on human rights and democracy in Africa form part of the analysis. The discourse of Zehra Arat on democracy and human rights in developing countries is a useful contribution to the debate, as are the views of Rhoda Howard, Canadian scholar on human rights in Commonwealth Africa.

Protection of human rights in Africa is discussed, with emphasis on the problems inherent in the African Charter on Human and Peoples' Rights and the weakness of the African Commission in implementing the Charter. The role of the judiciary and the problems of implementing constitutional provisions are also analyzed. An assessment of human rights in contemporary Africa is undertaken. The role of human rights NGOs in conscientizing the masses is discussed. The various international instruments under which refugees are protected are looked at, with particular emphasis on the rights to be accorded asylum seekers. The cultural practices that infringe on the rights of women are examined. The need for women's participation in the political transformation of the continent is emphasized. The rights of the child are examined and many of the problems facing the African child are highlighted.

An in-depth survey of Nigeria's transition to democracy is undertaken, including an analysis of the problems that have plagued the seven-year-long process. The role played by poverty, illiteracy, money, and corruption are analyzed within the context of the impact of the Structural Adjustment Program (SAP). A new phenomenon has emerged in the political discourse on democratization since the beginning of the 1990s. That is the idea of convening a national conference to pave the way for multiparty democracy. Though mainly an experiment in French African countries, many in English-speaking Africa have been calling for a national conference to discuss the myriad problems facing their countries. I will evaluate the problems and prospects of convening a national conference, especially in light of the developments in Zaire and Togo.

I conclude that liberal democracy can neither be consolidated nor sustained in Africa with its majority trapped in material and intellectual poverty. The challenge for the international community is to assist grassroots empowerment efforts which would replace the imperial and compradorial structures that exist within Africa. There must also be a new interpretation of democracy defined for Africans, by Africans. Unless human rights are given the same interpretation for all Africans, regardless of their class, ethnic affiliation, or religion, there will be no peace in Africa. As to the future of the continent, I underscore the role of the key players—Africans themselves—including those in the diaspora, the international community, education, and popular participation in saving Africa from the reemergence of military rule and from the dustbin of history.

NOTES

1. *Commonwealth Currents* (1992), p. 2.
2. Claude Ake, "As Africa Democratises," *Africa Forum* 1, no. 2 (1991): 13.
3. Ibid.
4. Zehra F. Arat, *Democracy and Human Rights in Developing Countries* (Boulder, Colo.: Lynne Rienner Publishers, 1991), p. 71.
5. René Dumont, *Pour L'Afrique J'Accuse* (Paris: Plon, 1986), p. 339. Translated from its original French by the author.
6. Ibid., p. 257.
7. Arat, *Democracy and Human Rights in Developing Countries,* p. 4.
8. Rhoda E. Howard, *Human Rights in Commonwealth Africa* (Totowa, N.J.: Rowman and Littlefield, 1986), pp. 45–46.
9. *Sunday Tribune,* January 31, 1993, p. 5.
10. *African Concord,* January 11, 1993, p. 9.
11. *Sunday Tribune,* January 31, 1993, p. 5.
12. Robert K. Dornan, "Greedy African Dictators Stealing $Billions We Give to Feed Starving People," *National Enquirer* (February 2, 1993), p. 31.
13. Ibid.
14. *Mission to South Africa: The Commonwealth Report.* The Findings of the Commonwealth Eminent Persons Group on Southern Africa. Foreword by Sjridath Ramphal (London: Penguin Books for the Commonwealth Secretariat, 1985), p. 23.

Chapter 1

Governance in Africa

At this critical stage in the social, political, and economic evolution in the lives of Africans, it is necessary to examine the past to learn more about themselves and to find a pathway ahead. It is equally important for those interested in Africa to do further research. Governance has recently emerged as another fad in development parlance, but we must first be clear about what we mean by governance. For the purpose of this work, I define governance as a political process whereby those in authority make decisions for the benefit of the citizenry. Such a process existed in traditional Africa. This chapter seeks to answer such questions as: What can Africans today adopt from the past that can be useful in sustaining democracy and good governance for this generation and the next? Are the current brand of leaders in Africa a reflection of past socialization? We must begin by examining the political structure and patterns of behavior of the rulers and the ruled during precolonial, colonial, and postcolonial Africa.

PRECOLONIAL AFRICA

Governance is not a novel idea to Africa. I will discuss governance in traditional Africa by examining three of the most noted African kingdoms: the Mali Empire, the Benin Kingdom, and the Zulu Empire. As far back as 1352 one of the greatest travellers of medieval times, Ibn Battuta, noted that in Mali, "the negroes are seldom unjust, and have a greater abhorrence for injustice than any other people." He noted that their ruler showed no mercy to anyone who was guilty of the least act of injustice. Battuta noted that he was impressed with the justice and efficiency of the government and the good order it maintained. He also noted that Mali was a rich, prosperous, peaceful, and well-ordered empire with effective government and organized communication.[1]

Anthropologists have concluded by their evaluation of the songs of griots (oral historians) and other historical records that the Mali Empire was one of the most outstanding kingdoms in Africa. From their accounts, the Mali Empire under King Sundiata Keita operated as a congress in which the warriors, intellectuals, and artists exercised power under the authority of the king. The warriors were responsible for the security of the kingdom and they selected candidates for the throne. Laws were applied through the clans of the marabouts (clairvoyants/astrologers) and they were assigned the roles of judges. The intellectual clan advised the king through their griots. The intellectual clan were the spokespersons and advocates of the society; they had power to dismiss or dethrone the king if necessary. All major decisions were made by the royal court, which was comprised of individuals from all of the clans as well as representatives of various organizations including youths, women, family heads, and cooperative organizations. Every subject could participate as long as he or she went through the marabout, but womens' opinions could only be expressed through their brothers.

In the Benin Kingdom, the powers of the former kings were limited by those of the traditional leaders. In the Yoruba Kingdom, the chiefs played a primordial role in governance at the time. In most of the kingdoms, the basic modus operandi was a sharing of power between the king and the chiefs who represented various groups. Within the hierarchical structure and division of power, both slaves and ordinary people had freedom of speech, freedom to appoint their representatives, and freedom to criticize the king.[2]

In the Zulu Empire, while the right to life was respected, historians claim that there was oppression of the citizenry. For example, marriage could only be contracted between the ages of thirty and forty and was seen as a compensation and not as a right to citizens.[3] It is noted that before the reign of Chaka (1816–1828), founder of the Zulu Empire, a democratic tradition had existed in the traditional family setting.

The argument as to whether or not governance in traditional African society was democratic, or to what extent it was, is a controversial one. While many experts agree that in traditional Africa governance was by and large democratic, there are some who hold the view that the society was undemocratic. Osita Eze acknowledges that "African chiefdoms and empires were more or less 'democratic' in the sense that rarely did the will of one man, whether chief or king, determine the fate of those societies."[4] However, he cautions against romanticizing the democracy of traditional Africa. Another scholar, Claude Ake, also makes the claim that

Traditional African political systems were infused with democratic values. They were invariably patrimonial, and consciousness was communal; everything was everybody's business, engendering a strong emphasis on participation. Standards of accountability were even stricter than in western societies. Chiefs were answerable not only for their actions, but for natural catastrophes such as famine, epidemics, floods and drought.[5]

Noted Nigerian political scientist Eme Awa informs us that the political system in traditional Africa was expected to assure social justice for all people. He points out that traditional African society operated on the basis of participatory democracy. "Decision making was recognized as a joint activity and all the people had equal rights to participate in it, thus everybody was offered the opportunity to be informed properly of the problems of the political system and their probable solutions."[6] Other African scholars[7] argue that traditional Africa was democratic, and that consensus decision making was the basic modus operandi.

The argument in the opposing camp is that the ruling kings and chiefs encouraged class domination, and that unequal participation existed. Scholars, such as Badejo and Ogunyemi, argue that traditional Africa was far from democratic and egalitarian. They contend that the powers vested in obas (kings), chiefs, kings, or emirs allowed them to oppress the lower class and unjustly take their lands, use them as slaves, and even engage in wanton and needless taking of life. In such cases democracy as government of the majority did not exist. In addition, the notion which implies equal rights for all human beings regardless of social class was not practiced.[8] They further contend that the checks and balances in place to curb the actions of the obas were exercised by the ruling class. They point out that the majority of the population played little or no role in the removal of the oba. Moreover, they opine that such checks and balances were actually used to protect the ruling classes themselves.

Joy Mukubwa Hendrickson is yet another scholar with the view that traditional African society was undemocratic. She forcefully argues that human rights were abused by kings who at times would kill their subjects by sheer whim. There were occasions when wives were buried with husbands, twins were killed at birth, and thrashing or killing of a disobedient child or an unfaithful wife was allowed.[9] Hendrickson also laments that "claims to be treated in a certain manner are still made with reference to one's position in a society which varied according to age, sex and position in a well defined kinship structure."[10] She also points out that people were not always free to emigrate as some scholars claim. For example,

Among the Tswanna, a man is rarely allowed to depart peacefully with all his moveable property. . . . If his intention becomes known to the chief, his cattle may be confiscated. . . . At times punitive expeditions were sent after those who managed to leave and often it was only after fighting and bloodshed that they either made good their escape or were compelled to return and suffer the penalty.[11]

Rhoda Howard[12] is also of the view that there has been an overexaggeration of the notion of the consensual nature of traditional African politics. She points out that the Ashanti leadership in Ghana operated on a quasi-feudal bureaucracy. She also points to the existence of castes of untouchables among the Igbos in Nigeria and the Masai in East Africa.

Conclusion

Traditional Africa had its shortcomings, and there are reasons to believe that there were some undemocratic practices as well as gender discrimination. Nonetheless, both politically and economically today's Africa has seriously regressed. The misery and squalor in which the poor wallow today, amidst the affluence of the few, did not exist then. Much of the traditional basis has been destroyed and replaced with western structures, and there is conflict in marrying the two. While today's leaders are elected through a western model, they see themselves as kings and therefore rule by traditional methods. This is done by corrupting traditional leaders who wield influence among the people. The leaders remain alienated from the masses. Consequently, the grassroots population feels no connection to their national leaders. Their loyalty is to the village chiefs and obas with whom they interact, and these are the people the national leaders use to manipulate the masses.

What can today's Africa incorporate from the past to achieve good governance? Today's Africa needs the type of morality that existed then, which eschewed greed and ensured a humane existence for everyone. There should be checks and balances built into the system to ensure accountability from leaders. Also, the absence of political rivalry worked well then. Perhaps Africa needs to find a mode of governance that entails not political rivalry, but a decentralized mode of governance.

COLONIAL AFRICA

Colonial Africa, in my view, refers to those African countries which were conquered by European empires and divided up at the Berlin Conference in 1884, following which colonial masters brought peoples of various tribes, cultures, and nationalities under the central control of European authority, mainly for the purpose of exploitation.

The impact of colonialism on the protection of human rights is best summarized by Minasse Haile's account:

Colonialism has contributed to the poor record of human rights in Africa. Human rights were not part of the Western law brought to Africa. The colonial government in Africa was "authoritarian to the core," and its legacies in the areas of civil, political, and personal security rights, and in the administration of judicial rights were clearly undemocratic. . . . The state and the law were used to regulate and coerce. Colonial courts were used to enforce taxes and impose servitude on the African peoples as part of the apparatus of control. . . . The colonial state in Africa also created other situations that now militate against the adequate observance of human rights, for example, [a] very high degree of social stratification and the maintenance and intensification of parochial, tribal identities.[13]

Among the evils that Haile has highlighted, the stratification of society and the tribal problem militate against the establishment of democracy in Africa. With the partitioning of Africa, tribes and other groups were disorganized and now find themselves scattered in several different boundaries from one country to the next. This has created an open ground for tribal warfare and difficulty for any form of integration. It also makes it more difficult to have a homogeneous civil society which is necessary for the establishment and sustenance of lasting democracy. Other scholars such as Rhoda Howard point out that the right to life was not respected, and economic rights were abused. Workers were not permitted to unionize until the 1920s and they had very few rights. She also notes that thousands of Kenyans were expelled from their lands to make way for white settlers and African farmers were prevented from growing profitable crops such as coffee, which would be in direct competition with white farmers. Howard states that "the colonial state assumed no obligation for economic development until 1939 . . . nor was there any notion that the British should ensure in their colonies even the limited range of social welfare provisions that existed at home."[14] Osita Eze succinctly sums up the influence of British and French rule in this way:

All the colonialists were interested in exploiting the colonies and this over-concern with siphoning off their resources was the ultimate determinant of their policies. Differences in the method of achieving this objective were based on the philosophical and historical experiences of the colonisers. The French and Belgian practice of attempting to transform Africans into Frenchmen or Belgians was only partially successful . . . while the British approach . . . created a body of "elite" with Anglo-Saxon values. Thus in all the colonies . . . there emerged a ruling "elite" who shared Western values and traditions and who in most of these countries have formed bridgeheads of imperialism.[15]

POSTCOLONIAL AFRICA

Since the early 1960s, when most African countries gained independence, governance in most parts of the continent has been punctured by selfish greed, corruption, denial of fundamental human rights, and arbitrariness in leadership decision making. Postindependence Africa abounds with dictators, tyrants, despots, and self-styled life presidents who for the most part languish in the blood of anyone who dares to oppose them. According to Nwabueze's account, most African countries have experienced at least one military coup since independence. He notes that Nigeria, Benin, Ghana, Niger, Guinea, Mauritania, and Uganda have had at least five coups each; Sudan and Mali have had four coups each; Burundi, Comoros, Central African Republic, and Sierra Leone all have had three coups each; Egypt, Ethiopia, Lesotho, Madagascar, and Algeria have had two coups each; while the remaining African countries have had one coup each.[16]

A survey of the political terrain reveals that the will of the people has been emasculated by fascism almost everywhere on the continent. In Gabon, President El Haji Omar Bongo, who has held on to power for twenty-four years, continues to cling to power in spite of the clamor for new leadership. In Ivory Coast, President Felix Houphouet-Boigny held sway for thirty-one years. When elections were held in the early 1990s, he declared himself the truly elected leader despite allegations of massive rigging. President Boigny remained at the helm of his country until his demise in December 1993, at the age of ninety. Leadership of Ivory Coast is now in the hands of Henri Konan Bédié. Hastings Kamuza Banda made himself president for life and refused to submit to the clamor for democratic change in Malawi until recently, when he was forced to accede to international pressure. Before this book went to print, elections were held in Malawi, and Banda was voted out and replaced by Bakili Muluzi. In Burkina Faso, President Blaise Compaore continues his grip on the people with his dictatorial style. In Zaire, Mobutu Sese Seko has ruled like a tyrant since 1965. When a national conference was convened in 1990, Mobutu defied the will of the Zairean people for democratic leadership and continues to cling to power. The performance of Eyadema in Togo is almost a carbon copy of Zaire's Mobutu.

President Kenneth Kaunda was also accused of suppressing opposition and, in spite of twenty-eight years in power, initially rejected calls for democratization. When he finally gave in to the demand for democracy, he was voted out of power and leadership in Zambia was handed to Frederick Chiluba in 1991. In Zimbabwe the government of President Robert Mugabe is accused of intimidating Joshua Nkomo into accepting the position of vice president in order to silence him as a democratic opposition leader. In Kenya, President Daniel arap Moi was accused of leading an inept and impotent government by crushing all opposing voices. Noted among his victims is the world-acclaimed writer, Ngugi Wa Thiongo, who was banned from his native country. In a surprising twist, when Moi was forced to call elections in December 1992, his ruling party, the Kenya African National Union (KANU), was reelected into power. There have been reports that opposition candidates were physically harassed, prevented from holding rallies in key sections of the country, and disparaged on the government-controlled radio and television. More significantly, Moi is accused of withholding the identity cards of as many as one million Kenyans, thus disenfranchising them from voting.[17] Consequently, the people of Kenya continue to live under the tyranny of Daniel arap Moi.

The history of Central Africa has seen General Jean-Bedel Bokassa crown himself Field Marshall in 1966 and later declared himself life president. As Bokassa moved from title to title, so also did the heads of his political opponents roll. By the late 1970s Bokassa crowned himself emperor, with limitless power. The situation in Equatorial Guinea was another sad spectacle. General Marcias Nguema openly eliminated any opposition, while the people lived in terror of his machete-wielding death squads.

In Nigeria there have been several attempts to install democratic governance. These attempts were short-lived. The first regime failed in 1966, and later events led to a traumatic civil war when the Biafrans, disgruntled over their treatment in a united Nigeria, decided to secede. The other attempt at democratic governance failed in 1983. During the thirty years since Nigeria became independent the country experienced eight military coups. A more recent attempt at civilian rule was aborted after its president, General Ibrahim Babangida, cancelled the results of elections held on June 12, 1993.

Governance in postindependence Africa has reduced the continent to a state of hunger, disease, and squalor. All over Africa, there can be seen the tragic spectacle of failed leadership and mass poverty. That is the situation that the current democratization is expected to rectify. However, the current brand of leaders cannot be trusted to bring genuine democracy to Africa. It is their authoritarian style that keeps them in power. As Shivji correctly puts it: "Imperialism is a negation of all freedom, of all democracy. . . . In Africa this has been proved true to the hilt as we have seen that most authoritarian regimes and military dictatorships derive their support from imperialism. Therefore the present stage of the revolution in Africa is defined essentially as an anti-imperialist, democratic revolution."[18]

The changes needed to ensure that democracy and human rights are achieved and sustained in Africa call for a collaborative effort between an enlightened civil society and those outside the continent who are committed to improving the human condition in Africa. Though at times Shivji's tone appears to be blunt and harsh, I concur with his argument that

the historic task of democracy, the task of constituting a civil society, falls squarely on the shoulders of the working people of Africa. The task can be fulfilled only in opposition to the state of the compradorial classes—the neo-colonial state. By definition the neo-colonial state has tended, for its own reproduction, to usurp and obliterate the autonomy of civil society and therefore the very foundation of democracy. It is within this formation that rights struggles, like other democratic struggles, have to be waged.[19]

One group of Africans who have already been forced to organize along the lines of Shivji's argument is the black majority in South Africa living under apartheid. This struggle stands apart because of the uniqueness of the problems of apartheid. It was a rulership that inflicted gross abuse on a section of mankind while the international community attempts to promote universal human rights. We will now discuss the realities of living under such a system, and the role of Nelson Mandela in the struggle against apartheid. We will assess the efforts of the international community and the Organization of African Unity (OAU) to bring an end to that oppressive form of governance. Finally, we will attempt to look into the crystal ball to see what post-apartheid South Africa would be like.

APARTHEID

Kill a dog or bird in a protected area and you go to jail. Kill a white man and you hang. But kill a black man, it's all right.

Miriam Makeba[20]

The evils and injustices of apartheid have been aptly revealed in that statement by Makeba as she painfully recalls the ordeal of black South Africans. South Africa is the only country in the world which is ruled by an oligarchy based on color. Political rights for majority blacks are totally disregarded. Parliament is reserved exclusively for whites. The lower house is elected by whites only. The South African blacks and coloreds have been excluded from provincial councils. Even in the homelands the participation of Africans in legislative activities is subject to the veto powers of the Minister for Bantu Education.

The economic rights of blacks in South Africa were viewed with the same disregard as political rights. Osita Eze gives an account of the magnitude of the injustice by noting that the economy is firmly controlled by the white minority; blacks simply form a pool of labor for white exploitation.[21] The Native Labour Regulation Act and others comprising the Bantu Laws Amendment act of 1967 are all geared to ensure that blacks remain at the lower end of the job ladder. In addition, blacks are required to seek employment through the labor bureau and are only allowed to keep their jobs for as long as the labor bureau permits them to do so. At times, banning orders may result in forcing workers to leave a job in a particular area affected by the ban. He points out that members of different races were paid different wage rates and the unions were subjected to so much restriction that it rendered them ineffective. He adds that any slight wage increase over the years for blacks was wiped out by high inflation, while the whites continued to enjoy an increased standard of living.

South African journalist Joe Thololoe explains that in the academic year 1987–1988 the South African government spent 595 rand on the education of an indigenous South African child. It spent R1,508 on that of a colored child, which is three times the amount spent on an indigenous South African child. It spent R2,015 on an Indian child in South Africa and R2,722 on a white child, which is five times the amount spent on an indigenous African child.[22] In terms of wage distribution Thololoe reveals that in 1987 the average income of whites was R14,880; that of Indians was R4,560; colored R3,000; and that of an indigenous African was R1,989—which represents less than one-seventh of what the whites earned.[23]

In both political and economic rights the apartheid regime in South Africa has violated all the fundamental human rights guaranteed individuals in the UN's Universal Declaration of Human Rights. Apartheid is a contravention of the right to life and security of person (Article 3); the right to be free from torture, cruel or degrading treatment, and punishment (Article 5); the right to recognition as a person before the law and to be given equal protection by the law (Article 6 and 7); the right to freedom of movement and residence within the borders of one's state and the right to leave the country and return (Article 13); the right to own property and not to be arbitrarily deprived of this property (Article 17); the right to freedom of expression (Article 19); the right to freedom of assembly (Article 20); and the right to take part in the government of one's country (Article 21). Apartheid also contravenes Article 25 of the UN declaration, which guarantees everyone the right to a standard of living adequate for the health and well-being of themselves and their families. The right to education guaranteed in Article 26 is also violated.

Although South Africa is signatory to the UN Charter, the provisions of the Charter have never been promulgated as law in South Africa. In addition, South Africa is not signatory to the Universal Declaration of Human Rights nor the Covenants on Civil and Political Rights and Economic, Social and Cultural Rights. Therefore, the courts could not protect citizens against human rights abuse. Blacks had nowhere to seek redress, so they resorted to defiance.

Opposition to Apartheid Within South Africa

Blacks in South Africa have challenged the apartheid regime since 1912. How-ever, other groups[24] emerged over the years. These include the African National Congress (ANC), which drew its support from the Congress of South African Trade Unions (COSATU); the United Democratic Front (UDF), which drew support from a number of civic associations; the South African Communist Party (SACP), which projected a communist ideology, and the Pan African Congress (PAC). Other groups in the homelands formed separate resistance movements. One such group is the Zulu-based Inkatha Freedom Party (IFP), led by Man-gosuthu Buthelezi. (This resistance group has become a thorn in the flesh of the democratization exercise in South Africa, as we will discuss later.)

In March 1960 PAC leadership called for the boycotting of the use of pass-books. Black males in particular responded overwhelmingly to this call. Joe Thol-oloe expressed their sentiments, which could well be understood.

We were tired of carrying the badges of our oppression. We were tired of being hunted down by police in our own motherland simply because we did not have the "right" to be in urban areas. We were tired of being allowed into the urban areas only for as long as we were employed and useful to the white society. And we were tired of being sent back to the "homelands" to die of old age and poverty.[25]

During the demonstration police opened fire, killing sixty-nine people, some of them children. This incident (the Sharpeville Massacre) drew global indigna-tion and condemnation. In part, it was the beginning of the end of the heinous system. International pressure mounted to end apartheid. What is noteworthy here is that the people were conscientized and committed enough to face bullets. The people wanted *change*. That is the difference between the struggle in South Africa and elsewhere on the continent. The grassroots are not involved; they are still in a state of apathy. Also, the struggle in South Africa had effective leadership. The ANC, led by Walter Sisulu, Oliver Tambo, and Nelson Mandela, was ex-emplary. Arrests and imprisonment became commonplace for these men. Man-dela demonstrated the type of fortitude and wit that is worth mentioning. During the trial in 1962, in which Mandela and the other leaders faced treason charges,

Mandela was asked to make his plea. He replied, "The government should be in the dock, not me. I plead not guilty."[26] Later on in his historic self-defense, Mandela kept the court spellbound for over four hours as he turned the trial into a political spectacle. As part of his defense submission, Mandela stated,

During my lifetime I have dedicated myself to this struggle of the African people. I have fought against white domination, and I have fought against black domination. I have cherished the ideal of a democratic and free society in which all persons live together in harmony with equal opportunities. It is an ideal which I hope to live for and to achieve. But if needs be, it is an ideal for which I am prepared to die.[27]

Such commitment is rare in common men. Mandela paid a significant price; he suffered incarceration for twenty-seven years of his life. And in other ways, he has been robbed of what is considered a normal existence.

The Role of the UN Against Apartheid

The UN attempted to address the human rights violations in South Africa by isolating the regime. The UN General Assembly passed a number of resolutions isolating South Africa. It called on the international community to impose sanctions on South Africa. However, most of the UN's efforts were not effective. Among the permanent five in the Security Council, their economic interests prevailed over the human rights of blacks in South Africa. The other hindrance was that the UN's resolutions were not binding. This is a significant area of weakness in the organization. Despite the good intentions of the General Assembly resolutions, the UN did not have sufficient clout to make its resolutions stick. For instance, the Independent Expert Study Group reporting on sanctions in South Africa noted that Japan, West Germany, the United Kingdom, the United States, and Italy remained South Africa's biggest trading partners. There was some trade with countries in the Southern African Development Coordination Conference (SADCC), but "total SADCC trade was less than that of any single one of the big five trading partners."[28] Even though SADCC countries would undergo hardship if sanctions were imposed on South Africa, SADCC leaders pointed out that if sanctions were to be effective it was necessary for the industrialized countries to impose sanctions. SADCC leaders felt that despite expected hardship, the cost would be worth it. They were convinced that comprehensive sanctions would end apartheid quickly, so that the cost need not be borne for long. More importantly, they felt that the cost would be much less than the more than one million people killed and the material damage of over $60 billion caused by South African destabilization.[29]

The Role of the OAU Against Apartheid

All OAU member states isolated South Africa and many of the liberation forces in South Africa found training grounds in such countries as Zambia, Ghana, and

Tanzania. Many of the member states pledged financial support and offered other assistance to liberation forces in South Africa. OAU member countries also pressured other governments which still had diplomatic ties with South Africa to sever their relationships. OAU members also resolved to assist refugees from South Africa and granted them scholarships, educational training and, where possible, employment in the public service of other African countries. Yet, there remains an interesting irony to this scenario. Not all African countries severed ties completely with South Africa. Many of the leaders are themselves dictators and have awful human rights records; they require the protection of a well-trained military for their own security. They therefore have depended on South Africa to train their bodyguards.

While apartheid in South Africa has always been indefensible by any human standards, one must still consider the consistency of OAU member states in condemning human rights violations on the continent. It is hypocritical for the OAU to have brought South Africa before the UN and the eyes of the world when President Mobutu and President Gnassingbe Eyadema committed the most vicious abuses against the people of Zaire and Togo and stalled the process of democratization for over two years while the OAU remained indifferent to what was going on. The OAU lacks personalities with the type of integrity to give leadership. When it comes to human rights atrocities it is a matter of who is fit to cast the first stone.

The way the apartheid issue was handled both at the international level and the regional level (by the OAU) underscores much of the argument that human rights tenets are most often rhetoric. Changes are now coming to South Africa because the grassroots men, women, and children, with effective leadership, challenged the system and were prepared to sacrifice their lives for freedom. The resilience of the oppressed in South Africa in their struggle for human rights demonstrates what can be achieved when the grassroots are conscientized. Ultimately, it is the people themselves who will be the defenders and protectors of their human rights.

Democratization in South Africa

> Our people demand democracy. Our country, which continues to bleed and suffer pain, needs democracy. It cries out for the situation where the law will decree that freedom to speak of freedom constitutes the very essence of legality and the very thing that makes for the legitimacy of the constitutional order.
>
> Nelson Mandela[30]

The attempt to democratize South Africa is a welcome move. However, the move to democratize a country deeply traumatized by the inhumanity of apartheid is one fraught with apprehension, mistrust, and setbacks. South African society has been deformed by apartheid, and the wounds of blacks run deep. Therefore, the challenge of democratization in South Africa is without doubt a herculean task.

As preparations toward democratization in South Africa got under way, most of the resistance groups retained their identities but recognized the paramount role of the ANC. This was not the case for the Inkatha Freedom Party. Their leader, Buthelezi, ensured that he secured a place at the negotiating table and disagreed with the ANC on almost every issue. The rivalry escalated into a bloody power struggle between supporters on both sides. At the same time, security forces in South Africa were accused of fueling the violence. So far this issue has not been handled with much success. The transition has been plagued with violence and banditry among the two rival factions—and this does not augur well for post-transition South Africa.

Post-Apartheid South Africa

Governance in a new South Africa must ensure that the human and democratic rights of each individual are respected, protected, and guaranteed.[31] Therefore, South Africa will be faced with the challenge of psychological reorientation among blacks and whites to bring about justice and national reconciliation. Whites, who enjoy almost all of the country's economic resources, will have to share their economic power while blacks will have to heal and forgive.

If democracy is to survive in a post-apartheid South Africa, a new regime should implement policies to reduce poverty and inequality among the various racial groups. There should be land redistribution, mass education, and training for most of the population and improved social services. More importantly, the entire public administration should be reorganized to accommodate anti-apartheid programs and policies. All such changes will require the political will of policymakers.

At this point in time it is difficult to predict how things will develop in South Africa. Even after elections are held it is likely that the rivalry between the ANC and the Zulus will continue. The appetite for power in some like Buthelezi will not be quenched overnight. At the same time, there are other groups such as PAC to contend with. It is difficult to foresee one leader emerging who can bring all the warring factions together. The whites will also have to be accommodated in a democratic dispensation. The future South Africa could still be explosive if the ethnic question is not dealt with. In addition, I foresee a mass exodus of whites from South Africa, particularly the hard-line conservatives who are prepared to kill to hold onto the status quo. When faced with the reality of black majority rule, as the whites were in the former Rhodesia in 1980, they will drive their luxury cars to the airport, set fire to them, and leave South Africa.

Conclusion

Nelson Mandela has gained notoriety as a distinguished crusader for social justice in the eyes of the world because of his selfless sacrifice. All along Mandela demonstrated exemplary fortitude of mind amidst obstacles that could weaken the moral strength of any ordinary human being. The only thing Mandela stood to gain from his dedication to the freedom of black South Africans was either a life sentence or the noose around his neck. Notwithstanding this threat, Mandela sustained perseverance to overcome all the obstacles that confronted him. Mandela demonstrated leadership that others in Africa should emulate. The task ahead for Africa is a long struggle for change. More leaders of this caliber are needed to come forth and educate, conscientize, and lead the masses rather than isolating them until they need their votes.

Events in South Africa as it attempts democratization bear similarity to what is happening in other parts of the continent. The same black-on-black violence unleashed in South Africa is unleashed in other parts of Africa in the form of the economic violence unleashed on the majority poor by the comprador ruling class. In addition, the ethnic tensions in South Africa demand the same palliative cure as elsewhere on the continent. The feudal structure has bearing on events unfolding in South Africa as well as in other parts of Africa. Since the Zulus traditionally held power, they are unlikely to accept rulership coming from another tribe, and this is largely responsible for the struggle between Buthelezi and the ANC. Africa cannot be genuinely democratized and exist in peace unless the people themselves control the productive forces and all groups, including minority groups, are involved in decision making that affects their lives. For South Africa, a decentralized form of federation might better serve the various ethnic groups who are making their own demands during the process of transition.

NOTES

1. J.D. Fage, *A History of West Africa* (London: Cambridge University Press, 1969), p. 24.

2. Tachable Zacharie, "Is the Protection of Human Rights and Democracy Strange to the African Tradition?" paper delivered at a conference on "Human Rights and Democracy in Africa, Yesterday, Today and a Vision of Tomorrow," organized by Human Rights Africa, in Ota, Ogun State, Nigeria, March 26–28, 1991.

3. Ibid.

4. Osita C. Eze, *Human Rights in Africa: Some Selected Problems* (Lagos, Nigeria: Nigerian Institute of International Affairs, 1984), p. 12.

5. Claude Ake, "Rethinking African Democracy," *Journal of Democracy* 2, no. 1 (Winter 1991): 34.

6. Quoted in Olusegun Obasanjo and Akin Mobogungie, eds., *Elements of Democracy* (Lagos, Nigeria: ALF Publications, 1992), p. 46.

7. See Kenneth Kaunda, *A Humanist in Africa* (London: Longmans, 1966), pp. 24–25. See also Osisioma B.C. Nwolise, "Africa's Problems with Democratisation: An Overview," in Ayo Fasoro, Deji Haastrup, and Femi Otubanjo, eds., *Understanding Democracy*, proceedings of a conference organized by African Democratic Heritage Foundation (ADHERE) and held at the University of Ibadan Conference Centre, August 19–20, 1991, published by ADHERE, 1991, p. 104.

8. See Babafemi Badejo and S.A. Ogunyemi, "Integrating the Past with the Present: A Futile Exercise?" in John A. Ayoade and Adigun A.B. Agbaje, eds., *African Traditional Political Thought and Institutions* (Lagos, Nigeria: Centre for Black and African Arts and Civilization [CBAAC], 1989), pp. 175–186.

9. Joy Mukubwa Hendrickson, "Rights in Traditional African Societies," in Ayoade and Agbaje, eds., *African Traditional Political Thought and Institutions*, pp. 19–43.

10. Ibid., p 35.

11. I. Schapera, *Government and Politics in Tribal Societies* (London: C.A. Watts and Co., Ltd., 1963), p. 154. Quoted by Joy Mukubwa Hendrickson in Ayoade and Agbaje, *African Traditional Political Thought and Institutions*, pp. 21–22.

12. Rhoda E. Howard, *Human Rights in Commonwealth Africa* (Totowa, N.J.: Rowman and Littlefield, 1986), p. 20.

13. See Minasse Haile, "Human Rights, Stability and Development," pp. 591–592 as quoted in James Silk, "Traditional Culture and the Prospect for Human Rights in Africa," in Abdullahi Ahmed An-Naim and Francis M. Deng, eds., *Human Rights in Africa: Cross Cultural Perspectives* (Washington, D.C.: The Brookings Institute, 1990), pp. 293–294.

14. Howard, *Human Rights in Commonwealth Africa*, pp. 9–10.

15. Eze, *Human Rights in Africa*, p. 21.

16. See "30 African Countries Hit by Coup, Says Nwabueze," in *The Guardian* (Lagos), September 18, 1992.

17. *Time*, January 19, 1993, p. 24.

18. Issa Shivji, *The Concept of Human Rights in Africa* (London: CODESRIA, 1989), p. 70.

19. Ibid., p. 71.

20. Miriam Makeba with James Hall, *Makeba My Story* (New York: NAL Penguin, 1987), p. 20.

21. Eze, *Human Rights in Africa*, p. 112.

22. Joe Thololoe, "Human Rights Abuses in South Africa" in Kathleen Mahoney and Paul Mahoney, eds., *Human Rights in the Twenty-First Century* (Utrecht, The Netherlands: Kruwer Publishing, 1993), p. 43.

23. Ibid.

24. See Pauline H. Baker, "South Africa's Future," *Journal of Democracy* 1, no. 4 (Fall 1990): 7–24.

25. Thololoe, "Human Rights Abuses in South Africa," p. 43.

26. Ronald Harwood, *Mandela* (New York: NAL Penguin, 1987), p. 100.

27. Ibid., p. 110.

28. *South Africa: The Sanctions Report Documents and Statistics*. Submitted by The Independent Expert Study Group, ed. Joseph Hanlon (London: Commonwealth Secretariat, 1990), p. 299.

29. UNICEF 1989:38. Quoted in *South Africa*, p. 300.

30. Nelson Mandela, *Journal of Democracy* 1, no. 4 (Fall 1990): 32.

31. South African legal expert Albie Sachs makes an excellent contribution to this debate in *Protecting Human Rights in a New South Africa* (New York: Oxford University Press, 1990). Sachs insists that the new constitution must be for all South Africans, oppressors and oppressed alike. He urges that the cultural diversity of South Africa must be accommodated and the rights of individual citizens respected. See in particular "The Last Word—Freedom," pp. 184–191.

Chapter 2

Emerging Concepts

With the end of the Cold War, western powers insisted that authoritarian regimes embark on democratization anchored in human rights and popular participation. Since development efforts were a failure in the "lost decade" of the 1980s, the West felt that installing liberal democracy was the appropriate prescription to end the increasing poverty, corruption, and human rights abuses which many Africans suffered under authoritarian regimes. So far the process which began in 1990 has shown few positive signs of real change.

When development efforts started in the 1960s donor agencies predicted that growth in per capita GNP would result in development. Thus began the arrival of a plethora of technocrats who joined the development set to advise Third World countries on how to "do" development as perceived through the GNP paradigm. During all this, mothers in developing countries were advised to forego breast feeding and replace breast milk with lactogen (produced by western multinationals). Local beverages were replaced by a Coca-Cola culture. Basic farming tools were abandoned for tractors and huge machines, which eventually were abandoned for lack of maintenance and lack of skills in how to use them. After thirty years, the results have been grossly disappointing. Africa in particular has become increasingly poverty-stricken, and today is at the brink of extinction. A number of factors can be attributed to such massive failure. I for one have refused to exonerate African leaders for their role in Africa's underdevelopment (an argument developed in Chapter 3). In addition, the western approach to development in Africa, which insists that "my way is the best way," has proven destructive to Africa. Western aid is presently tied to multiparty democracy and, despite their meager contribution at this stage, there is still reluctance on the part of western donors to avoid making the same mistakes as in the past. Liberal democracy is not likely to bring about the development that Africa needs. Now is the time to rethink the process. Democracy must be redefined if it is to have real meaning for majority Africans.

In this chapter, I present my definition of democracy, and I undertake an examination of liberal democracy as to its feasibility as a solution to Africa's political problems. Questions are raised such as: Is the African society in a state to effectively operate as government *of* the people *by* the people? Is the universality of human rights rhetoric or reality? Does democracy guarantee protection of human rights? An assessment is made of the current debate among African scholars as they search for a homegrown model of governance.

DEMOCRACY DEFINED

Over the years, democracy has been given various definitions by philosophers, theoreticians, and policymakers. Many have adopted a definition of democracy that they hope will solve their problems, assist economic progress, or influence public opinion. Most Africans today live under the dictatorship of material poverty.[1] Democracy in Africa must therefore be a marriage of the political and economic. In this case, I define democracy as a system of governance which allows people to freely elect their leaders and hold them accountable, and which provides opportunity for the greater number of people to use their human potential to survive in dignity. Africans need improvement in their lives, and it can only come from their capacity to make demands on their leaders. The democracy I refer to here is specifically about empowerment at the grassroots level. Average working-class Africans must be able to organize and spearhead a people-centered transformation of institutions and values which will result in political and economic democratization. The notion of democracy is ever-changing. For this reason it is necessary to look at the historical development of the concept.

Early western scholars embraced the definition of democracy as government of the people, by the people, and for the people, which was first advanced by President Lincoln in his Gettysburg Address in 1863. Later on, other scholars offered different interpretations of democracy. Some saw democracy not as a way of governing, but as a system which allows citizens to control those who govern. MacIver for one avers that "Democracy is not a way of governing, whether by majority or otherwise, but primarily a way of determining who shall govern, and broadly, to what ends . . . the people, let us repeat, do not, and cannot govern; they control the government."[2]

Kenyan scholar Peter Anyang Nyong'o expresses a similar view by stressing that "democracy is not about what governments do; it is about what people do to make their governments accomplish things for the common good."[3] Philippe Schmitter and Terry Lynn Karl also perceive democracy in a similar fashion. They define modern democracy as "a system of governance in which rulers are held accountable for their actions in the public realm by citizens acting indirectly through the competition in cooperation of their elected representatives."[4]

Other philosophers have proffered different ideas on the concept of democracy.[5] For example, in ancient Greece, Pericles, who was one of the greatest democratic statesmen of all time, instilled in the Athenians that patriotism, civic responsibility, and fulfillment of one's civic obligations are necessary for the success of democracy. This noble ideal is still a sine qua non for democracy, but such values are lacking in present-day Africa. While many are quick to exercise civic rights, they fail to recognize it is accompanied by civic duties. This is largely due to the fact that the state in Africa has failed to meet the needs of the masses. Therefore, there is no loyalty toward the state. Also, the ruling class gives no leadership by example on this matter because all they do is plunder the state.

In Britain the signing of the Magna Carta in 1215 and the Bill of Rights in 1689 became the pillars of democratic ideology. These two historic documents postulated that in a democracy power should be mainly in the hands of the people, while royal power should remain limited.

Further development of the ideology of democracy includes the arguments of several noted philosophers, such as Jean Jacques Rousseau, John Locke, and John Stuart Mill. While some scholars were concerned with representative government, others like Rousseau were more concerned with effective participation in the political process. Rousseau, in his famous discourse *The Social Contract*, contended that government was a covenant between the sovereign and the citizen. Therefore, the state existed primarily to protect those people to which it owed its existence. Rousseau also opined that only legitimate government should be respected[6] and where the government failed to fulfill its obligations it should face the people's revolt. Stressing the importance for equality in sharing the nation's resources, Rousseau argued that no citizen should be so rich that he can buy another, while no one should be so poor that he is forced to sell himself.[7] Rousseau further postulated that individuals should be regarded as equal in rights, and that only in a forum in which the whole citizenry is allowed to participate in the affairs of the state is true democracy being practiced.[8] For such reasons he opined that the size of modern nations would make genuine democracy seem impossible.

I would dismiss the argument as to whether the size of a nation-state has any impact on democracy; nonetheless, the rest of Rousseau's argument holds much relevance in light of the realities of today's Africa. It raises such questions as: Is anyone so poor that he/she is forced to sell him/herself? Is anyone in Africa so rich that he is able to buy another? To whom does the state in Africa owe its existence, and is it protecting those people? Ultimately the question can also be asked: Have governments in Africa been fulfilling their obligations? None of these ideals exist for the majority poor in present-day Africa. We can then take the question further and ask: Is the current democratization movement taking place in Africa likely to change the situation for Africa's majority?

Another contribution to the philosophy of democracy came from John Locke, who, like Rousseau, contended that government was based on a contract and that those who rule must be cognizant of the inalienable rights of the people. Locke argued that people must be allowed to express their opinions on the policies of government. The people should also participate in enforcing government decisions and ensuring that the basic law which enshrines their inalienable rights must never be abrogated. He contended that all legitimate governments rest upon the consent of the governed.[9]

John Stuart Mill was a staunch defender of liberty. He contended that no opinion should be silenced. "All of mankind," Mill asserted, "has no justification in silencing even the voice of one dissenter."[10] In his view, "If the opinion is right they are deprived of exchanging error for truth; if wrong, they lose what is almost as great a benefit, the clearer perception and livelier impression of truth produced by its collision with error."[11]

Although these philosophers have offered varying conceptions of democracy, the central theme is that democracy should be government of the majority, and government should be accountable to the people. MacIver's definition reflects an empowered majority and speaks directly to the writer's notion of government *of* the people *by* the people. This approach is not taken with any illusion that a society can be entirely democratic, in which case I commend Rousseau's brilliance and foresight when he said: "If there were a nation of Gods, it would govern itself democratically. A government so perfect is not suited to men."[12] Democracy as practiced in the West has its inherent weaknesses. There is poverty and deprivation in the North as well as in the South. Also, with all the progress of the feminist movement in the United States, a woman is yet to be elected president. Yet, democracy is at work in the United States. It was the voice of the people that led the United States Senate to move to impeach President Nixon during the Watergate scandal. The problem in Africa is that there is no voice of the people. What in fact operates is the tyranny of the minority (i.e., the ruling elites and their cronies who support their rapacious lifestyles by exploiting the masses).

There is yet an even more important aspect to this debate, which appears to have been overlooked in the case of Africa. Liberal democracy was actually desired because western society had already achieved a level of development, particularly in the market economy. In this regard, C.B. Macpherson has been illuminating.

Liberal democracy is a late product of market society; the first need of the market was for the liberal state, not a democratic one. . . . The democratic franchise was added only when the working-class that had been produced by the capitalist market society had been strong enough to get into competition; strong enough to demand that it should have some weight in the competitive process. Thus liberal democracy is the unique product of . . . successfully developing market societies.[13]

Kenneth Bauzon also enlightens readers on this issue. He points out that greater political freedoms and more open political systems that operate in the West are not accidents of history. "They are definite outgrowths of a long process of evolution and institutionalization consciously pursued by historical forces under unique conditions that enabled the seed of individualism to grow and prosper."[14]

How then can the reverse be applied to Africa? For one thing, liberal democracy resulted from capitalism and Africa does not have that kind of history. The conditions that favored liberal democracy in the West do not exist in Africa, and Africa does not have the time. Africa needs the type of democracy that will address Africa's present social, cultural, and economic realities.

DEMOCRATIZATION

Democratization is conceptualized as "the process of transforming a group, community, or state into a democratic entity."[15] When a society attempts to democratize it aims to achieve an arrangement which operationalizes the following:

1. Supreme power is vested in the hands of the people through their elected representatives.
2. Laws are established which guarantee political equality.
3. The democratic spirit is put into practice.
4. People are legally empowered to determine who governs and what policies and programs those who govern should pursue.
5. Laws and machineries are in place to ensure that those who govern are responsible, responsive, and accountable to the people who bear the weight of their governance.
6. People can participate fully in the management of their affairs.
7. Respect and promotion of fundamental human rights and freedoms.
8. The making of laws by the people or their popularly elected representatives, thus ensuring there is justice in society.
9. The rule of law (not rule of man).[16]

Is the present African society in a state to put these tenets into practice? We will examine the application of liberal democracy in Africa to arrive at an answer.

DEMOCRATIZATION IN AFRICA

The liberal concept of democracy includes: (1) the civil society, (2) the state system, and (3) the ideals of democracy, these being freedom, equality, justice, and fraternity. Careful examination reveals that these do not operate for the benefit of the greatest number of citizens.

The Civil Society in Africa

Most of the intellectual reasoning agrees that the transformation of Africa's political landscape will be undertaken by civil society. Larry Diamond underscored the significant role of civil society in the democratization process.

Civil society is a crucially important factor at every stage of the process of democratization. ... The construction of democratic institutions and processes in Africa's authoritarian re-

gimes will in most cases have to begin, and always have to proceed in large measure, as a
"bottom-up" phenomenon. For this to happen, however, popular organizations must themselves be "bottom-up" and truly popular in character. This means they must have strong
roots in local communities, meaningful participation by members, relatively democratic
internal processes and structures, and substantial autonomy from the state.[17]

If civil society in Africa is to accomplish the task before them as Diamond
outlines it, there are some problems that must be addressed. The groups comprising civil society (i.e., professional bodies, workers' unions, women's organizations, student associations, and other interest groups) must provide input into
the system to ensure that democracy delivers social justice. However, a huge
portion of African society cannot have effective input into the system. Over 50
percent of Africans are illiterate, and the majority are devastated by poverty, disease, and despair. Consequently, those who provide input into the political system
are the intellectual elites who often use the masses to garner access to power for
their own selfish ends. African leaders are not in touch with people at the village
level, so traditional rulers play a significant role in the political process. However,
many of the traditional leaders, corrupted by the political leaders, improperly exert
their influence on the villagers. Traditional rulers dictate how the community
should vote; they are often the ones to ignite ethnic rivalry and to order that
fightings be stopped. The task here is to educate the grassroots to think for
themselves.

Civil society is also not homogenous. Cohesiveness is a vital factor in forging
national movements that can result in the kind of people power that forces dictators from power, as was witnessed in the Philippines. For example, after the
annulment of the June 12 elections in Nigeria in 1993, the Yurobas in the south
were clamoring for the installment of the democratically elected leader. The
Hausa Fulanis in the north were largely silent (and to some extent in agreement
with the annulment, since it protected their long-standing dominance of Nigeria's
political landscape). The Ibos, on the other hand, remained on the fence, quick
to point out that they were reviled during the Biafran war. Even though the cause
was just, they did not come together to act. Africans are firstly committed to their
family and then their tribe. National interests are third in this exact order. This
also reflects a larger problem for African integration.

Michael Bratton observed that there are hopeful activities within civil society
in Africa. Groups of average working Africans come together to protect their
interests, and there is usually a high level of commitment to their association.
Much of this is the result of the hardship Africans face, which is aggravated by
structural adjustment. For example, market women form associations to ensure
that government does not charge exorbitant rates for stall rental, or that transportation fares are not too high. Bratton also pointed out that village communities
receive support through the old boys' network that links political and economic
elites to their home schools and villages.[18] This is one area in which finances are
redistributed to help in community development. These are positive signs for civil

society in Africa. But while people collaborate to ensure their economic survival, the average African is not sufficiently conscientized politically to be prepared to make sacrifices for the national good. That is a major hurdle.

The State System

The main problem with the state system in Africa is that there is no real separation of powers. While separation of powers is recognized in the constitutions, it is not practiced in reality. Rousseau puts such a scenario in its appropriate context when he notes that "the prince and the sovereign being the same person constitutes, so to speak, a government without government."[19] What exists in Africa is absolute power. Written constitutions in Africa are based on western values, but African leaders rule as traditional chiefs and kings and do not subordinate to written law. That is another area of confusion. The constitutions are also adopted without input from the masses; therefore they are not designed to suit the interests of the working class. The legislature, the judiciary, and the executive are all controlled by authoritarian leadership. In examining these bodies, one needs to find out how members are selected to these bodies and whether the lower members of society are found among them.

The composition of the legislature does not reflect the grassroots. It is not comprised of people from different levels of society, and there is usually an underrepresentation of women. Members of the legislature are drawn from the upper class, so oftentimes the welfare of the common man is ignored. Laws are often unjust and enacted to perpetuate oppression. As Rousseau noted, with civil society man acquires the moral freedom to be the master of himself, and "obedience to a law one prescribes to oneself is freedom."[20] The judiciary is usually selected from members of the legal profession, and they are often more concerned about legal technicalities than social justice. Added to that judges are not allowed to adjudicate without political interference. As Osisioma Nwolise aptly states, "The judiciary is completely powerless and useless to the people in the struggle for democratisation, preserving human rights and even promoting the rule of law especially in the face of military rule."[21] The military, police, and security agents, who should protect the people from internal disorder and outside invasions, often act as enemies of the people. Security forces often regard dissenting voices as a threat to the status quo and resort to dubious activities to prop up existing regimes. Nwolise made a statement that not too many would dispute: "If the defence and security forces acted as agents of the people rather than agents of the ruling class . . . the dictators, tyrants and butchers in Africa would have long ago been driven off the throne and the societies democratised."[22]

The state administration is often corrupted. Regional and local governments do not adequately meet the needs of the people. Career bureaucrats who collect revenue and disburse expenditures are often bribed to hand out contracts. They are also expected to award contracts to their kinfolk as part of their responsibility to tribe and family. If bureaucrats misspend money allocated for housing, education, health, and so on, the government can be embarrassed but it is the masses who bear the brunt. Since the local government operations directly affect the grassroots, this tier of government requires careful scrutiny. Local governments exist for two main reasons: the democratic principle and the development principle. If they are to be held accountable, then one should ask whether the rural people are given opportunity to take part in government. Are the local government councilors genuine representatives of the people or did they bribe their way into power? In terms of development, we need to find out whether basic infrastructure such as roads, water supply, health clinics, and schools are being provided. Is the money allocated to providing these necessities being properly channeled? Can the people demand accountability from their leaders?

Reports of studies indicated that money being pumped into many of the local governments for development purposes are not having any impact on the lives of ordinary individuals. The only people who can change this situation are the oppressed people themselves. This situation will not be changed by a top-down hierarchical structure. The bureaucrats are the ones who benefit from the status quo. Therefore, change at the local government level is crucial to transforming Africa. Here is where empowerment must begin. People at the grassroots must receive literacy training. Basic infrastructure must be provided, not as a result of being a "good boy," but as the end-product of democracy. Only an enlightened and empowered popular movement will articulate such demands.

The Ideals of Democracy

The tenets of liberal democracy espouse equality of all individuals before the law and the state, the freedom and dignity of the person guaranteed through human rights, the respect for a constitution as the fundamental law of the land, and primarily the power of the people to decide their leadership through universal suffrage and free and fair elections. Majority Africans have not been educated about the ideals of democracy and are often ignorant about rights as well as duties. How then can they ensure that these tenets work? For instance, the majority have no interest in freedom of the press, so when government muzzles the press the only people who argue are the elites who are trying to wrest power from one another. Poverty-stricken people are often so concerned with mere survival that they have no concept of freedom. As Franklin Delano Roosevelt said, "necessitous men are not free." As things now stand, the average person might be bribed to vote, but that has nothing to do with appreciating the values of democracy. In terms of equality one needs to ask: Are all citizens equal before the law? Do all children have access to primary education? Are all capable young people given an opportunity to work for a living? What one discovers is that certain privileges remain the right of a few who continue to be indifferent to the plight of the majority.

If fraternity is at work in a society, then each person should consider others as fellow citizens and work with them. This is one aspect of African culture that has eroded with modernity. People have become less cohesive and more stratified. In fact, African society today is largely two groups—the haves and the have-nots. The haves do not consider the masses their brothers in any way; they only find the need for the masses when they need access to power. The have-nots are equally suspicious of the haves and, in fact, rather than fraternity, what really exists is fury on the part of the suffering masses and fear on the part of the oppressive minority. William Godwin tells us that

Democracy restores a man to a consciousness of his value, teaches him, by the removal of authority and oppression, to listen to the dictates of reason, gives him confidence to treat other men as his fellow human beings, and induces him to regard them no longer as enemies against whom to be on his guard, but as brethren whom it becomes him to assist.[23]

Such type of social interaction will only emerge in Africa when the inequities caused by the exploitative and parasitic class structures are removed. To this end, majority Africans will need to be enlightened enough to cross ethnic barriers and collaborate in a collective struggle that will transform the continent.

DEMOCRATIC TRANSITION

The injustices of authoritarian rule usually undermine the social contract between the rulers and the ruled and result in a movement toward democracy. This was the case for Africans throughout the Cold War, but at that time no one was prepared to listen to cries of injustice. However, the present transition to democracy began largely as an outcry against economic discontent. Pressure for change mounted among interest groups and the church. The church in Africa has often been vocal on matters of social justice because this has been the institution that worked hard to deliver welfare services to the masses. We will define democratic transition to see whether the definition applies to the ongoing process. We will then discuss the role of the West and the models of transition in Africa thus far.

A group of African scholars at a meeting organized by the Africa Leadership Forum defined democratic transition as "a systematic process of change in the political institution and process based on the values of democracy."[24] When we apply the values of democracy to the ongoing process in selecting a government and the conduct of elections in Africa, it becomes evident that the current transition in Africa is a political transition, and *not* a democratic transition. Moreover, majority Africans cannot apply the values of democracy because they have not been educated about such values.

In their discourse, "What Democracy Is . . . and Is Not," Philippe Schmitter and Terry Lynn Karl point out that what distinguishes democratic governments from undemocratic ones are norms that condition how these persons attain power and the checks and balances that hold them accountable for their actions.[25] This is crucial to the ongoing process of transition in Africa. Can the majority who are in ignorance and squalor impose checks and balances that will hold leaders accountable?

Yusuf Bangura has identified three major processes that are central to democratic transition from authoritarian military and one-party regimes: the demilitarization of social and political life, the liberalization of civil society, and the democratization of the rules governing political and economic competition.[26] During the current democratization movement in Africa, it is important to consider all of these factors. Is civil society free and functioning? Are political parties set up and governed democratically or are they dominated by the power elite? Can such a process produce a democratic government? Furthermore, will the current democratization exercise result in a subsequent demilitarization of social and political life? The role of the military, particularly in Zaire and Togo, has been a significant hindrance to the transition program.

The Role of the West in Africa's Political Transition

The democratization exercise in Africa is being pursued at this time because the West demanded it. Few would argue that Africans need accountable government, but what is important is whether the demand will go beyond multiparty elections. Elections are only a beginning, and results thus far indicate that it has brought very little change in leadership. When demands were made for democratization in Africa, the West neglected to take into consideration the huge financial resources it would entail. Democracy is more than buying thousands of ballot boxes; there is need to build new structures or to transform existing ones to make for accountable and just leadership at all levels of government. Such considerations were not part of the western agenda for Africa. At the same time calls were made to democratize, aid flows were diminished and directed to the eastern countries. Africa needs mass literacy and improved material condition to achieve lasting democracy. Africa is a continent that is in ruin, and its redemption will need further assistance from the West. The question then is: Will the West see Africans through? As Gilbert Keith Bluwey argues, "The West, having literally plodded African liberals into engaging these dictators to a test of legitimacy through the ballot box, have a moral obligation not to abandon the liberals in mid-stream and thus turn them to the Kamuza Bandas as meat fit for crocodiles, or to be dealt with as rats by the Arap Mois."[27]

The greatest contribution the West can make to democracy in Africa is to assist in laying a sound foundation for the development of a democratic culture. While the West was calling for democratization, human rights, and accountability, the current brand of ruling parasites stashed enough money in western banks and dummy corporations to ensure that they "lived happily ever after." All this was done at a time when those same governments were implementing structural adjustment measures. Simultaneously, the West decreased funding to NGOs that usually worked at the grassroots level to alleviate the misery of the poor. Consequently, the plight of majority Africans has increasingly worsened since the democratization exercise was initiated. The other repercussion politically is that the current brand of leaders are the ones with huge sums of money to fight elections and bribe the masses, while the opposition for the most part does not have equal amounts of finances. That is reflected in the election results we have seen so far. In this case there is need for serious rethinking of the process.

The current exercise is imperiled because it was externally imposed and elite-driven, while the majority remains dormant. It will not change much, except to allow for more political rivalry. Bluwey suggested that western countries should agree on a mechanism whereby they could measure what progress each African country was making towards democratization. He proposed that the following questions should form part of a checklist:

1. Are the views of opposition parties represented on the state media (radio, television) and national newspapers?
2. Can private groups opposed to the government hold public meetings and rallies without police permit?
3. Are public officials legally protected from public criticism?
4. Are there laws which allow public officials to order the detention or imprisonment of another person without laying formal charges against such an individual?
5. Does the government consult with identifiable political groups before making appointments to key electoral positions?
6. Does the government consult with identifiable political groups in deciding on the transition timetable?
7. Is the incumbent government interested in contesting the impending elections?
8. Who writes and who promulgates the constitution?[28]

Though these ideas are useful for the conducting of elections, Bluwey also commits the same error. Nothing in this list suggests that the people be involved at the grassroots level. For example, he never asked: Are the political parties themselves democratically organized? The change that Africa needs cannot come about by merely electing a government through the ballot box and ensuring that opposition parties are allowed to exist. It is simply catering to the same groups of people, and that will not change the oppression of the masses.

If the West is serious about democratization and human rights in Africa, there must be a willingness on its part to work with Africans as they search for a political arrangement that is suited to the needs of Africans. At the same time the West should:

1. Assist grassroots education programs in human rights and democratic development;
2. Wage war on poverty by funding projects initiated by grassroots communities themselves;
3. Assist in institution-building within NGOs working at the grassroots level.

Still, there remains an equally important consideration—the democratization of the rules governing political and economic competition vis-à-vis Africa. To what degree is the West prepared to democratize the rules of economic competition when it comes to trade with African countries? Are the fora in which the price for Africa's raw materials being fixed themselves democratic? Have the IMF conditionalities under structural adjustment eroded the power of African leaders to make decisions that would benefit their people? Several scholars,[29] among them Carol Lancaster and Richard Joseph, contend that the IMF conditionalities are intent on external aid agencies dictating governance in Africa. They argue that the deepening African crisis has resulted in the erosion of African self-governance in the economic and fiscal spheres. Claude Ake expressed his frustration with the international financial institutions (IFIs) in this way: "They (the IFIs) think that political variables can simply be treated as an engineering problem and 'factored in' to improve the effectiveness of their structural adjustment programs, and thus that they can avoid changing their overall approach to development. . . . This is a dangerous error."[30] The key question in all this is: How do such situations impact the establishment and consolidation of democracy in Africa?

Models of Transition in Africa

The ongoing transition in Africa has taken different forms. Writing in the *Journal of Democracy*, Richard Joseph has identified seven models of democratic transitions:

1. The national conference
2. Government change via democratic elections
3. Co-opted transition
4. Guided democratization
5. Recalcitrance and piecemeal reforms
6. Armed insurrections culminating in elections
7. Conditional transitions[31]

The national conference lends itself to popular participation, dialogue, and openness. It has been attempted in a number of French countries, but the success of its initial attempt in Benin Republic did not carry over to other countries as was expected. A number of African leaders have frustrated the exercise. With the guided model, some military leaders remained at the helm and steered the transition to democracy, as in Nigeria and Guinea. In other cases, some leaders have reluctantly moved to piecemeal reforms, as in the case of Ghana and Cameroon. In countries such as Uganda and Ethiopia, armed insurrections have culminated in elections. In rare instances, such as in Algeria, leaders maintain the power to interrupt, delay, or abort the democratization exercise.

So far the transition which began in 1990 has resulted in only a few countries making the full transition from authoritarian or single-party rule to democratically elected leadership. Among them are Benin Republic, Zambia, Cape Verde, Sao Tome and Principe, and Madagascar. The Chiluba government in Zambia imposed a state of emergency after less than two years in office. None of the models have proven to be an easy path, and whether or not they can sustain democracy is uncertain. The national conference holds out the best hope for grassroots participation and therefore could sustain lasting democracy in Africa. The experiment was elite-initiated and directed, and this was one of its major pitfalls. Africans need to undertake further research on this model and benefit from errors made which resulted in the standoff in Zaire and Togo for almost two years.

Obstacles to Democratic Transition

The structures that should be in place to augur a democratic process of transition are nonexistent in Africa. The statement does not mean that democratization should not have been initiated in Africa until the structures were built. The writer's emphasis is that the exercise started at the wrong end. Democratic transition in Africa is externally imposed and administered by a top-down bureaucracy, completely alienating the masses. That is what is essentially wrong with the transition process in Africa.

Samuel Huntington's observations of newly emerging democracies provide some useful insights. He notes that some of the major obstacles to democratization include:

1. The lack of experience with democracy in those countries that operated under an authoritarian system.
2. The lack of real commitment to democratic values on the part of political leaders.
3. Reluctance of long-standing authoritarian rulers to accept democratic reforms.
4. Cultural values inherent in such religion as Islam.
5. Poverty.[32]

In Africa, the lack of real commitment on the part of political leaders poses a serious impediment. However, poverty remains the most serious threat to democracy. As Huntington pointed out, "most poor societies will remain undemocratic so long as they remain poor."[33] At present, majority Africans are mired in material and intellectual poverty. Democracy in Africa will have to include successful poverty alleviation measures. If economic problems are not addressed, democracies will be shortlived. (The challenge posed by poverty to the sustenance of democracy in Africa will be discussed later on.) Other impediments to democracy lie in the practice of the ideology itself. As Diamond pointed out, there are paradoxes that pose problems for the practice of democracy and threaten its survival in most developing countries.[34]

Interim Governments

Scholars such as Yossi Shain and Juan Linz have posited that "whether, when and how interim governments can lead toward competitive multi-party elections depends on their origins and way they handle the problems that confront them, particularly the issue of democratic legitimacy."[35] This is precisely the dilemma of most of the interim administrations in Africa as the democratization exercise continues.

The interim administrations set up during the national conferences in Zaire and Togo suffocated due to their lack of legitimacy. The interim leaders were rendered powerless since it was unclear who was really in charge. The leaders whom the interim administrations were trying to unseat had long legitimized their military rule and considered themselves as the only ones with legitimate power. While the ruling class struggled for change, the interim leaders had no broad-based support throughout the country. The biggest problem was that they did not have the support of the military. This led to a tug of war between the authoritarian leaders (Mobutu and Eyadema) and supporters of the national conference. During the stalemate, the nation's business was at a standstill while soldiers unleashed terror on society. In the end it was the poor who suffered most.

Incumbent caretaker governments faced similar problems. General Babangida set up a caretaker government in Nigeria between January and August 1993 and appointed the governor of the Central Bank, Ernest Shonekan, as the executive head of state. At the same time, Babangida remained head of the National Defence Security Council. Shonekan had no power to act on matters of national importance. His administration was powerless to deal with the falling naira or to address the escalating high prices and hardships that Nigerians were undergoing. Worse still, the national assembly which was duly elected was given "no go" areas, disallowing them from addressing political or economic issues. If those who were elected by the people could not act, it was obvious that Shonekan, who was handpicked by Babangida, had to play by Babangida's rules. The problem which confronted the elected members of the Nigerian national assembly shows the apathy within the population. And it is not unique to Nigeria. The people elected those members and yet, one man supported by a few gun-toting men in uniforms could disallow elected representatives from acting on matters vital to the people. The situation in Africa will only be altered with mass education and grassroots empowerment. It is the people who must rise en masse against such arbitrary actions by military leaders.

Power sharing is particularly of interest in light of the ongoing process in South Africa. The biggest problem in this case is the ability of leaders to restrain the more radical elements in their own ranks. The rivalry between the Zulus and members of the ANC does not lend itself to a successful power-sharing arrangement. Attempts to work out such an arrangement between the de Klerk regime and the ANC was thwarted by the hard line of PAC and the staunch opposition and violence by the Zulus. These events scuttled the efforts at power sharing in

South Africa. Where it stands apart is that in each factionalized group the people at the grassroots were enlightened and acted to ensure that the results got them a stake in any final arrangement.

For the most part, interim governments in Africa have not had much success. Interim leaders lacked popular support. A key factor in their success would be to woo the military to their side or successfully engineer a split in the military ranks. Material condition is also reflected here. Soldiers back the individual who has money to bribe them to do his bidding, and interim leaders would not likely be in charge of huge sums. In many cases, they are set up to administer the country after its treasury has been emptied. Some interim leaders were handpicked to be rubber stamps for military dictators who were not genuinely committed to democratization. Interim leaders needed broad-based grassroots support, but the people would first have to be politically enlightened and empowered to struggle for change.

HUMAN RIGHTS DEFINED

The definition of human rights has been a controversial topic among scholars. The interpretation of scholars such as Henkin and Cranston is seen as idealistic philosophical constructs in the eyes of scholars such as Shivji. Liberal thinkers conceptualized human rights as rights individuals possess by virtue of being human. According to this view, the mere use of the nomenclature "human" implies that all human beings have them equally and in equal measure regardless of age, sex, race, social class, talent, or religion. Louis Henkin, in *The Age of Rights*,[36] posited that human rights are universal moral rights that are fundamental to human existence and can neither be transferred, forfeited, or waived. They are demands or claims individuals or groups make on society and are deemed essential for individual well-being, dignity, and fulfillment. They are universal and belong to every society regardless of geography, history, culture, ideology, or political or economic system. From the African perspective, it is easy to question the universality of such a definition with respect to women, children, slaves, and minority groups.

Maurice Cranston was equally idealistic. In his view, "A human right is something of which no one may be deprived without a great affront to justice. There are certain deeds which should never be done, certain freedoms which should never be invaded, some things which are supremely sacred."[37]

In the view of Charles Humana, human rights are laws and practices that have evolved over the centuries to protect ordinary people, minorities, groups, and races from oppressive rulers and governments.[38] This is a narrow view which fails to take into account those persons who do not fall into any of these categories. Shivji criticizes such philosophical viewpoints, arguing that

Human rights ideology . . . has historically played a legitimising or mobilising role in the struggle of classes to either rally for certain specific changes or legitimise the status quo.

And at no time, either philosophically or conceptually, has it applied to all human beings, for the very concept of "human" has varied historically and socially.[39]

Shivji argues that from the African perspective the human rights debate should be historically situated and socially specific. He also contends that any debate conducted on the level of moral absolutes of universal humanity is not only fruitless but ideologically subversive to the interests of the African masses. He argues that the conception of human rights must be rooted in the perspective of class struggle. He further contends that "the right-holder need not be an autonomous individual but a collective: a people, a nation, a nationality, a nation group, an interest/social group, a cultural/oppressed minority."[40] In his view, right should be seen as a means of struggle. In this case, " 'right' is not seen as a standard 'granted' as charity from above but a standard-bearer around which people rally for struggle from below."[41]

Shivji's tone is unpretentious and what some might brand radical, yet his central argument deserves careful thinking. Empowerment of the grassroots is in fact the way out. According to the liberal paradigm, human rights are demands an individual makes on the state, but in Africa the state has failed the people. Western powers anticipated that the democratization movement would bring change and reverse the losses of development in the 1980s, but that has not happened. Since the exercise was initiated, little has changed in Africa. Economically, Africans are undergoing even greater hardship due largely to structural adjustment programs. African masses have no choice. Improvement can only come from education, conscientization, and mass struggle that will transform the entire fabric of African society.

The African Concept of Human Rights

Human rights in the African context is mainly based in communal rights. The rights of the group are primordial as opposed to the rights of the individual. In her discussion of human rights within the African context, Rhoda Howard points out that there are three elements in the African concept of human rights:

1. The group is more important than the individual.
2. Decisions are made by consensus rather than by competition.
3. Economic surpluses are redistributed and not based on making profit.[42]

James Silk[43] argues that the emphasis on groups is arbitrary since groups by their very nature do not exist without the individual in them. Asante shared a similar view, noting that "both strong government, rapid economic development, high standards of living and internal security are ideas which are meaningful only in so far as they enrich the lives of individual citizens."[44] There has been wide debate among scholars[45] as to whether Africa has a tradition of human rights. Wai and M'Baye[46] argue that Africa in fact has a tradition of human rights and that the concept is not unique to the West. Shivji attacks this approach which, according to him, "fails to understand the correct material and philosophical basis of certain community-oriented conceptions and practices in some of the more or less classless societies in Africa; portrays these as human rights and endeavours to prove that they are similar to Western human rights."[47] He sees it as cultural inferiority and questions further the need for Africans to show that they are human.

Despite all the arguments of African and western scholars, two things are essential to the debate on the African concept of human rights: human dignity and access. The following statement by Barrington Moore speaks directly to the individual African.

There are two kinds of "human dignity rights" which, I believe, any person living in a small-scale, communal, non-modern society would want. . . . The first is a right . . . to a fair share of the community's economic resources. Along with this is the need . . . to feel secure in one's kinship or social system and in one's exercise of custom, ritual, culture; the need to feel that those who have power have some legitimacy and are not arbitrary.[48]

Dignity for Africans translates into ensuring a humane existence for each other. The elderly are cared for in the family, and the more privileged family members share their good fortune with the family. This is the social safety net that has ensured the survival of African families and communities. Values such as respect for elders are stressed among all groups. In some communities there are Age Grade structures; in some groups the younger ones must prostrate before their elders before speaking to them. However, individuals can be overburdened by the rules of the group. It is necessary to ensure individual protection. For example, women in families, children, and minorities should be protected within their own groups. What groups require of individuals in the name of dignity might include some rituals that are injurious to the individual. To preserve one's dignity, one simply toes the line. As Africans attempt to marry traditional values with modern concepts, these are some areas in which changes are likely to be made. However, these changes must be suited to African society because the notion of individual rights can be taken to the extreme, as is the case in the West. As a result, that society has lost control. Parents, teachers, and those in authority find their backs against a wall as children overassert their individual rights and continue to flout moral direction. Too much emphasis on individual rights has produced chaos in the West. If Africa can boast of only one thing, it is its humanism. That to my mind Africa must keep. African society cannot pursue the liberal path of the West, because the price society pays is too high. Africans cannot allow materialism to replace humanism.

The Development of the Human Rights Philosophy

The concept of human rights developed from the basis of natural law, but as society evolved natural law gradually diminished. Philosophers such as John Locke argued that human rights were conferred by God. While in legal discourse a right is only recognized if it is justiciable; nonetheless, ardent naturalists at one time argued that man-made laws must conform to the natural law. The outcome of this debate was to make a distinction between the rights of man and the rights of the citizen. The rights of man are those a person enjoys by being a member of the human race, while the rights of the citizen include the political, economic, and social rights one enjoys by virtue of being a member of society.

Another group conceptualized the term human rights to be those rights that form part of a positive legal system and were derived from either the will of the state or the command of the sovereign. The socialist stance is that human rights are part of a legal system, and that law is the instrument of the ruling class which is supported by the coercive force of the state to secure and safeguard the dominant.

Contemporary human rights are based on Article 55 of the UN Charter.[49] The Universal Declaration of Human Rights was proclaimed on December 10, 1948, and was intended to secure universal and effective recognition and observance of the rights and freedoms it lists. The UN provides an International Bill of Human Rights which includes three documents: The Universal Declaration of Human Rights, The International Covenant on Civil and Political Rights, and The International Covenant on Economic, Social and Cultural Rights.

Civil and political rights include, among others, the right to life, liberty, and security; the right to nationality and equality before the law; freedom of thought, conscience, and religion; freedom of opinion and expression; the right of assembly; freedom of association; the right to a fair trial; the right to participate in one's government; the right to self-determination; freedom of movement and choice of residence; freedom from slavery and forced labor; and the right to seek and enjoy in other countries asylum from persecution. In addition, it stipulates that there should be full consent of intending spouses in a marriage.[50]

Economic, social, and cultural rights include the right to work; the right to fair remuneration; the right to just working conditions; the right to belong to a union; the right to adequate standards of living; the right of everyone to be free from hunger; the right to equal pay for equal work; the right to social security; the right to paid maternity leave for pregnant women; the right to education; the right to participate in the cultural life and enjoy the benefits of scientific progress; and copyright protection, among others.[51]

While civil and political rights were accepted even before the nineteenth century, economic, cultural, and social rights were guaranteed by the UN in 1966. The development of economic rights can be traced to Karl Marx's criticism of capitalism. Another set of rights known as "third generation" rights include the right to development and the right to a healthy environment. The right to development declares the right of the state to pursue policies aimed at socioeconomic development while at the same time affirming the right of the individual to development.

THE RELATION BETWEEN HUMAN RIGHTS AND DEMOCRACY

Article 21 of the Universal Declaration of Human Rights stipulates that everyone has a right to take part in the government of his country, and sets out that this should be expressed by periodic elections held by secret vote. Since democracy is based on the right of the people to decide who should govern them and how, democracy falls within the scope of political rights. The important question in this work is whether democracy will secure protection of human rights in Africa. At this point there is not enough empirical evidence on that. However, Zehra Arat has presented some findings that are instructive.

Democracy is not a have/have not attribute of political systems and where a political system falls on the scales of democracy depends largely on the extent to which it recognizes and enforces civil and political rights. Thus in the presence of democratic structures, the more strongly civil and political rights are reinforced in a society, the more democratic it becomes.[52]

This argument is proven by the egregious human rights violations committed by authoritarian regimes in Africa. Uganda's president, Idi Amin, Central Africa's emperor, Jean-Bédel Bokassa, and the apartheid regime in South Africa are among the most notorious. The degree to which citizens enjoy democratic rights determines the measure of human rights protection those citizens enjoy, since both concepts are interdependent and mutually self-reinforcing. Democracy provides a climate in which there is freedom of expression and majority participation. This encourages public debate on issues such as policy direction, rights, the structure and control of political parties, and other issues affecting the citizenry. In this case there is a mechanism for checks and balances. It also makes it possible to enact laws to safeguard citizens against the violation of their human rights. However, though democracy and human rights might be related, they are not identical. Human rights principles are selectively applied. For instance, a democracy like India would claim to protect human rights, but for which group? What human rights ideals apply to the caste of untouchables in India?

Democratic conditions allow for better human rights protection, but democracy is not an end-all to human rights violations. Democratic governments often violate the human rights of women and minority groups within their societies. Canada claims to be a democratic country, but the native peoples have long claimed that their rights are abused. The French in Quebec are seeking language rights protection. Moreover, a government can be elected by majority vote and not be committed to human rights. For instance, in January 1992, the Islamic

Fundamentalist Movement in Algeria came close to being elected because they had majority vote. According to the tenets of liberal democracy, they should have formed the government. Had that been the case, it was almost a certainty that the government would have embarked on repressing the rights of religious minorities as in the Sudan because such groups believe that society should be organized in a certain way. Existing democratic governments in Africa show disregard for human rights. Botswana has long been admired as a stable democracy in Africa, yet Amnesty International[53] accused the government of human rights violations against the Basarwa ethnic group.

The Charter of Paris for a New Europe states that democracy is the best safeguard of freedom of expression, tolerance of all groups of society, and equality of opportunity for each person. It also adds that respect for human rights is an essential safeguard against an over-mighty state, and their observance and full exercise are the foundations of freedom, justice, and peace.[54] While much of the emphasis is on civil and political rights, should a democratic government not be accountable for economic rights? Is a government which fails to protect the prosperity of the masses a legitimate government? Rousseau said one evidence of a good government is one in which the people prosper. In his words, "All other things being equal, the government under which, without external aids . . . the citizens increase and multiply most, is infallibly the best government. That under which the people diminish and wastes away is the worst."[55] Africans need a democracy that protects and promotes both political and economic rights. Only when this is achieved can Africa be considered truly democratic.

AFRICANS SEARCH FOR HOMEGROWN DEMOCRACY

There are serious limitations to liberal democracy as a viable option for much of the African continent. In *The Real World of Democracy*, C.B. Macpherson (1965) posits that there are three concepts of democracy: the liberal concept, based in capitalism; the modern communist concept, based on rule by the proletariat; and the democracy of the newly independent, underdeveloped countries.[56] Macpherson explains that

The third concept . . . rejects the competitive ethos of the market society and sees no need for the competitive system of political parties. But while it thus adopts the pattern of the one-party state, it rejects the communist idea that where a people has broken away from capitalism the post-revolutionary state must be a class state. It sees instead the possibility of operating immediately as a classless society and state. Democracy, in this view, becomes immediately rule by the general will.[57]

Now more than ever Africa needs rule by the general will and general prosperity to avert the annihilation of the continent. The task at present for Africans is to determine and define the form of governance suited to Africa's culture and tradition. What may well emerge is a different mode of governance from one region to another as each country comes to grips with its unique realities. As Ake argues, what Africa needs is the kind of democracy, self-reliance, and popular control necessary for development.

What it calls for is not liberal democracy, but self-determination. Government of the people, by the people. It calls for democracy in the sense of being a decision-maker, not in the Western sense of merely choosing among prospective decision makers. . . . The democracy which the movement is groping for is a fusion of the economic and the political, an arrangement by which the people become the means as well as the end of development.[58]

Essentially the debate in Africa is on two fronts, political and economic. While Africans search[59] for an effective form of governance, they are also seeking new direction economically. According to Osita Eze, irrespective of the present crisis in socialism there still exist today two dominant "democratic" systems, capitalist democracy and "socialist democracy."[60] In a capitalist democracy the liberal freedoms such as freedom to vote and be voted for are guaranteed. While such a system allows political freedoms, economic justice remains unrealized. The majority continue to be marginalized, while control and ownership of the means of production remains in the hands of the few. In this case it is impossible for the majority to participate fully in the political process, notwithstanding that their political rights are guaranteed on paper. Eze also points out that in a socialist democracy the workers, peasants, and the masses control the economy and government. The government owns and operates business in the interest of people. Civil, political, socioeconomic, and cultural rights are guaranteed, although there are limits to political freedoms. However, he cautions that both capitalist democracy and socialist democracy produce different effects and do not lend themselves totally to popular democracy.[61] Capitalist democracy is antithetical to empowerment of the masses, while socialist democracy is equally unfavorable because, while its intent was to raise social consciousness and liberate the masses, the system has derailed from its original objectives.

Kenneth Bauzon does not see the failure of socialism to mean that capitalism is the best economic arrangement for the Third World. In fact, he argues that there is no affinity. As he sees it, "the failure of socialism in one place neither confirms the success of capitalism in another nor gives reason to foist it over those whom it has already victimized."[62]

African scholars are, however, still unclear as to what path the continent should pursue to ensure its economic survival. Looking inward does appear to be a realistic and wise option. As one scholar puts it:

Today more than ever, Africans must make an effort to think for themselves instead of being content to adopt models from outside. The failure of the socialist experiment in Eastern Europe must not be equated with the success of the Western model. Our salvation lies elsewhere. In the face of the shifting political and economic alliances in Europe and

Western countries generally, the unification of Africa has become the number one priority.[63]

Unification of Africa might be easier said than done because of the colonially imposed boundaries and ethnic alliances that have been entrenched over the years. It seems almost impossible for Africa to exist as a unified entity. However, there is need for economic integration, and efforts should be made to pursue this more vigorously. Whichever way things go, both political and economic structures in Africa must be built from the bottom up, not the reverse. Majority Africans must be empowered through their own initiative to decisively shape the political economy. Africans themselves should decide what form of socioeconomic organization they should have, who should govern, and with what powers and constraints. The role of women is central to this process. Not only are women in the majority, but they have borne the brunt of the economic crisis in Africa as mothers, homemakers, and mates. African women have demonstrated leadership and resilience in times of misfortune. Their human qualities give them a solid grasp of the human needs in society. Women are therefore in good stead to take the helm in reversing the devastation of the African continent and its peoples.

Most Africans are agreed that governance in Africa should emerge from a process in which some traditional principles that are relevant to present-day African society are grafted to some of the values of liberal democracy. This ought to be the present preoccupation of Africans from the villages to the presidential palaces as each group brainstorms and evaluates the best way forward.

NOTES

1. Richard L. Sklar, "Democracy in Africa," in Richard L. Sklar and C.S. Whitaker, *African Politics and Problems in Development* (Boulder, Colo.: Lynne Rienner Publishers, 1991), p. 261.

2. R. MacIver, *The Men of Government* (New York: Macmillan, 1947), p. 198. Quoted by Osisioma B.C. Nwolise, "Africa's Problems with Democratisation: An Overview" in Ayo Fasoro, Deji Haastrup, and Femi Otubanjo, eds., *Understanding Democracy,* proceedings of a conference organized by African Democratic Heritage Foundation (ADHERE) and held at the University of Ibadan Conference Center, August 19–20, 1991. Published by ADHERE, 1991, pp. 97–113.

3. Peter Anyang Nyong'o, "Africa: The Failure of One-Party Rule," *Journal of Democracy* 3, no. 1 (Winter 1992): 92.

4. Philippe Schmitter and Terry Lynn Karl, "What Democracy Is . . . and Is Not," *Journal of Democracy* 2, no. 3 (Summer 1991): 75–88.

5. For a contemporary African definition, see Olusegun Obasanjo and Akin Mobogungie, eds., *Elements of Democracy* (Ogun State, Nigeria: Africa Leadership Forum Publications, 1992), p. 2.

6. Jean Jacques Rousseau, *The Social Contract,* trans. Maurice Cranston (London: Penguin Books, 1968), p. 53.

7. Ibid., p. 96.

8. Ibid., p. 113.

9. John Locke, "Second Treatise on Government 1690," in *The Human Rights Reader 1989* (New York: Penguin Books, 1989), pp. 62–67.

10. John Stuart Mill, *On Liberty* (1859), trans. Gertrude Himmelfarb (New York: Penguin Books, 1974), p. 76.

11. Ibid.

12. Rousseau, *The Social Contract,* p. 114.

13. C.B. Macpherson, *The Real World of Democracy* (Toronto: Canadian Broadcasting Corp., 1965), p. 35.

14. Kenneth E. Bauzon, ed., *Development and Democratization in the Third World: Myths, Hopes and Realities* (Washington, D.C.: Krane Russak, 1992), p. 2.

15. Nwolise, "Africa's Problems with Democratisation," p. 98.

16. Ibid., pp. 102–103.

17. Larry Diamond, "Prospects for Democracy in Africa," in *Beyond Autocracy in Africa,* working papers for the inaugural seminar of the Governance in Africa Program, Carter Center of Emory University, Atlanta, Georgia, February 17–18, 1989, pp. 25–26.

18. Michael Bratton, "Civil Society in Africa," in *Beyond Autocracy in Africa,* p. 29.

19. Rousseau, *The Social Contract,* p. 112.

20. Ibid., p. 65.

21. Nwolise, "Africa's Problems with Democratisation," p. 109.

22. Ibid.

23. As quoted in "The Essence of Democracy," *Royal Bank Newsletter,* November–December 1991.

24. Obasanjo and Mobogungie, *Elements of Democracy,* p. 2.

25. Schmitter and Karl, "What Democracy Is . . . and Is Not," p. 81.

26. Yusuf Bangura, "Authoritarian Rule and Democracy in Africa: A Theoretical Discourse" (Geneva: United Nations Research Institute for Social Development, 1991), p. 2.

27. Gilbert Keith Bluwey, "Democracy at Bay: The Frustration of the African Liberals," In B. Caron, A. Gboyega, and E. Osaghoe, eds., *Democratic Transition in Africa* (Ibadan, Nigeria: Institute of African Studies, 1992), p. 48.

28. Ibid., p. 49.

29. For various viewpoints on this issue, see Michael Lofchie, "Perestroika without Glasnost"; Carol Lancaster, "The Governance of Africa by Aid Donors"; Carolyn Sommerville, "The Informal Governance of Africa"; and Richard Joseph, "The Informal Governance of Africa by Development Agencies," in *Beyond Autocracy in Africa,* working papers for the inaugural seminar of the Governance in Africa Program, Carter Center of Emory University, Atlanta, Georgia, February 17–18, 1989. For various views on the debt problem see Paul Vallely, *Bad Samaritans: First World Ethics and Third World Debt* (New York: Orbis Books, 1990) and Richard Lombardi, *The Debt Trap: Rethinking the Logic of Development* (New York: Praeger, 1985). See in particular chapter 7, "Aid Policy and Third World Development."

30. Claude Ake, "Rethinking African Democracy," *Journal of Democracy* 2, no. 1 (Winter 1991): 32–44.

31. Richard Joseph, "Africa: The Rebirth of Political Freedom," *Journal of Democracy* 2, no. 4 (Fall 1991): 13–17.

32. Samuel P. Huntington, "Democracy's Third Wave," *Journal of Democracy* 2, no. 2 (Spring 1991): 12–34.

33. Ibid., p. 33.

34. Larry Diamond, "Three Paradoxes of Democracy," *Journal of Democracy* 1, no. 4 (Summer 1990): 48–60.

35. Yossi Shain and Juan J. Linz, "The Role of Interim Governments," *Journal of Democracy* 3, no. 1 (Winter 1992): 73–88.

36. Louis Henkin, *The Age of Rights* (New York: Columbia University Press, 1990), pp. 2–5.

37. As quoted by Osita Eze, *Human Rights in Africa: Some Selected Problems* (Lagos, Nigeria: Nigerian Institute of International Affairs, 1984), p. 5.

38. Charles Humana, *World Human Rights Guide* (London: Hutchinson, 1983), p. 7.

39. Issa Shivji, *The Concept of Human Rights in Africa* (London: CODESRIA, 1989), p. 50.

40. Ibid., p. 71.

41. Ibid.

42. Rhoda E. Howard, *Human Rights in Commonwealth Africa* (Totowa, N.J.: Rowman and Littlefield, 1986), pp. 17–23.

43. James Silk, "Traditional Culture and the Prospects for Human Rights in Africa," in Francis M. Deng and Abdullahi Ahmed An-Na'im, eds., *Human Rights in Africa: Cross-Cultural Perspectives* (Washington, D.C.: The Brookings Institute, 1990), pp. 290–328.

44. Ibid., pp. 296–298.

45. See Rhoda Howard, "Group Versus Individual Identity in the African Debate on Human Rights," in Deng and An-Na'im, *Human Rights in Africa*, pp. 159–183. See also Claude E. Welch, Jr., and Ronald Meltzer, eds., *Human Rights and Development in Africa* (Albany: State University of New York Press, 1984).

46. See Keba M'Baye and Buraine Ndiaye, "The OAU," in Philip Alston, ed., *The International Dimension of Human Rights* (Westport, Conn.: Greenwood Press; Paris: UNESCO, 1982), p. 583. See Dunstan M. Wai, "Human Rights in Sub-Saharan Africa," in Adamantia Pollis and Peter Schwab, eds., *Human Rights: Cultural and Ideological Perspectives* (New York: Praeger, 1979), pp. 115–144. Virginia Leary also tries to show that Africa does have a tradition of human rights. She posits that the concept of human dignity can be expressed as social justice or human rights. It simply happened that the West has chosen to express human dignity by adopting the notion of human rights. See Deng and An-Na'im, *Human Rights in Africa*, p. 5.

47. Issa Shivji, *The Concept of Human Rights in Africa*, p. 44.

48. Barrington Moore, Jr., *Justice: The Social Bases of Obedience and Revolt* (White Plains, N.Y.: M.E. Sharpe, 1978), ch. 1, "Recurring Elements in Moral Codes." Quoted by Rhoda Howard in "The Full Belly Thesis: Should Economic Rights Take Priority Over Civil and Political Rights? Evidence from Sub-Saharan Africa," *Human Rights Quarterly* 5, no. 4 (November 1983).

49. David P. Forsythe, *Human Rights and World Politics* (Lincoln: University of Nebraska Press, 1981), p. 8.

50. United Nations, *The International Bill of Human Rights* (New York: United Nations, 1988), pp. 5–7.

51. Ibid., pp. 12–16.

52. Zehra F. Arat, *Democracy and Human Rights in Developing Countries* (Boulder, Colo.: Lynne Rienner Publishers, 1991), p. 4.

53. Amnesty International, 1993 Report (London: Amnesty International, 1993), p. 73.

54. Charter of Paris in *Twenty-Four Human Rights Instruments* (New York: Columbia Center of Human Rights, 1993).

55. Rousseau, *The Social Contract,* p. 130.

56. Macpherson, *The Real World of Democracy,* p. 36.

57. Ibid.

58. Claude Ake, "The Feasibility of Democracy in Africa," *Daily Times,* October 19, 1992, p. 7.

59. Africa Leadership Forum in Nigeria has convened a number of conferences to spearhead efforts toward resolving Africa's political crisis. See its report on a Conference on Democracy and Governance held in Ota, Nigeria, November 29–December 1, 1991. See also ALF Conclusions and Papers Presented at Conferences of the Africa Leadership Forum on Sustainment of Democratization and Good Governance in Africa, Cotonou, Benin Republic, October 5–6, 1992, and Challenges of Leadership in Democracy and Good Governance in Africa, Nairobi, Kenya, March 10–12, 1993.

60. Osita Eze, "Is the Protection of Human Rights and Democracy Strange to the African Tradition?" paper delivered at a conference on "Human Rights and Democracy in Africa, Yesterday, Today and a Vision of Tomorrow," organized by Human Rights Africa, Ota, Ogun State, Nigeria, March 26–28, 1991.

61. Ibid.

62. Bauzon, *Development and Democratization in the Third World,* p. 9.

63. See Diomansi Bombote, "Democracy in Africa: Which Form Will It Take?" in *Development and Cooperation* (February 1991): 9.

_____

Chapter 3

Human Rights in Africa:
An Assessment

The despots who have ruled in Africa since independence have been mainly concerned with consolidating their hold on power. As a result, they have used the coercive organs of the state to deny both political and civil rights to their subjects. While that is the sad picture of civil and political rights, the problems of underdevelopment have made economic, social, and cultural rights a mere illusion for most Africans. As Adebayo Adedeji states,

The ideals contained in the international and regional bills of human and peoples' rights remain ideals precisely out of the reach of the overwhelming majority of the people in Third World countries, particularly in Sub-Saharan African countries. In most of these countries, pervasive lack of democracy, over-centralization of power and impediments to the effective participation of the majority of the people in political life of their countries have been the order of the day.[1]

Prior to independence, African leaders such as Ghana's Kwame Nkrumah led the struggle for self-determination to end the abuse of their colonial masters. However, soon after these leaders assumed control, they too began to abuse their power. Since independence, Africa has seen the tragic disregard for human lives displayed by the likes of President Idi Amin in Uganda, General Marcias Nguema of Equatorial Guinea, General Jean Bedel Bokassa of Central African Republic, General Samuel Doe of Liberia, and others who have unleashed a reign of terror on their own people.

A survey of civil and political rights on the entire continent reveals a disturbing picture. In spite of the march toward democratization, many governments continue to kill, torture, detain citizens illegally, and muzzle them with repressive laws. There are bad laws almost everywhere on the continent, from the heinous laws enacted as pillars of apartheid in South Africa to the arbitrary decrees in Nigeria, to Zaire in Central Africa, and to Egypt and Sudan in North Africa. There are emergency laws which give unlimited powers to executives and negate the fundamental rights of their citizens. In addition, the judiciary is often corrupt because the courts are poorly funded and influence peddling among judges is commonplace all over the continent. Most citizens mistrust the decisions of the judiciary because they lack independence. The problem also stems from the hardships judges face as the crisis deepens on the continent. They operate in a monolithic structure because there is no real separation of powers. Therefore, judges tend to be malleable in dealing with cases in which the government is charged with human rights abuses. It is a matter of "who plays the piper dictates the tune," and judges too must secure their livelihood. Consequently, victims of human rights violations often find the fallout of poverty stalking them at every level of society.

During the immediate post-independence era, human rights in Africa saw further expansion among the various interest groups who waged the struggle for independence. Unfortunately, since the decade of the 1980s Africa has regressed on all fronts. For example, Amnesty International reported in 1992 that human rights abuses in present-day Uganda under President Yoweri Museveni would surpass the era of President Idi Amin. Governments affix their signatures to international covenants as well as the African Charter on Human and Peoples' Rights. They also enshrine human rights provisions in their constitutions; yet, human rights are honored more in the breach than in the observance.

This chapter will examine political rights, in particular freedom of the press and political participation. We will also examine economic rights and look at factors militating against the realization of economic rights in Africa. The disadvantages African women face due to cultural and traditional practices are examined, as well as the need for women's participation in the leadership of the continent. Emphasis will be placed on the need to ensure that rural women have a voice in the agenda for change. The rights of children are examined in relation to the plight of the majority of African children regarding their access to basic needs (i.e., food, primary health care, and basic education). The plight of refugees will also be examined.

POLITICAL RIGHTS

The UN Covenant on Civil and Political Rights requires all member states signatory to the covenant to allow their citizens the right to freedom of thought (Article 18) and expression (Article 19), the right to peaceful assembly (Article 21), the right to associate (Article 22), and the right to participate in the conduct of public affairs (Article 25). I would argue that although many African countries are signatory to the UN Covenant, those provisions are merely rhetoric.

Freedom of the Press

Liberal democracy rests on the notion that the press is free. It is the medium through which citizens participate in the affairs of government. The press should be free to transmit information to the citizens about the goings-on of the government as well as to criticize government activities. A free and competitive press encourages public debate, and should reflect the conscience of the people. To begin with, the press in Africa is not free.[2]

Article 9, Section 2 of the African Charter on Human and Peoples' Rights permits every individual the right to express and disseminate his opinions within the law. In this case, the press freedom granted in the African Charter is subject to the whims of Africa's dictators. Opinions must be expressed within the law, but there are bad laws. Such laws allow governments to harass editors, censor reporting, or simply take over organs of the press. Worse has befallen some journalists. Nigerian Dele Giwa was murdered in 1986, and many suspect that government security agents were responsible because Giwa was unearthing some embarrassing information. By 1991 two other Nigerian journalists met their demise in Liberia at the hands of forces loyal to Charles Taylor.

The Lawyers' Committee for Human Rights[3] reported that in the past five years the Kenyan government had used Section 52 of the Penal Code, which permits prepublication banning, to ban at least three publications—*Financial Review, Development Agenda,* and *Beyond.* The report also added that in September 1990 the government banned the *Nairobi Law Monthly* for almost a year. The government also imposed restrictions on the *Daily Nation,* preventing that newspaper from covering parliamentary debates following an article on government corruption in 1989. In early 1992 the Moi government impounded thousands of copies of *Society* magazine and later obtained a court injunction banning the magazine owners from publishing, distributing, or selling any issues. Similarly, journalists in South Africa have long borne the brunt of the apartheid regime.

The popular demands of the citizens will see to it that bad laws are changed; but majority Africans remain dormant, and do not make such demands. Absolute power is in the hands of the various governments. Another problem is that media persons face the brunt of poverty like anyone else, so many of them can be bought. In such cases they turn a blind eye to injustice.

The press can only be free in Africa when the people are free. At the same time, freedom of the people can be achieved with the help of the press. This is a crucial stage of evolution in Africa, and the press must be the vanguard. The press can help to transform Africa by:

1. Educating the grassroots;
2. Going to the people and bringing their concerns to the public eye;
3. Informing the people, in their local vernacular, about the goings-on in the country.

A free press is the only medium whereby the oppressed may be heard. As Alexis de Tocqueville noted in *Democracy in America,*

An oppressed member of the community has therefore only one method of self-defence, he may appeal to the whole nation; if the whole nation is deaf to his complaint, he may appeal to mankind: the only means he has of making this appeal is by the press. Thus, the liberty of the press is infinitely more valuable amongst democratic nations than amongst others.[4]

Presently in Africa, the majority are oblivious to the notion of liberty of the press. When governments muzzle the press, little or no reaction comes from the citizens. The only people who whisper their discontent are the elites who oppose the government. In a democracy, press freedom can only be safeguarded by an educated and well-informed populace. This is the challenge that the press in Africa must take on.

Political Participation

The right to participate is central to the nurturing of a democratic system of governance as well as to the evolution of appropriate human rights systems suited to Africa. Article 25 of the International Covenant on Civil and Political Rights guarantees everyone the right to take part in public affairs and to vote or be voted for. In addition, Article 13(1) of the African Charter on Human and Peoples' Rights states, "Every citizen shall have the right to participate freely in the government of his country, either directly or through freely chosen representatives." In Africa, the majority do not actively participate in policy decisions that affect their lives. Even though people vote in elections, the poor are often bribed. Many of them have not made analytical and critical decisions as to why they voted for an individual. Up until the late 1980s many African countries were either one-party states or military regimes, and such administrations allowed no room for active and vocal dissent. Leadership in Africa until recently saw Nigeria, Ghana, Togo, Burkina Faso, Benin, Liberia, Guinea-Bissau, Mauritania, Central African Republic, Rwanda, Burundi, Niger, Chad, Libya, Sudan, Ethiopia, Somalia, Mauritius, and Madagascar all under military rule. Guinea, Mali, Cameroon, Gabon, Congo, Uganda, Kenya, Zaire, Tanzania, Angola, Zambia, and Malawi were one-party states; Lesotho, Morocco, Western Sahara, and Swaziland were kingdoms. Algeria, Tunisia, Ivory Coast, Djibouti, Egypt, Namibia, Botswana, Zimbabwe, and Mozambique were multiparty states, while South Africa remained whites-only rule under its apartheid system.[5] From the beginning of the 1990s African governments have embarked on a democratization program by acceding to the demands of western donors for multiparty elections. We will now examine multiparty elections, especially in light of developments in those countries in which people recently voted.

Multiparty Elections in Africa

The right to vote imposes on me the duty to instruct myself in political affairs . . .

Jean Jacques Rousseau[6]

This statement by Rousseau would indicate that voters are knowledgeable about political goings-on and therefore make intelligent decisions when they go to vote. In such cases civil society should be literate and enlightened. Where that is not the case, to what extent are multiparty elections a viable solution? This is part of an ongoing debate as Africans search for political solutions. At a December 1991 conference organized by the Africa Leadership Forum on Democracy and Governance in Africa, participants reiterated that "Africa must be clear on the issue of multi-partyism in order to avoid the danger of equating multi-partyism with the practice of democracy."[7]

At the beginning of the democratization movement in Africa the hope was that multiparty elections would pave the way for real change. However, the exercise has only allowed the ruling party to engage its rivals politically. The incumbent leaders had no intention of changing anything, and that is the frustration of the exercise. Gilbert Keith Bluwey has been insightful as he explains the dilemma of African dictators.

As recent converts to liberal democratic politics, many of the African leaders are yet unable to leave the doors open to free and fair competitive politics. Many of them cannot see themselves in the role of ex-Presidents and private citizens in the fashion of Mathieu Kerekou, Kenneth Kaunda, Julius Nyerere or Leopold Sedar Sengor. Fear of restitution and retributive justice haunts several of them who had either abetted or ordered the assassination or torture of political opponents. Others have used the state machinery to despoil innocent citizens of their legitimate property holdings. The day of reckoning stares them menacingly in the face and drives them into committing further excesses in fruitless attempts to ward off the waves of change.[8]

There is yet another problem which has dogged the democratization exercise. Most of the political parties themselves do not operate democratically. In a democratically operated political party, all the positions should be filled by elections under free and fair conditions. Both the party's constitution and its manifesto must be drawn up with majority input. On account of illiteracy and ignorance in Africa, the opposite is the case. Political parties are operated by elites, most of whom are in pursuit of selfish interests. If the end of government is social justice for the majority, then political parties must reflect the views of all their members. The necessary structures must be in place at the constituency level to ensure that the party thrives on majority ideas rather than on party loyalties. The African majority is a long way from this stage.

It is still unclear whether multiparty election is the answer to the process in Africa. Though it is an improvement over the authoritarianism of the one-party state, there is no clear evidence that it is the alternative. Noted Nigerian political scientist Eme Awa points out some of the problems that could accompany a multiparty system in Africa:

1. There could be despotism or authoritarianism in a nation in spite of a multiparty system.
2. A multiparty system can exist and yet the same party always wins in the elections, thus disallowing the alternation of political power.

3. The incumbent party could have mismanaged the economy and yet, through its propaganda machinery, it prevents an alternative party with a different economic program from gaining power.

4. A multiparty system in which the major parties have their roots in their ethnic groups could exacerbate national conflict and retard development.

5. The multiparty system by itself is not foolproof against military intervention.[9]

Elections in Ghana, Kenya, and Cameroon have proven much of this argument to be correct. In almost every case, elections had opposition parties crying foul. In Cameroon, the election was followed by violent confrontation as citizens protested against electoral fraud. In Ghana, a cloud of uncertainty hung over the security of the Rawlings regime due to the maneuverings that accompanied the elections. In Kenya, the major opposition parties continued to dispute the legitimacy of the Moi government, claiming the elections were fraudulently conducted. In making a passionate plea for the installation of multiparty rule in Kenya, Gibson Kamau Kuria had this to say in 1991:

The democracy movement in Kenya would use the courts and the press to expose the hollowness of the government's claim that the one-party system can be combined with democracy, human rights and the rule of law. Strikes and demonstrations . . . will force it (the government) to concede the need for multi-party democracy in principle. Moi will then either flee the country, resign outright, or surrender all executive powers to an interim government formed by all Kenyan factions. This caretaker administration can then begin planning for multi-party elections and the restoration of democracy in Kenya.[10]

So far, the only thing multiparty election has restored in Kenya has been Daniel arap Moi.

For the most part, recently concluded elections in Africa have failed to reflect the wishes of the people. In almost every case, the incumbent party used the state machinery to retain its grip on the country. In addition, there has always been a multiparty system of government in South Africa, but as Nelson Mandela retorted during one of his trials, "For non-Europeans in South Africa, it is the most vicious despotism one could ever think of."

Some scholars suggest that a one-party state could be the answer for fragmented societies. Howard and Donnelly point out that competitive political parties could be a mere cover for intra-elite factional infighting in societies in which the majority of the people are still illiterate and disorganized.[11] The conduct of Nigerian "moneybags" leading up to presidential primaries in 1993 provided a typical scenario; the wealthy elites merely took advantage of the plight of the poor, illiterate masses.

Osita Eze explains that there is not necessarily any opposition between a one-party system and a democracy. He suggests that a well-structured one-party state, with a political party based on effective mass participation and support, is a real alternative for African countries.[12] V.O. Awosika urged Nigerians to reject multiparty politics and adopt a No-Party Electoral College System. In his words, "The No-Party Electoral Representative Democracy is definitely and beyond any shadow of doubt whatever the most viable political system at Nigeria's disposal."[13] He points out that the system lends itself to adaptability and versatility and would be equally applicable to a capitalist, socialist, or mixed economy. Awosika calls upon Nigerians and Africans to reject the multiparty system, adding that such a system is bad for any nation in the world where tribes form nation-states. He reiterates that "the existence of political parties super-imposed on a multi-tribal set-up in anywhere on this continent must be regarded as a CANCER in the body politic; capable of setting tribe against tribe, town against town, village against village, family against family and brother against brother ANYWHERE they are allowed to exist."[14]

Awosika's proposal appeared to be an appropriate mechanism for selecting leaders in Africa. It was brilliant and worked well in Nigeria until the Babangida administration replaced it with the National Electoral Commission (NEC). This is evidence that Africans have the capacity to arrive at solutions to their political problems. Some mechanisms might apply more readily to certain communities than others and might need to be fine tuned to suit a particular region. All emerging democracies have been tried and tested. African leaders need to be receptive to sound advice and apply new methods with patience and be ready to modify them until they fit.

If the multiparty process is deemed the best solution, the mechanism should be fine tuned. The number of political parties should be restricted to avoid fragmentation along ethnic lines. And governments should be restricted to two terms of office. Multiparty democracy is more likely to survive where the masses are educated and can make rational political decisions. In this way, they are less likely to be manipulated by selfish, unscrupulous office seekers.

ECONOMIC RIGHTS

> Necessitous men are not free men.
>   Franklin Delano Roosevelt[15]

The International Covenant on Economic, Social and Cultural Rights guarantees all people the right to work, the right to fair remuneration, the right to just working conditions, the right to belong to unions, the right to adequate standards of living, the right of everyone to be free from hunger, the right to equal pay for equal work, the right to social security, the right to paid maternity leave for pregnant women, the right to education, and the right to participate in the cultural life of the community, among others. So far economic rights have eluded majority Africans. There has been increasing hunger and deteriorating health services, and education has seen a dangerous decline due to lack of funding. Africa's economic growth rate of about 1.5 percent[16] is the world's lowest. The near 600 million people in Africa have a combined gross national product of less than $150 billion.[17] Africa's population is growing at a rate of 3.2 percent annually while its food production is 20 percent lower than it was over twenty years ago, when its population was half its present size.[18] Any increase in wealth in Africa through donor aid or economic boost (such as Nigeria experienced during the oil crisis or gains from the 1991 Gulf War) ends up in the coffers of the parasitic elites. None of this has trickled down to the poor. Therefore, it requires more than a top-down, externally imposed democratization movement to turn this situation around.

While civil and political rights require restraint on the part of the state, economic rights require positive action. For this reason some argue that African countries do not have the resources to make economic rights a reality. I do not share this view. I will discuss economic rights within the context of underdevelopment. My point of departure will be the three aspects of underdevelopment in Commonwealth Africa as suggested by Rhoda Howard: (1) the internal aspect, which includes poor infrastructure, inadequate planning, the exploitation of the agricultural sector for the sake of industry, and insufficient human capital; (2) the external aspect; (3) the human dimension (i.e., the actions of African rulers).[19] I will focus on the external aspect and the human dimension. Much of the argument surrounding the role of external actors is anchored in the dependency thesis—unfair trading practices, the role of multinational corporations, and so on. I will discuss the impact of the debt problem as well as unfair trading practices. The actions of African rulers have contributed to the underdevelopment in Africa to a disturbing degree. I will refer to this as the role of the vampire state in Africa's underdevelopment. I intend to show how actions on the part of Africa's ruling class could stimulate development on the continent.

The Impact of the Debt Problem

By the end of 1990 Africa's debt stood at an estimated $272 billion.[20] Arrears on the foreign debt in Africa rose from $704 million to $10.7 billion between 1980 and 1989.[21] Debt relief in Africa has been minimal and had little impact. For example, in 1990 Sub-Saharan Africa paid about $10 billion[22] in debt repayment while it gained less than $100 million[23] through debt cancellation. In May 1993, *The Economist* reported that Africa's debt has more than tripled since 1980, and that Africa spends four times more on the interest on its debts than on health. According to *The Economist*, this is how debt servicing affects the economies of these countries:

Burundi, a wretchedly poor country manages to service almost all of its debt, but doing so gobbles up 30% of its budget each year. Moreover, in order to keep up payments on their debts, governments use up scarce foreign exchange. Uganda spends two-thirds of all the foreign currency it earns from exports on servicing its debts. The average share of Sub-

Saharan Africa is about one-fifth. The price of these outflows of foreign exchange to the west in billions of dollars is unsurfaced roads, unpurified water and untreated illness.[24]

The debt burden will be discussed in more detail in Chapter 8, where we will examine the obstacle poverty poses to the establishment and sustenance of democracy in Africa.

Unfair Trading Practices

African countries have long been dependent on foreign trade to generate foreign exchange and for economic growth.[25] Over the years, there has been an imbalance of terms of trade between agricultural and industrial products.[26] Terms of trade have been changing adversely for the food- and mineral-producing nations; for example, the number of tractors to be obtained from a given quantity of cocoa or coffee or copper continued to decline.[27] African economies feel the ripple effect each time there is a drop in the world price of their commodity, and prices have declined steadily since 1980. Rhoda Howard notes that the average price level of the 1980s was 15 to 20 percent below what it was in the 1960s and in the second half of the 1970s. Between 1977 and 1981, Tanzania's terms of trade deteriorated by 50 percent and its real material purchasing power declined by 18 percent.[28] Zambia's copper trade has seen drastic decline between 1974 and 1979, and purchasing power of export revenue was at times less than half of what it was in 1974.[29] Currently, the Chiluba administration faces a crisis because copper export has been reduced to almost nil. Ghana's economy suffers each time there is a drop in the price of cocoa on the world market. Yet African countries have no control over such changes because they have no voice in international trading fora. As René Dumont argues,

All the agriculture of the rich countries (Europe, North America, Japan, etc.) are vigorously protected. In Brussels there is much talk about the production cost of wheat, milk, beet sugar, olive oil and wine. No one ever talks about the production cost of coffee, cocoa, tea and tropical oils, rubber or cotton. The priority is evidently Western domination which perpetuates inequalities between Africans. And those inequalities continue to emerge every time there is a change in regime. The jungle state, peripheral economy, and starving people are the three rules that have governed the world ever since.[30]

Shivji makes a similar contention as he launches a stinging attack on M'Baye's idea of a right to development. "Underlying the right to development is a conception which sees development/democracy as a gift/charity from above rather than the result of struggles from below. On the international plane, it is based on an illusory model of co-operation and solidarity (a la M'Baye). This is like crying for the moon, for how can there be solidarity between a rider and a horse?"[31]

Not many would disagree that imperialism and western hegemony have contributed to the sad state of Africa. However, some of Shivji's argument pertaining to Africa's underdevelopment reflects bias on his part since he fails to castigate those greedy African leaders who have plundered Africa and contributed to its ruin. At this point, it would be more beneficial for Africans to avoid romanticizing colonialism and place much of the blame where it belongs—on the shoulders of the leaders of the vampire states in Africa.

The Role of the Vampire State in Africa's Underdevelopment

Africa has been hemorrhaging from the plunder of billions of dollars stolen by its greedy, unscrupulous leaders. There are allegations that over the past twenty years African leaders stole over $100 billion.[32] The state in Africa has failed to implement policies needed to ensure the basic needs of the masses are met. As Rhoda Howard points out, "sub-Saharan African societies, like all other societies, are stratified by social class, and the elites who formulate economic policy may well be doing so in their own interests, not in the interest of the malnourished masses."[33] There is ample evidence of this fact. For example, Theirry A. Brun found that in Africa, "the rich get richer, the poor get poorer: malnutrition and obesity increase at the same rate."[34]

African leaders show little concern for the people. When it comes to development plans, there has been much talk and little or no action. For example, the Lagos Plan of Action (1980) was a blueprint for economic development in Africa and held much promise. Unfortunately, it has been left to gather dust. African leaders later argued for the Declaration on the Right to Development, and action is still pending on their part. In 1991 African leaders, at the commonwealth meeting in Zimbabwe, agreed to the Harare Declaration.[35] In the Declaration they pledged, among other things, to promote democracy and human rights, equal rights and opportunities for all citizens regardless of race, color, creed, or political belief, and equality for women, along with sustainable development and poverty alleviation. What have the African people received so far? Increased hardship from structural adjustment and continued restriction of human rights.

Meanwhile, much of the money earmarked for development assistance continues to be stolen or misspent. Many African leaders simply pursue whatever pleasures their hearts desire. Mobutu, for example, reportedly flies his hair stylist into Zaire from the United States more than once a month, and continues to lavish in luxury. President Felix Houphouet-Boigny built a vatican in Ivory Coast—interestingly enough, neither the donor agencies nor the people of Ivory Coast questioned how the building was financed. In Nigeria, the country with Africa's largest population, teachers are more often on strike than in the classroom because the government fails to pay salaries. At the same time, local chiefs and obas are given cars valued at millions of naira as gifts. There has been no significant outcry demanding that the strikes end, because the rich either send their children to private schools or educate them abroad. And the masses, who are really the ones affected, have no voice. This justifies Shivji's criticism concerning the right to development.

The "State" here has been presented out from a fairy-tale as the embodiment of all virtues and interests of the people which, needless to say, flies in the face of historical evidence and is certainly nowhere close to the real-life authoritarian states of Africa used ruthlessly by imperialism and compradorial ruling classes in the exploitation and oppression of the African people and nation.[36]

If Africans could recover as little as one-third of the wealth that has been stolen by their kleptomaniacal leaders, there would be development in Africa. For example, by the end of 1992 Nigeria's external debt stood at about $30 billion. Meanwhile, numerous reports disclosed that just about ten families in Nigeria could pay off that debt.

Yet, most Nigerians suffered even greater hardship as a result of increasing austerity measures. The average Nigerian faced increases in the cost of food and transportation, further deterioration of infrastructure, and spiralling inflation. At the same time, there was total chaos in schools and universities as government faced off with teachers and university dons over increased salaries and improvement in teaching resources.

All of these factors resulted in an increased crime rate—the only area that affected the rich. They were forced to take more precautions, such as building higher fences and adding barbed wire and live electrical wires to their property. At this point some of the poor became valuable to them. They were charged with keeping the other poor, who had turned to robbery and violence, away from the abusive elites by being gatekeepers. The robbers began to snatch the luxury cars of the elites as they cruised the streets, causing many of them to ride in simpler cars as a disguise. But one would hope that the desperate actions of the poor would cause the elites to reflect deeply on the consequences of their own greed and injustices. It is within this context that I argue that economic rights are realizable in Africa. The capacity to do so remains largely the initiative of Africa's parasitic ruling class. They have the means to improve schools and universities, pay teachers better salaries, improve health delivery services, and set up improved farming methods to boost agricultural production. We must also take into account that the information age has bypassed Africa. That too can be addressed.

When African leaders press for improvement in international arrangements, they are not genuinely representing the masses; they are merely looking out for themselves. As a result, western powers are reluctant to write off Africa's huge debt, fearing that the masses will not be the ones to benefit. Their misgiving is expressed in the following statement in *The Economist:*

If the West would be confident that full debt forgiveness would automatically be matched by growth in spending on things like schools and clinics, then the zeal with which it pursued debt-forgiveness might be greater. But the conviction too often remains that any extra money in the government's pot will somehow find its way into the pockets of the country's leaders.[37]

Yet, there is reason to wonder about the sincerity of such concerns. Western governments remain loyal to most of Africa's sit-tight leaders and welcome Africa's stolen billions into their banks. Undoubtedly, if there is to be any genuine development in Africa, the onus is on the African working class.

The Right to Development

The Human Development Index for 1992 revealed that an estimated 26 percent of rural dwellers in Sub-Saharan Africa have access to safe water. More than half the population has no access to public health services, and many are afflicted by tropical diseases. Malaria kills hundreds of thousands of children each year. The adult literacy rate is 45 percent, while there are only eleven literate females for every twenty literate males. An estimated 100 million people were unemployed in 1989 while another 100 million were underemployed. Real wages fell by one-third between 1980 and 1989 and have continued to decline. For majority Africans the right to participate in policies affecting their lives is the key to their development; therefore, development is a political issue. As the Human Development Index noted, "countries that rank high on political freedom also rank more highly on the development scale. Political freedom unleashes the creative energies of people which leads to higher level of income and progress."[38]

The Declaration of the Right to Development (1986) describes development as "a comprehensive economic, social, cultural and political process, that aims at the constant improvement of the well-being of the entire population and of all individuals on the basis of their active, free and meaningful participation in development and in the fair distribution of benefits resulting therefrom."[39] The Declaration supports the right of individuals, groups, and peoples to participate in all aspects of development, the right to respect for civil, political, economic, social, and cultural rights, and the right to an international environment in which all these rights can be fully realized. Africans may use this Declaration to challenge western attitudes toward development, but African countries lack the clout needed to make changes to the international economic order. At the same time, African leaders themselves do not aim for the constant improvement of the population, and economic benefits are far from being shared equitably. Therefore, this Declaration appears to have joined the band of other human rights rhetoric.

Development in Africa will need radical changes in policies, both externally and internally. As Joe Clark points out, "We cannot demand democracy and deny development. Democracy is not secured by building parliaments or observing polling booths. Democracy and human rights require a foundation of belief and a foundation of development."[40]

The Right to Food

Food shortage in Africa is a perennial problem. The problem is a result of several factors, such as drought, civil war, and lack of correct food initiatives on the part of governments. Although in 1974 the World Food Council made a commitment to end hunger within a decade, food self-sufficiency continues to elude Africa. According to the World Food Programme, thirty million people in Africa required food aid in 1991.[41] The food agency noted that while some improvement in harvests were recorded in many Sub-Saharan countries, the food situation remains critical, particularly in the Horn of Africa.[42] There are serious food supply difficulties in Ethiopia, Somalia, and Sudan, as well as in Angola, Liberia, Malawi, Mozambique, and Sierra Leone.[43] Most of these countries are ravaged by civil war.

The right to food, like other economic rights, is not justiciable, even though there has been much debate on the subject.[44] While some experts argue the right to food from the perspective of the moral right to basic sustenance, others look for the legal justification and mechanism whereby a citizen can hold a government accountable. Henry Shue argues that the right to food correlates to a duty on behalf of the actors to ensure that adequate nutrition is available. In this case there should be

1. Duty not to eliminate a person's only available means of subsistence;

2. Duty to protect people against deprivation of the only available means of subsistence by other people; and

3. Duty to provide for the subsistence of those unable to provide for their own.[45]

The right to food is guaranteed in a number of international covenants, such as the four Geneva Conventions and their two Protocols of 1977.[46] However, Article 25(1) of the International Covenant on Economic, Social and Cultural Rights makes it more definitive. It states that "everyone has the right to a standard of living adequate for the health and wellbeing of himself and his family, including food."

Who should be held responsible to ensure the right to food? Phillip Alston points to the involvement of four main categories of actors: (1) the states in respect of their domestic duties; (2) states in respect of their external duties; (3) individuals; and (4) the international community.[47] Asbjorn Eide[48] explains that the role of the state at the primary level is to respect the freedom of individuals to take necessary actions, such as using the resources of their country to secure food. At the secondary level the state is obliged to protect its citizens' freedom to use their own resources from more powerful economic interests and multinational corporations. Laws should be enacted to protect against dumping of hazardous products on areas in Africa, and the interest of the nationals must not be compromised or sold out to multinational corporations. Many Africans feel that progress in their countries has been stunted because the policymakers, who should be the protectors, at times front for multinational corporations in exploiting the country's resources. Where its role as protector fails, the state is obliged to actually fulfill the obligations of the right to food. It could (1) provide opportunities for those who have no access to resources and (2) give food aid or provide social security.[49]

In Africa the state has failed both to protect and to provide. Food security has been a victim of poor planning. As Howard points out,

> Comprehensive economic policy-making, therefore, requires flexibility and freedom of debate, as well as a real understanding of African complexities, rather than ideological myths whether right or left. Yet in Africa, economic policies are often made by executive fiat, with no room for debate; such decisions often result in dramatic swings in policies when failures must finally be rectified or in interference by multilateral lending agencies. Nowhere are the effects of poor planning more tragic than in food production and distribution.[50]

Any effective plans for food self-sufficiency must involve the people from its initial stage. Peasants must be consulted to ensure that rural development plans suit their needs. This can only happen when the grassroots are empowered to defend their own interests.

At the international level, the UN General Assembly Resolutions 34/46, 35/179, and 36/133 call for a new international economic order to ensure that the right to food is realized. If the UN resolution is to be realistically applied, then the duties as expressed by Henry Shue would be operationalized in the following manner:

1. The duty to avoid depriving would mean that actors involved have a duty to avoid international policies which deprive other states of their means of subsistence or which promote an inequitable distribution of world food supplies.

2. The duty to protect from deprivation indicates that there is a duty to ensure that international trade and aid policies contribute, in a large measure, to the equitable distribution of world food supplies.

3. In honoring the duty to aid the deprived, those states who realize food surplus are duty bound to contribute to emergency buffer schemes and to assist in cases of internationally declared emergencies.[51]

Notwithstanding such provisions, food supply is only given band-aid measures during famine. Otherwise, all the talk of eliminating hunger remains rhetoric. Some experts, such as Canada's Donald MacDonald, argue that the food problem is a product of a very elaborate transnational economic system. He notes that often the economic reality of food trading is fundamental for the economic situations of most countries. In such circumstances social issues and human rights responsibilities become peripheral.[52] Some argue that policies in the West contribute to damaging food supply in other countries. For instance, Charles Brockett[53] contends that U.S. policies in Central America deprived citizens the right to food because of its support for a government that destroyed peasants and the country's source of food production. René Dumont argues that IMF and World

Bank policies diminished the food supply in Ethiopia, the Sahel, and Somalia and aggravated famine and malnutrition in the 1980s.[54]

I agree with MacDonald that to break the cycle of inertia regarding the right to food, this aspect of human rights must be contemplated within the larger issues of economic rights, self-determination, participation, and equality.

Workers' Rights

Article 23 of the Universal Declaration of Human Rights guarantees the rights of workers. Other provisions are made for workers by the International Labour Organization (ILO) in Conventions No. 87 and No. 98.

According to Convention No. 87, workers and employers have the right to join organizations of their own choosing without previous authorization. It further guarantees workers and employers' organizations "the full right to draw up their constitutions and rules, to elect their representatives in full freedom, to organize their administration and activities and to formulate their programmes."[55] Convention No. 87 specifically states that public authorities should refrain from any interference which would restrict the right of workers to organize or impede the lawful exercise of this right. It goes even further and stipulates that "workers' and employers' organizations shall not be liable to be dissolved or suspended by administrative authority."[56]

Convention No. 98 protects workers from intimidation by employers. It provides that workers shall enjoy adequate protection against acts of anti-union discrimination in respect to their employment. The convention also protects workers against acts calculated to make the employment of a worker subject to the condition that he shall not join or shall relinquish trade union membership. More significantly, it protects workers from dismissal in case their union membership requires their participation in activities outside working hours or during working hours, with the consent of their employer.[57]

When workers' rights are abused, trade unions take action. For this reason, trade unions are one of the most important political organizations available for ordinary people to achieve their fundamental human rights. Trade unions protect and defend workers' right to a decent standard of living as well as their rights to assemble, to speak out, and to strike. Actions initiated by trade unions on behalf of their own members frequently have favorable repercussions on nonunionized sectors of the working poor. Through trade unions, both subsistence rights to better wages and political rights to freedom of association are achieved. Trade unions enjoy the support of civil society, and oftentimes they are allied with professional organizations, academic affiliations, and other human rights groups.

Despite legal provisions and the various international conventions protecting workers, trade unions in Africa are not allowed to operate freely. They are often placed under government control and subjected to political interference. Some governments have imposed a single trade union structure, and this violates the workers' right to establish or join an organization of their own choosing. The right to strike is either prohibited or severely restricted in some countries, including Angola, Mozambique, Tanzania, Ethiopia, Somalia, Libya, Mauritania, Equatorial Guinea, Chad, Congo, Rwanda, Seychelles, Cameroon, and Gabon.[58] In some countries the government has extensive powers to interfere in collective bargaining.

While trade unions are harassed under one-party leadership, there is little evidence that the current democratization exercise will change much. One-party states might be more draconian, but most leadership co-opts union leaders, and in such cases they fail to articulate the interests of union members.[59] For instance, there was widespread discontent among workers with the leadership of Pascal Bafyau of the Nigerian Labour Congress. Nigerian workers were disgruntled over Bafyau's unclear stance on Babangida's constant manipulations with the transition program. Most Nigerians felt Bafyau could not be trusted and they lost confidence in his leadership. In another situation involving the Academic Staff of Nigerian Universities (ASNU) and the Babangida administration, lecturers argued that the government had succeeded in "settling" (a term used for buying off) most of the other union leaders except the leader of ASNU. Since the government failed in this attempt, the impasse dragged on with government reneging on signed agreements. Finally, the government threatened to dismiss the striking lecturers and flouted court orders restraining the administration from executing the dismissal action.

As Howard has observed, the extremely poor economies of Commonwealth Africa make government inducements powerful tools because trade union officials are often not as well paid as in other countries. She correctly notes that "Given the underdeveloped, politically unsophisticated, and co-opted nature of most African trade unions, a liberal human rights stance in favor of protecting their visible (if not real) exploiters is highly unlikely."[60] The stance of the ASNU in Nigeria is exceptional. At the same time, the government's action underscores the reality that the road ahead for actualizing workers' rights in Africa is a rocky and frustrating one.

The right of workers to organize is seen as a threat to the ruling class, which benefits from exploiting workers. As Shivji points out, the African ruling class compensates for its economic weakness and political instability by denying its peoples the right to struggle and organize in opposition, protest, and revolt.[61] Workers' rights, like other economic rights, are not justiciable and are mere provisions on paper. Just governance in Africa will only emerge from a structure that is anchored in people power.

THE RIGHTS OF WOMEN AND CHILDREN

Women embody a source of unrecognized potential in Africa, despite the declarations of intent. In sheer numbers, they account for more than half of the population. Through their involvement in production, especially in agriculture, and their unique role in social reproduction, they are essential to Africa's development.[62]

Women's rights should be accorded priority in the debate on democracy and development in Africa, because women's participation as the majority group is essential to development in Africa. The United Nations Convention on the Elimination of all Forms of Discrimination against Women (1979) is the omnibus document advancing women's rights. The African Charter also provides for women and children in Section 18(3), stating that "the State shall ensure the elimination of any discrimination against women and also ensure the protection of the rights of women and children as stipulated in international declarations and conventions." These provisions have not had much impact on the lives of most African women. Women in Africa are not in a position to make decisions that will impact the future of the continent. Many of the educated ones lack the finances, and the majority are too busy trying to feed starving families to be concerned about political issues. At the same time, it is important to bear in mind that improving women's lot is directly linked to the entire ongoing evolutionary process on the continent. Women's issues should be men's issues as well, because what is needed in Africa is collective struggle, not merely gender-specific issues. Efforts should be concentrated on reorientation of the entire society to work toward what is just for both men and women. Development in Africa requires a collaborative effort, with all its human resources working toward a common goal (i.e., the survival of the continent and its peoples).

Many of the problems facing African women are brilliantly summarized by Miriam Matembe of Uganda as she urges the women to mobilize and demand their human rights.

> . . . You are at the centre of production
> But are at the periphery of benefits
> You hold half of the world
> But own nothing
> You have no property
> You have no home
> You have no children.
> . . . You are a woman
> And a human being
> All human beings have rights
> and so do you.[63]

Women in Africa are abused through customary laws, traditions, and societal norms. There are discriminatory laws, polygamous relations, child marriages, genital mutilations, and other forms of abuse. There is also a significant gender gap in terms of political and economic power.

Discriminatory Laws

Women in Law and Development Africa (WiLDAF) has identified four common legal problem areas for women in Africa: family, property, employment, and violence.[64] In the area of family matters, women often do not know their rights in marriage. The divorce laws favor men and they are often awarded custody of the children. In cases where men must pay maintenance, they are often slow in making payment. Gender discrimination in marital laws has resulted in the continued pauperization of women.

Because of the traditional belief that women may not own land, women often receive inadequate inheritance, and the courts are usually unsympathetic to them. Under customary law, women do not inherit their husband's land, and a daughter is deprived of inheriting her father's property. However, women can be inherited like property. In Nigeria, for example, in the case of *Ogunkoya v. Ogunkoya*, the Lagos Court of Appeal held that "wives are also regarded as chattel who are inheritable by other members of the family of the deceased under certain conditions."[65]

Tax laws in many African countries prevent a married woman from claiming tax relief for her children unless there is expressed permission from her husband. This law disregards the fact that women shoulder much of the responsibility for raising the children. In cases where parties are divorced or separated, women continue to suffer such discrimination. There are also cases in which the husband claims for the wife, even though he might be contributing nothing to her maintenance.

Forced marriage is another discriminatory practice under customary law. In many African countries young girls are forced into early marriages and have no say in choosing a partner. This is a contravention of the UN Convention on the Elimination of Discrimination Against Women, which stipulates that in marriage women shall have the same rights as men to enter into marriage and to freely choose a spouse; shall enjoy the same rights and responsibilities as men during marriage and its dissolution; shall enjoy the same rights and responsibilities as men in matters relating to children; shall enjoy the same rights as men regarding guardianship, wardship, trusteeship, and adoption of children; shall enjoy the same rights as men in choosing family name, profession, or occupation; and shall enjoy the same rights as men with respect to acquisition, enjoyment, administration, and disposition of property.[66]

Early betrothal denies young girls the opportunity to complete their education. Consequently, they remain illiterate as adults and continue to lack both political and economic empowerment in their communities. Another disturbing consequence of child marriage is that many of these girls bear children at a very young age and experience complications during labor, which results in many suffering from vesico vagina fistula (VVF), an opening between the vagina and the bladder which causes a woman to lose control over her bladder functions. Those women who are afflicted with VVF become social outcasts as both their husbands and, at times, their families abandon them.

Domestic violence and rape are not criminal offenses in Africa, and the police and courts are unsympathetic toward women.[67] Whenever such matters are brought before the courts, women are often ridiculed by unscrupulous judges. For such reasons women are often reluctant to press charges against their violators. In summer 1991, a group of boys in Kenya were angered because the school administration did not pay the necessary fee for their participation in an inter-school athletic competition. They urged the girls to join them when they decided to go on a rampage, and the girls declined. Consequently, the boys burned down the building where the girls had sought refuge. Many of the girls were crushed to death as they suffocated under the rubble. It was reported that seventy-one girls were dead and nineteen were raped. When the case was brought to trial in 1992, the boys were acquitted of the manslaughter charge.[68]

Police Discrimination Against Women

Speaking on "The Challenge of Promoting Women's Rights in African Countries," Florence Butegwa drew attention to the fact that "having rights on paper is not going to help women if they cannot exercise them."[69] On numerous occasions, women are frustrated by police when they make an attempt to exercise their fundamental human rights. Butegwa explained that "members of the police force often refuse to accept and to record a complaint from a woman against her husband or member of her family."[70]

Police often obstruct women's rights in other areas of law as well. Although there is no law in Nigeria forbidding women from standing as surety for a person in police custody, the police in Nigeria have made it their own law to deny women the right to bail. I had a rude awakening when I came face-to-face with the "police law" when I attempted to assist a casual worker in our organization whom police had been holding in custody for several days. I was informed that police would not accept me because I am a woman. That such an incident took place in 1993 shows how much education is needed. Again, it is the failure of human rights organizations to work to educate government agencies and to persuade governments to include women's rights training in police education.

Injurious Traditional Practices

In some countries in Africa a woman is subjected to various forms of inhumane treatment on the death of her husband to prove she did nothing to contribute to her husband's death. Such practices involve shaving the woman's head, isolating her in an empty room, feeding her through a cubicle like an animal, and subjecting her to rituals such as drinking the water used to bathe the dead husband's body. Some women die while undergoing the ritual. Individuals who practice such rituals must be educated to see the dangers and futility of such rituals.

Women are often at a disadvantage in childless marriages. In a case where the husband might be the inadequate partner, at times he may pack away the first wife, marry a new wife, and arrange for her to bear him a child through a surrogate male, unknown to the first wife.[71]

Women Under Islamic Religion

The Islamic religion allows a man unilateral divorce. A man can divorce a woman for no reason except that he wishes to do so. The man has sole custody after divorce and even when he dies, the child becomes the responsibility of his closest male relative. According to the words of the Koran, Allah has ordered that

Male heirs shall have twice the amount given to female ones. If there are female inheritors, numbering more than two, they will receive half of it. The rest is to go to the community. Father and mother of the deceased each receive one-sixth of the estate if there is a child. If the testator has left no child, and his parents are the only heirs, the mother will receive only one-third, the rest to go to the father. If the testator had brothers the mother receives one-sixth. . . . Half of what your wives leave belongs to you if they die childless. If they have children one-fourth of the estate belongs to you; the wives receive one-fourth of your estate if you die childless. But if you have children the wives receive only one-eighth of your estate.[72]

While Muslims accept this as part of their religious tenet, the main problem lies in how it is applied from one Islamic state to the next. In this case, women can work toward improving this unfair situation by educating society. Such changes involve psychological reorientation of values and attitudes.

The Economic and Political Status of Women in Africa

Seney Diagne addresses the economic plight of women in these words. "We know for a fact that more than two-thirds of our agricultural commodities are produced by African women, but they own only five per cent of the continent's wealth, at best."[73] Women in Africa continue to work between ten to fourteen hours a day, facing shortages of water and a lack of primary health care. Even though they are overworked, they cannot space out their children since they have no control over their own reproduction. The economic crisis in Africa has also placed greater burdens on women as heads of households.[74] Since unemployment has increased and farm income is unreliable, most men have neglected their family responsibilities, thus leaving women to manage the feeding and education of the children. At least 80 percent of women in Africa are illiterate[75] and unprepared for the enormity of the household and societal responsibilities that have been thrust upon them.

Men have traditionally held the reigns of power and will be unwilling to vacate their position of dominance. As Angela Davis Powell correctly points out, "Sexism has survived through the ages because it embodies privileges that men are unwilling to surrender. . . . The willingness of women to believe that men will repudiate all dominance over us in the name of socialism—or any other—without a fight, is putting the ultimate victory of feminism in danger."[76]

Men in contemporary Africa pay lip service to women's rights, but they are slow to change. It is not unusual for educated men to make such statements as, "My wife can only be as liberated as I can tolerate her to be." This means his food must be ready when he needs it, and she must never dare ask him to baby-sit the children so she can attend a political meeting. However, as men recognize the need for two incomes to meet the high cost of living, they have begun to give way to greater participation of women. Also, the state of leadership in Africa calls for the ingenuity, foresight, and resourcefulness of women to turn things around, and men have begun to recognize that. The psychological reorientation needed will come through education and persuasion rather than through an atmosphere of conflict.

Some of the hurdles women face in their bid for political power often come from the influence of the extended family. In-laws and other family relations place much guilt on those women who seek positions of power that, at times, may call for changes in how domestic chores are handled. All this substantiates Powell's argument that "Sexism will not die out unless people are conditioned and propagandized from childhood into anti-sexism just as surely as the present system and previous generations were indoctrinated into sexism."[77] Over time, the change must come from a process of inculcating nonsexist values in men and women from childhood.

Presently, there is a huge gap between men and women in leadership positions in Africa. Up to June 1991, a survey indicated that women represented 12.2% of the Ugandan parliament; in Zimbabwe women comprised 12% of its MPs. In Tanzania women represented 11% of its parliament, and in Malawi 9.8%. Women made up 7.8% of the Gambian parliament, and in Namibia 6.9%.[78] Women in Africa comprised 2.7%[79] of the continent's parliaments.

Rhoda Howard correctly points out that women had greater political rights in traditional Africa. She reminds us that

Oral histories in West Africa recount stories of women chiefs' forming small states such as Mampong, Wenchi and Juaben in Ghana. Queen Amina of Katsina in Nigeria in the early fifteenth century received tribute from other chiefs. Also among the Igbos in Nigeria, women and men managed their own affairs and women's interests were represented at all levels. In 1929 Igbo women attacked the British Warrant Chiefs in what is widely called the "Aba Women's War" in protest over the imposition of taxes which would have abrogated women's traditional power.[80]

African women have lost much ground since precolonial times, both politically and economically.[81] Ali Mazrui opines that throughout Africa, there is inadequate planning for the empowerment of women in the political process. He points out that women who have had access to power, such as Ugandan Foreign Minister Princess Elizabeth Bagaya and the women ambassadors from Ghana and Tanzania, achieved this power more by default than by government design.[82] Mazrui suggests that a form of affirmative action[83] be put in place in Africa to facilitate the political involvement of women.

If Africa is to be rescued from the mire of poverty and penury, women must play a significant role in the development process. Leadership in Africa will require the expertise of its capable women. Oftentimes women are active at the grassroots level and then brushed aside in their bid for political office. For example, many women led the struggle against apartheid in South Africa while the men were in exile or in jail. However, in 1990, when negotiations began toward the transition to democracy, the same women who were soldiers in the army and community activists were considered unskilled to take on negotiations. At the same time, it was acceptable for men to learn those skills on the job. Women in Mali were at the forefront of the overthrow of President Moussa Troare in 1991, and then they were literally discarded while the reigns of power went to the men. Nigeria's capable women, such as Sarah Jibril and others, were also squeezed out of their bid for power during the 1993 presidential elections, largely for financial reasons.

Diagne suggests that women's bid for political power is hampered by three main obstacles: (1) Women's lack of self-confidence; (2) lack of solidarity among women, who are often involved in infighting among themselves; (3) women's lack of political knowledge and experience.[84] Diagne points out that in order to rectify this situation, women's organizations must encourage other women to gain the confidence to assume political leadership; literacy must be improved and women must receive political education.

The Role of Women's Organizations

The political and social mobilization needed for mass participation can only come about with dedication to majority women. Majority women in Africa dwell in the rural areas, and they should receive greater attention. Some of the vocal women have never met the rural women. When urban women speak they often have their own agenda, which does not correspond to that of the rural women. Like most other NGOs who seek western funding, women's NGOs in Africa organize seminars and conferences, but these cater to the knowledgeable urban women; rural women are not usually invited to listen and participate. To know the concerns of rural women, they must be included in these discussions. As Marlene Dixon wisely said, "women's liberation is a middle class movement. The voices of the poor working class women are infrequently heard."[85] Proponents of women's rights in Africa have not invested enough in the poor and illiterate women in the periphery. In matters of health, political enlightenment, or other issues there is a serious lack. Some young women are not even knowledgeable about their own biology. My own experience (as follows) substantiates this view.

A young girl in her mid-twenties approached me one day and asked the following question: "If I have my period and I wait until six days after and then have relations with a man, I won't get pregnant, will I?" On hearing this, I realized that she had misconceptions regarding human biology. If she waited six days and then began to have relations with a man, it was precisely the time that she ran the greatest risk of getting pregnant. I realized very quickly that explaining to her that there are days that she is not ovulating, and that this is the safe period, was something foreign to her. I had to resort to a calendar. I asked when her period began. I then placed Xs from the time the period began to about day twelve, and said to her, "these are times you can have relations with a man without getting pregnant." She insisted that she should wait for the five days during her period and begin counting afterwards. I informed her that the best thing to do is to look at a calendar the day her period begins and count from that very day. "Until about fourteen days from the beginning of your period, you are safe. From day twelve do not do anything with a man until about five days after that." I knew it would confuse her to explain that she is ovulating, so I took the shortest route and told her that immediately after the period is the very best time to have relations with a man. She still seemed confused. I realized she was not quite literate, and it seemed as though her idea of allowing six days to pass after her period was based on the taboo that during menstruation a woman is unclean. I had to insist that it is exactly during and immediately following menstruation that she can avoid becoming pregnant.

When she left, the thought struck me: What about AIDS? How would someone explain AIDS to her? If her sexual partner was also illiterate, he might not understand what she says about the disease. How could she tell him about condoms when men feel that they are supposed to dominate women? Then I realized that it is the role of those women's organizations that purport to be fighting for the cause of women to go to women in the rural areas and inform them. They can educate women and men in their local vernacular about such life-threatening diseases. How many organizations are offering literacy classes to the rural women? How many of the women's groups have seminars to which they invite men and women? Women's rights activists need to set up a machinery whereby they interact with the rural communities. Go to the rural women and get them to select a female representative from within their community. The urban women's organizations can organize seminars and training classes and train the rural representatives to become paraprofessionals in health care delivery, facilitators for literacy classes, team leaders for self-help projects, and so on. The village representative could also communicate the needs of the village women to the urban women's group. A careful survey revealed that many organizations that operate in the name of women do not impact grassroots women positively. In fact, in some cases rural women need to be rescued from some of these women's groups. One organization is referred to as "bitter life for rural women."

There are a few organizations which are making commendable efforts. Country Women Association of Nigeria (COWAN) offers family planning information, education, and services. They also aid rural women in skills development and offer loans. The Women's Health Research Network in Nigeria (WHERIN) runs workshops and seminars to help women with sexual and gynecological problems and fertility control, and advocate on behalf of women. In Algeria, an NGO called Women Living Under Muslim Law examines the actions of social forces which use religious tenets as instruments of repression against women. The main thrust of this NGO is to appraise strategies that women under fundamentalism can adopt to combat repressive state and customary laws. The Rape Crisis Centre in Cape Town, South Africa, assists women who are battered and sexually assaulted. The Centre also compiles statistics to highlight the magnitude of the problem and to lobby for change. The Ugandan Women Lawyers Association (FIDA–UGANDA) focuses on legal literacy training for rural women. FIDA–UGANDA operates from the viewpoint that if women know the law, they can use it to affect changes in their daily lives by confronting oppressive laws and customs that have resulted in women's subordinate status in society. The main areas targeted are marriage, divorce, child custody, property rights during marriage, and divorce and inheritance. On a continent-wide basis, Women in Law and Development Africa (WiLDAF) focuses on legal education and training. WiLDAF's emphasis is on legal rights awareness, grassroots NGO outreach, violence against women, and trafficking of women. The organization also addresses women's issues at both national and regional levels.

Clarice Davis, who undertook an assignment in 1991 to look at women's organizations in Africa, reported that most of the NGOs and associations have not effectively implemented their objectives.[86] Davis found that there were problems of inadequate funding, rivalry, and deficiency in group dynamics, as well as insufficient staffing. Since most of the women's organizations are run by volunteers, it affects the running of the organization because the hard economic times make it increasingly difficult for women to work for free. Problems of transportation and communication also make it difficult for these organizations to reach their intended beneficiaries in the rural areas. Many of the organizations also find there is lack of goodwill and support from member states, and this has curtailed their effectiveness.[87]

Conclusion

For women in Africa to realize their political and economic rights, there must be mental liberation of both men and women. In addition, it is important to recognize that the liberation of women in Africa is linked to the liberation of all of Africa's oppressed peoples. Both men and women suffer from the exploitations of the economic system that exists in Africa, except that women suffer additional forms of oppression based solely on gender. Women in Africa should be cautious to seek change in an atmosphere of cooperation, not of hostility. The vocal middle-class women need to change their approach to the issue of women's rights. They might appear to have a national agenda, but they cannot speak *for* village women without speaking *to* them. Otherwise, they are not truly representative voices of women.

Governments in Africa have not done enough to improve women's situation. Perhaps the underlying reason is that the dictators ruling Africa have been unconcerned about human rights at any level. However, some African countries have passed laws to end discriminatory practices against women, while others have clung to traditional practices, and as a result nothing much has changed. Joan Kakwenzire[88] noted that in all Francophone legal systems in Africa something had been done to rectify family laws discriminating against women. However, the efficacy of these laws has been hindered by illiteracy and lack of information.[89] In Islamic and Lusophone states some improvements have been made, even though they are not always fair to women. Anglophone countries, except Ghana, Tanzania, and Kenya, have no particular legal provisions regarding the family. Therefore, in most Anglophone countries women are still in a subordinate position in the family.

If governments are serious about improving women's lives, they are obliged to respect the international instruments to which they have affixed their signatures. Governments in Africa have long spent huge sums of money on arms and failed to improve the lot of more than half of the population. That is why it is imperative that women be part of the decision-making process in the new, transformed, and genuinely democratic Africa of tomorrow.

Children's Rights

The UN Convention on the Rights of the Child guarantees children a full range of human rights (civil, economic, social, and cultural) and calls for a healthy and safe environment, access to medical care, and minimum standards of food, clothing, and shelter to ensure the freedom a child needs to develop his or her intellectual, moral, and spiritual capacities. Added to these provisions, the heads of state of the OAU have adopted the Charter on the Rights and Welfare of the African Child, noting that "the child occupies a unique and privileged position in the African society . . . and that due to the needs of his physical and mental development, the child requires particular care with regard to health, physical, mental, moral and social development and requires legal protection in conditions of freedom, dignity and security."[90] OAU members stipulated that the child has the right to education (Article 11); to enjoy the best state of physical, mental and spiritual health (Article 14); and to protection from all forms of economic exploitation (Article 15). The charter also prohibits child marriage and calls upon states to enact legislation specifying the minimum age of marriage (Article 21[2]). The charter also calls upon states' parties to take all necessary measures to ensure that no child shall take a direct part in hostilities and to refrain from recruiting any child who has not attained the age of fifteen years (Article 22).

Most of these provisions are mere lip service. The African child is a victim of hunger, disease, illiteracy, lack of shelter, and early death. In Sub-Saharan Africa it is estimated that over four million children die each year, giving Africa the highest under-five mortality rate in the world.[91] Africa's children have been victims of civil strife and natural disasters. African women and children comprise the majority of refugees. According to UNICEF, infants and young children accounted for 1.2 million out of over 1.9 million deaths in southern Africa during the 1980s. In war-torn zones such as Ethiopia, between 40 and 60 percent of children aged one to three years die of malnutrition.[92] On the whole, there have been rampant violations of the UN Convention and the OAU Charter on the Rights and Welfare of the African Child. The basic needs of food, education, and health care are luxuries only enjoyed by those few African children born into wealthy families. The following poem by Rudolf Okonkwo paints an apt picture of the gross inequality of existence between the child born to the elite minority family and the child born among the majority poor.

African Children

Maybe you don't know
Kids wake up with empty stomachs
And attend school under mango trees
Writing brittle alphabets on slates
Singing songs to forget they are hungry
Maybe you don't know
Those kids belong to the lucky few
Kids actually wake up from dreamless sleep
Carrying oranges and groundnuts on sealed heads
Walking up and down some rugged streets
Hawking away their lives with their goods
Maybe you don't know
Those kids belong to the noble class
Kids actually wake up under the bridge
Glad they have escaped extinction once again
Get back into unholy tunnel of existence
Maybe you don't know
These same kids can move the mountain
If given a strong place to stand
For they are the gift of a continent
Long walloping in the darkness of ugliness
Maybe you don't know
Because you were never part of them
The children of Africa
Maybe
But that is what they are
Jewelleries left unrefined
Achievers wasting away
Children of Africa
Only heaven knows
When those stars will have their blue sky

Where they will live and shine
For now
In the dirty mud of mother Africa
Nothing can ever be achieved
Than more and more rusting
Day by day.[93]

The majority of African children lack proper nutrition even while in the mother's womb. Many of the young are victims of early childhood diseases. Most African children receive such inadequate health care that doctors now fear that the future generation of Africans could be a society of morons. As for education, many children are not sent to school. They are often used by parents as hawkers on city streets or sent to ply other trades to earn an income for their families. Those who do go to school often discover that teachers are underpaid, classrooms are overcrowded, and school supplies are often grossly lacking or nonexistent. In many cases there are no libraries, and school laboratories are often lacking in modern equipment. As for the right to food, oftentimes the African child only has a right to the food he earns himself. Whenever that is not the case, hunger, starvation, and sometimes death might be his lot.

By and large most of Africa's children suffer from the gross inequities that are pervasive within African society. Many have yet to start drinking potable water, enjoying proper education, receiving adequate health care, or eating nutritious food. Most African governments are signatories to the Conventions on the Rights of the Child. However, the efforts of organizations such as the African Network for the Prevention and Protection Against Child Abuse (ANPPCAN) have not resulted in many improvements in the rights of the African child. Governments set aside special days such as the Day of the African Child, yet little is being done. As far as I know, there are no truancy officers trying to get children off the streets and put them in school, and no one attempts to improve the conditions under which teachers have to work. For example, the political aspirants in Nigeria's 1992 presidential primaries spent billions of naira, but none of them donated anything to schools or hospitals. The government of Nigeria has not made it a policy to pay for medical services for children up to a certain age. One day I was eyewitness to a poor mother holding a child with both of its legs in casts. The mother was weeping because she could not afford to pay the bill. On personal investigation, the doctor disclosed that no children, regardless of age, are given health care at the government's expense. The doctor added that even if a child is two years old and has a broken limb the parents must pay the medical expenses. The question must therefore be asked: What has happened to the provisions of Article 14(1b) of the Charter on the Rights and Welfare of the African Child, which states categorically, "States parties to the present charter shall undertake to pursue the full implementation of this right and in particular shall take measures to ensure the provision of necessary medical assistance and healthcare of all children with emphasis on the development of primary health care"? At the same time one might also ask: Where were those politicians who were spending huge sums of money to win elections and have their turn at looting the country's treasury? In any case, what do they care about the rights of the child when their children are often not raised on the continent?

The woes of African children are directly connected to the plight of women as mothers. Discrimination against women results in a lack of education, a lack of basic health care and maternal health care, and a lack of economic empowerment, and thwarts their capacity to participate in the political process. Since mothers are responsible for the physical, mental, moral, and social development of children, their poverty-sticken state impedes the proper development of children. Until the rights of women are improved, the rights of children will remain largely unrealized.

THE RIGHTS OF REFUGEES

> Everyone has the right to seek and enjoy in other countries asylum from persecution.
>
> Article 14 of the UN Declaration of Human Rights[94]

Refugees undergo the most acute form of human suffering of all the despairing peoples of the world. Their ordeal ranges from fear of persecution in their own country, which usually precipitates their flight to other countries, to the accompanying destitution that is inherent in the poverty-stricken dilemma of most African countries. The United Nations High Commissioner for Refugees (UNHCR) explains the overwhelming magnitude of the problem in this statement:

In Africa today there are emergencies everywhere. The continent now has more than five million refugees. Many of them would be able to return home if we are able to assist them. We do not have the right to refuse them this assistance.[95]

Article 14 of the UN Declaration guarantees that everyone has the right to seek and enjoy in other countries asylum from persecution. Nonetheless, refugees face constant human rights abuses in countries where they seek asylum. They are often subjected to armed attacks and aerial bombardments, harassed by police and paramilitary units, and used as pawns by military rulers who deny aid workers the opportunity to bring food and aid to opposing factions. The efforts of relief agencies such as the International Red Cross and church groups are often restricted by government leaders who limit their movements in refugee areas.

Both the UN and the OAU make provisions for the fair and humane treatment of refugees. Following on the UN General Assembly Resolution 429(V) of December 1950, the UN adopted the Convention on the Status of Refugees. The Convention, which came into force as of April 22, 1951, defines the term "refugee" as a person who owing to well-founded fear of being persecuted for reasons of race, religion, nationality, membership of a particular social group or political opinion is outside the country of his nationality and is unable, or owing to such fear, is unwilling to avail himself of the protection of that country, or who, not having a nationality and being outside the country of his former habitual residence is unable or, owing to such fear, is unwilling to return to it.[96]

The Convention guarantees refugees freedom from discrimination on the basis of race, religion, or country of origin. It calls upon states to accord refugees treatment as favorable as that accorded to nationals in respect to freedom of religion, as well as religious education for their children. On matters relating to education, the Convention states in Article 22 that refugees should have the same access to elementary education as is enjoyed by their nationals. It further adds that states should accord refugees the same favorable treatment accorded to aliens with respect to access to higher education. States should also recognize foreign school certificates, diplomas, and degrees. Refugees should also be awarded scholarships.[97]

In Africa there are three main conventional provisions governing the treatment of refugees. The first is the instrument on the rights of refugees that governs those African states which are party to the 1967 Protocol. Second, the OAU Convention governs those states which are party to the OAU Convention and those states that are parties to the 1967 Protocol and OAU Convention. Third, the member states of OAU are expected to adhere to the UN convention guaranteeing fair treatment of refugees. The OAU convention expands on the UN definition of the term "refugee" to ensure that the criteria is wide enough to cover all of the refugee situations in Africa. The second paragraph of Article 1 of the OAU Convention states that

the term "refugee" shall also apply to every person who, owing to external aggression, occupation, foreign domination or events seriously disturbing public order in either part or the whole of his country of origin or nationality, is compelled to leave his place of habitual residence in order to seek refuge in another place outside his country of origin or nationality.[98]

For those African states which are not parties to any of the above-mentioned international instruments relating to refugees, their national laws and policies and their customary laws would be applied.

The Plight of Refugees in Africa Today

Most asylum-seekers receive a rude welcome in the countries where they seek refuge. Some are held in prolonged detention, or face physical assault, starvation, lack of proper medical care, and lack of potable water; many are denied employment. For most of these desperate people, their daily existence is a battle of survival. Among the victims of such crises, children suffer the most and comprise the largest number of victims. They are too young for long, exhausting treks, too weak to speak out when hungry and, being drastically malnourished, fall victim to the slightest virus. In Zimbabwe, the UNHCR estimates that there are more than 62,000 children under the age of eighteen in the five camps in the country.[99] In the camps in Kenya, children presented a sad spectacle. One account explains it this way.

At Walda, you do not see any children looking for affection. They are too weak and too hungry. The majority do not even have the strength to walk. In a makeshift hospital that resembles a ward for the dying, Kenyan doctors try to save some of them, but in most cases their efforts are in vain.[100]

The ordeal of Tchadian refugees in Nigeria was also painful and disappointing.[101] In 1992, the Civil Liberties Organization (CLO) accused the Babangida administration of deporting hundreds of Tchadian refugees who fled their country on account of the civil war. The CLO claimed that the deportation was masterminded by the Tchadian embassy in Nigeria in collaboration with the Nigerian police and army. The refugees were deported on the alleged fears of the Tchadian government that some of the influential exiles were supporting armed factions in the civil war in Tchad. The Nigerian government deported over three hundred Tchadian refugees, mostly males, leaving their families without breadwinners. At least forty-three of them were reported to have been killed by the Ndjamena government on return to Tchad. The CLO wrote to General Babangida as head of state and chairman of the OAU, asking him to use his office as chairman of the OAU to prevail upon the Tchadian government to stop the killings, but there was no reply. Even after the CLO obtained an interim order of injunction in the high court, the deportation continued.

Another twist to the refugee saga in Africa is that those tyrants who plunder their countries and engage in mass executions are received with open arms in other countries. Siad Barre, the former Somalian head of state, was given asylum in Nigeria, the same country that returned the Tchadians into the hands of a hostile government. Similarly, Mengistu Haile Mariam, after committing his atrocities in Ethiopia, was received with open arms in Zimbabwe. There are inequities in the application of the UN Convention and the OAU Charter. The rules of the game appear to differ depending on whether the asylum-seeker is a victim or a violator. What happens in Africa is that leaders remain mute when heads of state unleash their reign of terror and commit egregious human rights abuses against their citizens. At the same time, they are quick to offer asylum to the same ruthless individuals when their day of reckoning approaches.

The refugee crisis in Africa looms from Mozambique to Namibia, to Ethiopia, Somalia, and Liberia, as well as to displaced persons in Sudan. The alarming increase in the refugee population has further compounded the problem of poverty and destitution facing the continent. At this stage the refugee crisis has become a nightmare for humanitarian workers. In addition to the lack of adequate donor support of relief supplies, aid workers find it extremely difficult to mobilize assistance to refugees since many concentrate in remote areas which are difficult to reach.

The refugee problem is daunting all over Africa. In Liberia the civil war forced more than 750,000 to flee their homeland and seek refuge in neighboring countries. It is estimated that there are 227,500 refugees in Ivory Coast, 342,000 in Guinea, another 6,000 in Ghana, and smaller numbers in Nigeria, Gambia, and Mali.[102] Despite the existing laws which should protect refugees, the strained economic resources in many of these countries made it difficult to care for the large number of new arrivals. For example, in one case Liberian refugees outnumbered the number of inhabitants in a village in Ivory Coast. As a result, authorities became stricter in dealing with new arrivals and began to classify most Liberians as "tourists." Yet, many Liberians continued to flee because of the horror of the civil war.

The violence in Mozambique has also resulted in a large number of Mozambicans fleeing to neighboring Malawi. The exodus of Somalis into Ethiopia had seen a huge increase since 1988, when Somalis began to flee the country. There was also an increase of refugees into Kenya from Sudan, Ethiopia, and Somalia. While many were victims of war, the drought in Southern Africa in 1992 created a new crisis in the refugee saga in Africa.

Southern Africa was gripped by the most severe drought in its history in 1992. In Angola, Botswana, Lesotho, Malawi, Mozambique, Tanzania, Zambia, and Zimbabwe, the cereal harvests shriveled and the people faced starvation. In sending out an alarm, the UN World Food Programme warned that only a massive international relief effort would avert widespread starvation and famine. Mozambique was the hardest hit, since the drought only compounded the effects of years of civil war. That country had the world's highest child mortality rate, and one-third of the population was displaced.[103] The loss of crops and livestock, a lack of water, and a cholera epidemic resulted in a mass movement of people looking for food and water. In Ihambane province, women had to walk for a whole day to fetch water. Death from starvation and thirst was a common occurrence in the southern and central region, where there was almost total crop failure. An estimated three million needed emergency relief.[104] Of the eighteen million people who were threatened by the drought in the region, about two million[105] were refugees, most of them relying on food aid. At the same time, the crops of the estimated 250,000[106] Angolan refugee farmers in neighboring countries were also threatened, thus compounding the food problem.

While Zimbabwe was grappling with half of its population on the brink of starvation, it was still forced to handle the influx of Mozambican refugees who sought asylum in that country. The pressure of this influx caused added strain on the already scarce resources available in Zimbabwe. Supplies of available land, water, and firewood diminished daily in the ecologically critical areas around refugee camps. An estimated 30,000[107] refugees were said to have settled in the

Masowe River Bridge Camp while another 41,000[108] were in Tongogara Camp. The massive increase in population also took its toll on the surrounding vegetation. There was a shortage in the wood supply for building shelters and for fuel use. Not only that, but there was insufficient agricultural land to sustain the local population. The number of refugees in Zimbabwe's five rural camps increased from 97,000 in December 1991 to 113,000 six months later, and an estimated 3,500 arrived each month.[109]

As a result of the shortage of food, the Zimbabwean government adopted a policy of keeping the refugees in camps and ensuring that they had care and maintenance. The government also estimated that there was another one million[110] Mozambicans outside the camps who had spontaneously settled along the border.

Even though the long dry spell had caused a serious food shortage in Malawi, that country was still forced to contend with almost one million[111] Mozambican refugees who had fled their country. Malawi lacked the infrastructure to undertake massive relief operations, and relief workers encountered numerous problems in feeding the number of starving people. The resources of relief workers were severely strained, and there were problems bringing food into the country. The war in Mozambique resulted in the closure of Malawi from the east, and traffic in other ports in Tanzania and South Africa were often congested with supplies to other drought-stricken countries in the region. Such was the enormity of the refugee problem facing humanitarian workers in Africa during this period.

Displaced Persons

Another group of people forced to suffer from the consequences of man's inhumanity to man are those who have become displaced persons in their own homelands. Presently there are an estimated twelve million displaced persons in Africa.[112] Some of the poorest Sudanese are among this unfortunate group of people. Africa Watch reported[113] that the military government in Sudan has demolished the homes of approximately 500,000 of its poorest citizens. Since the government had neglected the rural areas, the displaced Sudanese were forced to flee to find sustenance in the city. Many of them sought refuge in three towns— Khartoum, Omdurman, and Khartoum North, where there is a concentration of services and economic opportunities. Since the capital was built to accommodate only a small population, there were hundreds of destitute people, some of whom were forced to crime, and racial tension increased.

The former residents of Maroko in Lagos, Nigeria are another group of displaced persons in Africa. In a similar case, the Nigerian government demolished the homes of the poor who lived in this slum area in Lagos. The estimated 300,000[114] inhabitants of Maroko occupied this slum area without any assistance from government in providing basic amenities, such as pipe-borne water, electricity, or proper roads. When the area became an eyesore to the elite residents in the nearby area, the government decided to demolish the site.

Despite protests from residents and the CLO, the government team levelled the residential site. The result was untold misery and anguish for the thousands of men, women, and children who once occupied the area. The CLO resisted the abolition of the site from the start and was caught up in legal wrangling with the Babangida government over the displacement. Almost two years later it was reported that only about 7 percent of those displaced persons had been resettled.[115]

Conditions for Guaranteeing Safe Return of Refugees

Faced with much despair and bewilderment, many refugees sometimes return to their country of origin or are even forced to do so. The UN guarantees refugees protection against forced return in the 1951 Convention, which prohibits refoulement (forcible return). In spite of this UN provision, thousands of refugees are returned to their countries of origin each year against their will. Where there is no international monitoring of returnees, the victims are often subject to life-threatening human rights abuses. The UNHCR has identified cases in which returnees have been executed. The UN General Assembly was forced to draw attention to those member states signatory to the 1951 Refugee Convention to honor their international obligations on the principle of refoulement. On a more optimistic note, however, an estimated 45,000 Somalians[116] were successfully repatriated in 1989. But there is pressing need for aid to assist returnees to do so safely.

In 1967, the UN General Assembly adopted a Declaration on Territorial Asylum prohibiting states from rejecting asylum seekers at their frontiers and prohibiting the forcible return of asylum seekers to states where they would be subject to persecution. The Convention also set forth a number of requirements[117] that should be met to ensure the safe repatriation of refugees. It also urges aid workers and decision makers in governments to abide by these guidelines.

Conclusion

With the exception of the drought that has recently wreaked havoc on food production in southern Africa, the refugee crisis in Africa is the result of the instability on the continent. The wars and inhumanities that produce refugees and displaced persons are rooted in sharing the paucity of resources that are available to the majority in those countries. The elites who control power usually exacerbate ethnic tensions among the poor who are competing for the crumbs, so to speak, while the minority bask in affluence. African leaders signed the OAU Charter on the rights of refugees and the various UN instruments, but these documents remain largely ineffective. For one thing, African refugees often find themselves in countries that are under such severe economic stress that the governments are not in position to respect the human rights provisions to which they have affixed their signatures.

In order to ensure that refugees receive humane treatment, some mechanism should be in place to help them. Most refugees in Africa will face economic hardship in countries in which they seek asylum unless the OAU establishes a special fund to help refugees. This would then ease the burden on the host countries, which for the most part are poverty-stricken themselves. Each country should set up refugee settlements and establish a mechanism to integrate refugees into society. Still, the ultimate problem to be addressed is putting an end to civil wars in Africa. Amos Sawyer of Liberia perhaps said it best on behalf of all refugees. "Our people are tired, and they want peace. We all have a moral obligation to end suffering now."[118] The current brand of leaders pay lip service to such words until their personal need for power is challenged. African leaders should put away selfishness and desist from fanning the flames of ethnic and religious tensions in order to serve their own ends. This will only be achieved by a complete societal reorganization in which leadership emerges from the bottom up.

NOTES

1. Adebayo Adedeji, "Promoting Economic and Social Rights Within Nations: Thoughts on African Development," paper delivered at the Second Ambassadors' Colloquium, organized by Human Rights Africa, April 21, 1992.

2. For details on the press in Africa, see *Attacks on The Press 1989: A Worldwide Survey* (New York: Committee to Protect Journalists, 1990), pp. 13–14; see also p. 123.

3. Lawyers' Committee for Human Rights, "Kenya," February 1992.

4. Alexis de Tocqueville, *Democracy in America* (1835), ed. and abr. Richard D. Heffner, 1956 (New York: New American Library, 1984), p. 308.

5. *Development and Cooperation*, No. 2/91 (Frankfurt: German Foundation for International Development, n.d.), p. 9.

6. Jean Jacques Rousseau, *The Social Contract*, trans. Maurice Cranston (London: Penguin Books, 1968), p. 49.

7. Report of a conference on Democracy and Governance organized by Africa Leadership Forum, Nigeria, November 29–December 1, 1991, Ota, Ogun State, Nigeria.

8. Gilbert Keith Bluwey, "Democracy at Bay: The Frustrations of African Liberals," in B. Caron, A. Gboyega, and E. Osasghae, eds., *Democratic Transition in Africa* (Ibadan, Nigeria: Institute of African Studies, 1992), pp. 45–46.

9. Eme Awa, "Strategies for Achieving Democratization and Good Governance in Africa," in African Leadership Forum, *Conclusions and Papers Presented at Conferences of the Africa Leadership Forum on Sustainment of Democratization and Good Governance in Africa* (Cotonou, Benin Republic, October 5–6, 1992), p. 53.

10. Gibson Kamau Kuria, "Confronting Dictatorship in Kenya," *Journal of Democracy* 2, no. 4 (Fall 1991): 115–126.

11. Rhoda Howard and Jack Donnelly, "Assessing National Human Rights Performance: A Theoretical Framework," *Human Rights Quarterly* 2 (May 1988): 214–248.

12. Osita Eze, *Human Rights in Africa: Some Selected Problems* (Lagos, Nigeria: Nigerian Institute of International Affairs, 1984), p. 59.

13. V.O. Awosika, *A New Political Philosophy for Nigeria and Other African Countries* (Lagos, Nigeria: African Literary & Scientific Publications, Ltd., 1986), p. 119.

14. Ibid., p. 127.

15. Franklin Delano Roosevelt, quoted in *The Human Rights Reader* (New York: Penguin Books, 1989), p. 313.

16. As quoted in *Daily Champion* (Lagos, Nigeria), January 20, 1993, p. 19.

17. Ibid.

18. Ibid.

19. Rhoda E. Howard, *Human Rights in Commonwealth Africa* (Totowa, N.J.: Rowman & Littlefield, 1986), p. 83.

20. *Africa Recovery* 5, no. 2–3 (September 1991): 24–25.

21. Ibid.

22. Ibid.

23. Ibid.

24. *The Economist* (May 1993): 46.

25. For an examination of the contribution of trade to economic development in developing countries, see "Trade, Aid, Industrialization and Economic Development," in Mangat Ram Aggarwal, *New International Economic Order: Interdependence and Southern Development* (London: Oriental University Press, 1987).

26. Howard, *Human Rights in Commonwealth Africa,* p. 74.

27. Ibid.

28. Ibid.

29. Ibid.

30. René Dumont, *Pour L'Afrique J'Accuse* (Paris: Plon, 1986), p. 11.

31. Issa Shivji, *The Concept of Human Rights in Africa* (London: CODESRIA, 1989), p. 82.

32. Robert K. Doran, "Greedy African Dictators Stealing $Billions We Give to Feed Starving People," *National Enquirer,* February 2, 1993, p. 31.

33. Rhoda Howard, "The Full-Belly Thesis: Should Economic Rights Take Priority Over Civil and Political Rights? Evidence from Sub-Saharan Africa," *Human Rights Quarterly* 5, no. 4 (November 1983): 475.

34. Theirry A. Brun in René Dumont, *Pour L'Afrique J'Accuse* (Paris: Plon, 1986), p. 320. Translated from the original French version by the author.

35. "Commonwealth Declaration of Human Rights," in *Development and Cooperation* 1 (1992): 7.

36. Shivji, *The Concept of Human Rights in Africa,* p. 82.

37. *The Economist* (May 1993): 46.

38. Kathleen Mahoney and Paul Mahoney, eds., *Human Rights in the Twenty-First Century: A Global Challenge* (Utrecht, The Netherlands: Kluwer Academic Publishers, 1993), p. 726.

39. United Nations, *Human Rights, the Realization of the Right to Development* (New York: United Nations, 1991), p. 9.

40. Joe Clark, "Human Rights and Democratic Development," in Kathleen Mahoney and Paul Mahoney, eds., *Human Rights in the Twenty-First Century*, p. 685.

41. World Food Programme, 1992 Annual Report (Rome: World Food Programme, 1992), p. 5.

42. Ibid., p. 9.

43. Ibid.

44. For an in-depth analysis of the argument see The United Nations, "Right to Food as a Human Right" (New York: United Nations, 1989).

45. Henry Shue, *Basic Rights: Subsistence, Affluence and U.S. Foreign Policy* (Princeton, N.J.: Princeton University Press, 1980), p. 53.

46. Phillip Alston, "International Law and the Right to Food," in Pierre Claude Richards and Burns Weston, eds., *Human Rights in the World Community: Issues and Action* (Philadelphia: University of Pennsylvania Press, 1989), p. 144.

47. Ibid., p. 147.

48. Asbjorn Eide, "Strategies for the Realization of the Right to Food," in Mahoney and Mahoney, eds., *Human Rights in the Twenty-First Century*, p. 465.

49. Ibid.

50. Rhoda Howard, "The Full-Belly Thesis," p. 471.

51. Alston, "International Law and the Right to Food," p. 149.

52. Donald MacDonald, "International Responsibility to Implement the Right to Food," in Mahoney and Mahoney, eds., *Human Rights in the Twenty-First Century*, p. 476.

53. Charles D. Brockett, "The Right to Food and International Obligations: The Impact of U.S. Policy in Central America," in George W. Shepherd and Ved P. Nanda, eds., *Human Rights and Third World Development* (Westport, Conn.: Greenwood, 1985), pp. 125–142.

54. Dumont, *Pour L'Afrique J'Accuse*, p. 248.

55. ICFTU, "The African Development Challenge," Pan African Conference Sponsored by Central Organization of Trade Unions (COTU) of Kenya and International Confederation of Free Trade Unions (ICFTU) in cooperation with the Organization of African Trade Union Unity (OATUU), Nairobi, October 25–27, 1989, p. 63.

56. Ibid.

57. Ibid.

58. Ibid., p. 61.

59. For a more detailed discussion see Richard Sandbrook, *The Politics of Basic Needs* (Toronto: University of Toronto Press, 1982).

60. Rhoda Howard, "Third World Trade Unions as Agencies of Human Rights: The Case of Commonwealth Africa," in Roger Southall, ed., *Trade Unions and the Industrialization of the Third World* (London: ZED Books, 1986), p. 243.

61. Shivji, *The Concept of Human Rights in Africa*. p. 103.

62. Marie-Angelique Savanne, "Women on the March," *Africa Forum* 1, no. 2 (1991): 18.

63. Quoted by Joan Kakwenzire in a paper titled "An Assessment of the Rights of Women and Children in Africa Today," presented at the Human Rights Africa's Conference on Human Rights and Democracy in Africa held at Ota, Nigeria, March 26–28, 1991.

64. Women in Law and Development Africa, *WiLDAF: Origins and Issues* (Washington, D.C.: OEF International, 1990), p. 13.

65. E.S. Olarinde, "Some Injuries to the Rights of Women and Proposed Remedies," paper presented at a workshop organized by Amnesty International and WORDOC on the theme "Women and Human Rights Abuse in Nigeria," at the Institute of African Studies, University of Ibadan, September 2–3, 1992, p. 5.

66. See United Nations, *Human Rights, A Compilation of International Instruments* (New York: United Nations, 1988), pp. 120–121.

67. Women in Law and Development Africa, *WiLDAF,* p. 13.

68. "Violence Against Women in Africa: A Human Rights Issue," *African Woman* (July–October 1992): 13–15.

69. Florence Butegwa, "The Challenge of Promoting Women's Rights in African Countries," in Joanna Kerr, ed., *Ours by Right: Women's Rights as Human Rights* (Ottawa: ZED Books, in association with the North-South Institute, 1993), p. 40.

70. Ibid.

71. See E.S. Olarinde, "Some Injuries to the Rights of Women," p. 3.

72. Clemens Ameluxen (translated by Henrietta Guethen), "Marriage and Women in Islamic Countries," *Human Rights Case Studies* 2 (1975): 97. Quoted by Eze, *Human Rights in Africa,* p. 151.

73. Seny Diagne, "Defending Women's Rights—Facts and Challenges in Francophone Africa," in Kerr, ed., *Ours by Right,* p. 43.

74. Ibid., pp. 44–45.

75. Ibid., p. 49.

76. Angela Davis Powell, quoted in Edwin Madunagu and Bene Madunagu, "Conceptual Framework and Methodology: Marxism and the Question of Women's Liberation," *Women in Nigeria Today* (London: ZED Books, 1985), p. 30.

77. Ibid.

78. *Commonwealth Currents* (June–July 1993): 3.

79. Ibid., p. 4

80. Howard, *Human Rights in Commonwealth Africa,* pp. 187–188.

81. The argument is attested to in the following historical accounts: Bolanle Awe, ed., *Nigerian Women in Historical Perspective* (Lagos, Nigeria: Sankore Publishers, Ltd., 1992) (see particular references to Queen Kambasa, Queen Amina, Mrs. Fumilayo Ransome-Kuti, and Adunni Oluwole); Elizabeth Ardayfio-Schandorf and Kate Kwafo-Akoto, *Women in Ghana* (Accra, Ghana: Woeli Publishing Services, 1990) (see reference to the enormous power of the Ashanti Queen Mother); see also Seny Diagne's reflection on the Akan and Lebous in Senegal during the precolonial era in "Defending Women's Rights."

82. See Ali Mazrui, "The Black Woman and the Problem of Gender: Trials, Triumphs and Challenges," The Guardian Lecture Series, delivered on July 4, 1991, p. 16.

83. Ibid., p. 17.

84. Diagne, "Defending Women's Rights," p. 49.

85. Marlene Dixon, "Ideology, Class and Liberation," in Margaret Anderson, ed., *Mother Was Not a Person* (Montreal: Our Generation Press, 1972), p. 229.

86. See CUSO Gender and Development Workshop Report, January 25–February 3, 1992. Leicester Peak, Freetown, Sierra Leone. Prepared for CUSO and the Coady Institute by the Association for Rural Development, Freetown, Sierra Leone. Published by German Adult Education Association.

87. Ibid.

88. Kakwenzire, "An Assessment of the Rights of Women and Children in Africa Today."

89. Diagne, "Defending Women's Rights," pp. 44–45.

90. ANPPCAN Charter on the Rights and Welfare of the African Child, pp. 12–13. Coordinated by Peter O. Ebigbo. Publication sponsored by Ford Foundation. Enugu, Nigeria.

91. *Africa Recovery* 5, no. 5 (September 1991): 34.

92. Ibid., p. 35.

93. Rudolf Okonkwo, "African Children," *The Punch* (Lagos), February 27, 1993, p. 20.

94. United Nations, Universal Declaration of Human Rights, Article 14.

95. *Refugees* (May 1991): 24.

96. United Nations, *Human Rights, A Compilation of International Instruments* (New York: United Nations, 1988), pp. 295–296.

97. Ibid. p. 302.

98. United Nations, "Human Rights, Human Rights and Refugees," UN Fact Sheet no. 20 (Geneva: United Nations, 1993), p. 9.

99. *Refugees* (July 1992): 13.

100. Ibid.

101. CLO, *The Campaigner* 1, no. 3 (April–May 1992): 3–4.

102. "Refugees," *Africa Watch*, October 21, 1991.

103. *Refugees* (July 1992): 13.

104. Ibid.

105. Ibid., p. 12.

106. Ibid.

107. Ibid., p. 13.

108. Ibid.

109. Ibid., p. 16.

110. Ibid.

111. Ibid.

112. *National Concord* (Lagos), July 29, 1991.

113. "Sudan: Refugees in their Own Country," *Africa Watch*, July 10, 1992.

114. "Maroko Three Years After," *Satellite Special* (Lagos) January 30, 1993, pp. 1–5.

115. Ibid.

116. *Refugees* (May 1991): 26.

117. *Refugees* (July 1992): 38–40.

118. *The Guardian* (Lagos), August 25, 1992, p. 8.

Chapter 4

The Protection of Human Rights in Africa

Originally, the protection of human rights in Africa had its basis in the African culture—thus, human rights has been influenced by communal norms and traditions. The underlying principle among African peoples was that the general law of the community was accepted by everyone, and people lived and shared together. Even though that was the general operation of society, one must be careful not to glorify the notion of rights in traditional Africa, because rights were abused then (see Chapter 1).

Contemporary human rights in Africa, as elsewhere, developed after the Second World War, when western countries drafted the UN Charter. The provisions of the Charter, which stipulate that all men are born equal and are guaranteed life and liberty, were considered to apply to all peoples of the world regardless of their national origin. In order to prevent a repeat of the gross inhumanity that was inflicted by the Nazis in the Second World War, the UN drafted the Universal Declaration of Human Rights. The provisions of the Universal Declaration, which took force in 1948, were considered applicable to all states signatory to the UN Charter.

Article 2 of the International Covenant on Civil and Political Rights makes human rights protection the obligation of the state by stipulating that

Each state party to the present covenant undertakes to respect and ensure to all individuals within its territory and subject to its jurisdiction the rights recognized in the present Covenant, without distinction of any kind, such as race, colour, sex, language, religion, political or other opinion, national or social origin, property, birth or status.

The Covenant further calls on those states whose legislature does not provide adequate human rights protection to "take the necessary steps, in accordance with its constitutional processes and with the provisions of the present covenant, to adopt such legislative or other measures as may be necessary to give effect to the rights recognized in the present covenant."[1]

As the concept of human rights developed, the human rights protection machinery expanded to the national, regional, and international levels. Protection of human rights at the international level falls directly under the arm of the United Nations Economic and Social Council (ECOSOC), which has established other agencies, such as the ILO, UNESCO, WHO, as well as the United Nations Human Rights Commission and the UN High Commission for Refugees. At the regional level, human rights protection in Africa is the concern of the African Commission on Human and Peoples' Rights, the Economic Commission for Africa, as well as human rights NGOs. At the local level, human rights are protected by the local courts. In this case judges determine human rights matters that fall within the purview of the local legislations. Where a case does not come within the appropriate law, the matter cannot be entertained.

As African countries attained independence, they drafted most of their Bill of Rights provisions in line with the stipulations in the Universal Declaration of Human Rights, particularly those states who drafted their constitutions with the cooperation of the UN. Somalia was the first country in Africa to enshrine provisions of the Universal Declaration in its constitution in 1950. This was followed by Cameroon in 1957, Guinea in 1958, and Togo in 1961.[2] Many other French colonies followed the same pattern as they attained independence. In the preamble of the constitutions of Niger, Mali, Ivory Coast, Madagascar, and Upper Volta, the governments pledged to adhere to the principles of the Universal Declaration of Human Rights.[3] As the English colonies attained independence they also drafted their constitutions, in which they guaranteed their citizens respect for fundamental rights and liberties in keeping with the UN provisions. Most of the constitutions of the African countries were influenced by the Universal Declaration of Human Rights, the European Convention, and the French Human Rights Declaration of the Rights of Man and Citizens. The constitutions of Ghana and Nigeria were influenced by the constitutions of India and Pakistan.[4] The question in terms of the protection of human rights is whether those states observe the provisions that are enshrined in their constitutions (this will be discussed later in this chapter).

In 1963 the member states of the OAU met in Addis Ababa and drafted the OAU Charter, which focused on three main issues—African unity, decolonization, and the elimination of racism. OAU member states also reaffirmed their commitment to the Universal Declaration of Human Rights at the time. One of the major aims of the OAU member states was "to achieve a better life for the peoples of Africa."[5] By 1979 the member states of the OAU mandated a group of experts to draft a treaty to protect human rights in Africa. The experts drew up a document called the African Charter on Human and Peoples' Rights, which came into effect in 1986. It is sometimes referred to as the Banjul Charter. We will now discuss the provisions and effectiveness of the African Charter on Human and Peoples' Rights, the constitutions, and the role of the judiciary in the protection of human rights in Africa.

THE AFRICAN CHARTER ON HUMAN AND PEOPLES' RIGHTS

Concern over human rights abuses in Africa grew out of the frustrations of many governments and peoples as leaders such as Idi Amin, Nguema, and Bokassa committed the most egregious human rights violations against their citizens in the 1960s and 1970s. By 1979 the Assembly of Heads of State of the OAU agreed that the OAU General Secretary should commence the process of establishing a regional commission on human rights. A committee was mandated to draft a charter which should reflect the African concept of human rights, and should take as a pattern the African philosophy of law and meet the needs of Africa.[6] The document should also recognize the value of international human rights standards that many African countries had already promised to respect. The Charter recognizes the rights of peoples, as well as emphasizes the duties of individuals to the community and the state.

Peoples' Rights

A marked difference between the African Charter and other human rights treaties is the provision for "Peoples' " rights. The argument is that African customary law places importance on the group or community in which an individual may express his identity, while exclusion from such groups would be deemed unacceptable. This is a reflection of the importance placed on the African concept of human rights. The provisions for peoples' rights include the right of colonized peoples to use any internationally recognized means to free themselves from domination. It further guarantees peoples the right to prevent the exploitation of their natural resources by foreigners, and gives them the right to enter into trade agreements and to protect and develop their wealth. In recognition of the importance of a clean, safe, and sustainable environment, the Charter guarantees peoples the right to protect their water supply, air space, and land from pollution and environmental degradation.

The African Commission on Human and Peoples' Rights

The machinery which has been established to enforce the provisions of the African Charter is the African Commission on Human and Peoples' Rights. The body is usually referred to as the Commission. Article 30 establishes the Commission within the OAU system, thus making the Commission the only institution set up by the Charter itself to ensure the observance of human rights by member states. The Commission is composed of eleven members elected from among Africans of distinguished character and with reputations of the highest integrity. Members are nominated by states parties to the Charter but elected by the entire OAU Assembly of Heads of State and Government (Article 33), to serve a term of six years (Article 36). Members should be individuals who are competent in matters of human and peoples' rights, who are impartial and have legal experience. They are expected to serve in their personal capacities rather than as representatives of governments (Article 31). Their functions are to promote and protect human and peoples' rights and interpret the African Charter. In addition, they are expected to perform any other tasks entrusted to the Commission by the Assembly of Heads of State and Government.

The Charter allows member states to file complaints to the Commission against other states. It is noteworthy that despite the abuses Mobutu and Eyadema inflicted on their people between 1991 and 1993, not one member state has ever filed an interstate complaint against these governments. A very likely reason is that they are not much better. This culture of silence among member states leaves the struggling masses at bay in times of difficulty. It also strengthens the argument that leadership in Africa must emerge from a collaborative struggle of the average working-class African.

How to File a Complaint to the Commission

Article 55 provides a channel for individuals and nongovernmental organizations to bring complaints of human rights violations before the Commission. The complainant could either be a victim of human rights violation by government or officials of a state that has ratified the Charter. An organization, such as a human rights body, can file a complaint on behalf of a victim who is unable to make the complaint. An individual or an organization who has extensive evidence that massive violations of human and peoples' rights have been committed can also file a complaint. There are seven conditions that should be met before a complaint can be considered. The communication procedure as set out in Article 56 calls for the following:

1. Identification of the complainant by name, even if anonymity is desired.
2. Compatibility with the Charter of the OAU and the African Charter.
3. The complaint may not be written in disparaging or insulting language.
4. The complaint may not be based on information gathered exclusively from media reports.
5. Exhaustion of all national remedies before a complaint may be filed.
6. The complaint must be submitted within reasonable time.
7. The complaint may not deal with cases already settled or which are being considered by another treaty-monitoring body.

Once the seven requirements have been met, the Commission informs the author of the complaint and the state party concerned that the case is being heard.

The state party is expected to send a reply to the Commission within four months. The reply should contain an explanation of the issues involved in the case, as well as the steps the state has taken to remedy the situation. The Commission will then send a copy of the reply to the author of the complaint. If the complainant submits additional information and observations concerning the matter within the fixed time limit, the Commission will then consider the merits of the complaint on the basis of all the information gathered. When the Commission has concluded its investigations, it is required to send its observations to the Assembly of the OAU, which may authorize it to publish its findings. This procedure leaves the victim at the whim of the government, who is often the violator. We shall develop this statement later.

Problems Inherent in the African Charter

There have been a number of criticisms regarding the efficacy of the Charter and the inability of the Commission in implementing the provisions contained therein. From my experience in human rights in Africa, most of these criticisms are justified, as will be shown in a few cases mentioned later. Another drawback is that the Commission has no clear mandate to interfere in the internal affairs of member states. The Commission cannot embark on its own fact-finding mission and can only arrange for peaceful settlement between states. What is more disturbing is that all reports, recommendations, and results of the Commission's investigations are confidential until such time as the Assembly of Heads of State and Government shall decide otherwise. Therefore, the deterrent effect of exposing and publicizing the wrongdoings of member states is nullified. Shivji expresses the frustrations which most Africans feel about the Commission in the following remark: "What then remains the Commission? . . . it is no more than a subcommittee of the Assembly of the Heads of State, the very body which has hitherto maintained its . . . solidarity of silence on one another's misconduct."[7]

The Charter does not provide for an African Court of Human Rights; therefore, breaches of human rights cannot be resolved by the judicial process. Article 62 of the Charter requires states to submit reports to the Commission every two years "on the legislative or other measures taken with a view to giving effect to the rights and freedoms recognized and guaranteed by the present Charter." The problem the Commission faces in this regard is that some states refuse to submit reports and where they do, the report might not indicate concrete measures taken to promote human rights. Not only that, but states can make laws and fail to enforce them.

Another restricting element of the African Charter is that almost all the rights have a "clawback" clause. The rights are qualified with such phrases as "subject to the law," "except for reasons and conditions previously laid down by law," "as recognized and guaranteed by conventions, laws, regulations, and customs in force," or "subject to law and order." The outcome is that it is the internal dynamics of legislations of governments that eventually determine the extent to which the rights stipulated in the African Charter are in fact rights.

By and large the Commission lacks enforcement capability, and many individuals who have sought protection from the Commission have been frustrated. Oftentimes member states fail to submit the reports which are the basis on which the Commission can act. Not only that, but the complaint procedure requests that the matter can only be brought before the Commission after all local remedies have been exhausted. Also, it is extremely difficult to pursue any case against the government (which is usually the main violator). The government uses its machineries to frustrate efforts at all levels. The victim often spends a great deal of money and wastes valuable time without much to show in the end. The following ordeal of a Cameroon couple is a typical illustration.

The husband in this family was a critic of the regime in Cameroon, so the government went after him. The husband was imprisoned on numerous occasions, and at one point spent over two years in imprisonment while attempting to appeal his sentence. Each attempt to process the papers through the courts was frustrated. For a period of over five years both husband and wife were often arrested on trumped-up charges and charged huge fines or prison terms. Finally, they were financially crippled. The wife had a business, and the court confiscated the business, claiming they owed the government. Then the government levied their home, taking all their furniture and quickly selling it at an auction sale. All their attempts to bring these matters before the courts were frustrated. If at one level of the judiciary they won the case, the government immediately appealed to the higher level. In most instances, after the couple filed cases against the government, the clerks at the court house would be unable to find any record that the complaint had been lodged. During all this ordeal one of their children died. The couple later fled to France, demoralized and financially bankrupt. From France, they brought the matter before the African Commission. By this time the harassment and legal wrangling had gone on for almost nine years. When the case was brought before the Commission, it was unable to deal with the case because the Cameroon government failed to submit its report, and the matter could not be pursued. After all these years of harassment and frustration, that couple found no justice at any level.[8]

By and large the Commission is seen as a toothless bulldog, incapable of protecting the rights of the ordinary individual. In a case such as this, NGO input is vital in ensuring that the Commission is an effective machinery for protection of human rights. And so far NGO input has been more or less negligible. Laurie Wiseberg of Human Rights Internet laments that formal input from human rights NGOs at the African Commission is limited. She points out that during the sessions, when Commission members question state representatives about their reports, the NGOs can only listen. That is a definite hindrance. If the facts about what is going on in the member states of the OAU are to be disclosed, the Commission needs to be briefed by local NGOs. As Laurie Wiseberg rightly stressed, "If the Commission is to tackle the question of protection, holding governments accountable for how they treat their own citizens, NGOs will have to feed it the information and ideas, and prod the Commissioners into action."[9]

The International Commission of Jurists (ICJ) also reiterates the importance of NGO input to ensure that justice is done. The Commission pointed out that "the part played by NGOs is beyond question since their direct daily contact with human rights problems makes them privileged sources of information."[10]

The oppressed in Africa need a mechanism of last recourse that is indeed effective, in which case it is heartening to note that the ICJ is set to establish an International Penal Court which would extend protection to individuals whose rights are violated. For instance, the Cameroon couple would have likely found justice at such a court if the machinery was in place. The International Law Commission has also finalized decades of work on a draft Code of Crimes against the Peace and Security of Mankind. The Code considers gross violations of human rights and grave breaches of humanitarian law as international crimes.[11] The International Law Commission is also presently considering the statute of a permanent International Criminal Court with jurisdiction over matters which appear in the Code. The Commission admits that politicization, selectivity, and confidentiality of procedures are the main obstacles hindering the effectiveness of the UN human rights work[12] and is set to address the problem.

The ICJ has reiterated that if human rights are to be universally respected, states must pay serious attention to the various human rights instruments and apply them adequately at the national level. The body expressed concern that international norms are insufficiently applied at the domestic level. The Commission pointed out that regional bodies, such as the African Commission on Human and Peoples' Rights, should become more instrumental in interpreting and designing mechanisms for the domestic implementation of human rights norms.[13]

The African Commission is one of the most important bodies on the continent, and it should function independently of the OAU member states. An African court of appeals should be established, and the clawback sections of the Charter should be made more specific. In addition, the Commission should set up machinery to propagate human rights so that knowledge can also be a deterrent factor in human rights protection. (In this case Amnesty International should be commended for taking up where the Commission has been lacking. The organization has produced a number of materials making the provisions of the Charter more comprehensible to the layman.) There is, however, optimism that things will improve. Demands from local and international human rights bodies for a more effective Commission are louder than ever before. Change is taking place in Africa, however slowly. If the Commission is better funded and is given greater autonomy, it will likely produce concrete results.

THE CONSTITUTIONS

Constitutionalism is not simply the provision of a written document, even one to which strict adherence is given. If the document does not provide for checks on government power, and if those checks are not then free to operate, then constitutionalism does not exist.[14]

A constitution is a document which codifies people's behavior. This depends on how society perceives certain behaviors and varies with cultural values. Constitutions also change with governments and over time. The effectiveness of a constitution lies in its ability to check the arbitrariness and indiscretion of wielders of political power. Since the constitution has defined limits which authority may not surpass, it has made it possible for citizens everywhere to enjoy their individual liberty. The question is, do all citizens enjoy the fundamental liberties as guaranteed in the constitutions in Africa?

Osita Eze is of the view that since a constitution is a program of action on how people should be governed, and which represents the relation between those who govern and the governed, the constitution is a mirror of the class structure that determines political philosophy and ideology. Constitutions are usually drafted by constitutional lawyers, and the politicians do not give lawyers free reign in drafting the document. In fact, as Duchacek notes, the politicians are the ones who have the last say. Duchacek points out that constitutions are basically political instruments. "However legalistic a national constitution of the land may sound, it basically deals with the hard core of politics, namely who leads whom, with what intent, for what purpose, by what means, and with what restraints."[15] Not only that, there are other factors that determine the enjoyment of constitutional rights; among them is whether the right is part of the preamble or embodied in the constitution itself. As Eze explains, once human rights provisions are placed in the preamble, objectives, or principles of a constitution, the rights provisions do not confer rights and obligations under common law jurisprudence and are therefore not justiciable. The effectiveness of constitutional human rights provisions are subject to certain limitations, according to Eze. These are:

1. Their location in the constitution;
2. The manner in which the relevant provisions have been formulated;
3. Machinery and procedures for determining the constitutionality of legislative or executive action;
4. The possibility of legal action and remedy for individuals who have been deprived of their constitutional right;
5. The degree of independence of institutions entrusted with deciding on human rights issues; and
6. Drastic changes which might lead to amendment or suspension of human rights provisions.[16]

Reference to human rights can be found in the preamble of several constitutions in the independent African states.[17] Most African countries have provisions in their constitutions to protect human rights. However, the problem lies in the application and the way in which the constitution is interpreted. Eze refers to a case in Tanzania to highlight the problem of interpretation. In the matter of *H. Adams v. E.A. P. & T.*, the judge decided that "the preamble to a constitution does not in law constitute part of the constitution and so does not form part of the law of the land."[18] In another instance, in a high court hearing in Nigeria in the matter of *Chief Victor Olabisi Onabanjo v. Concord Press of Nigeria Ltd.*, the High Court of Abeokuta held that "the preamble is part of the Constitution and may be used in order to ascertain the meaning but only when the preamble is clear and definite in comparison with obscure and indefinite enacting words."[19] The Court went on to declare that the preamble gives the intention of its framers and that it should only be resorted to in cases in which the constitution is ambiguous.

For Africans in former French colonies, the French jurisprudence is specific, and there is no need for ambivalence in interpreting the constitution. The French jurisprudence states that "French public law does not regard the provisions contained in the declarations of rights or the constitutional preambles as legal prescriptions of either constitutional or legislative nature."[20]

The problem with most of the constitutions in Africa stems from the way they were drafted at independence. Rhoda Howard points out that the constitutional negotiating process in Africa at independence appears to have been a ritual enabling all parties to be satisfied when independence was won and with the intention to make changes later on. She points to the weak central governments in a milieu in which the new nations needed political stability to necessitate nation-building. During negotiations the British were more concerned with compromising along the lines of political factions or ethnic groups, and Howard notes that such an arrangement was bound to produce conflict as soon as independence was attained.[21] She points to the subsequent civil war in Nigeria and constitutional changes in Ghana and Uganda as being directly related to the compromises made by leaders at the time of independence.

In expressing thoughts on "Constitutions and Human Rights in the Third World," Louis Henkin declares that "many a constitution is only hortatory, a 'manifesto,' 'a splendid bauble,' not higher law, and governments are not always and in all circumstances sensitive to constitutional declarations and promises."[22] He goes on to say that some of the Third World constitutions are limited by requirements for national unity, national security, national economy, public safety, protection of public health, or morals.[23]

The actions of many of the governments in Africa, particularly toward human rights activism, give substance to Henkin's statement. For example, Section 36 of the Nigerian constitution states, "the privacy of citizens, their homes, correspondence, telephone conversations and telegraphic communication is hereby guaranteed and protected." In Section 37 it states, "Every person shall be entitled to freedom of thought, conscience and religion," and in Section 38(1) the constitution states, "Every person shall be entitled to freedom of expression, including freedom to hold opinions and to receive and impart ideas and information without interference." Notwithstanding these provisions, members of the CLO, the Committee for the Defence of Human Rights (CDHR), the Campaign for Democracy (CD), and other human rights organizations have been repeatedly arrested and detained without being charged. Journalists and reporters have also been arrested in total disregard of the rights guaranteed in the constitution.

This situation is not unique to Nigeria. It is the modus operandi of most of the despots in Africa, and the present democratization movement has not produced much hopeful change. Those who have been succeeding themselves in recent elections continue to disregard the fundamental liberties guaranteed citizens in the constitutions. For example, arap Moi was reelected in elections held in December 1992 and, less than six months later, the editor of a church magazine was arrested for printing information that the Moi government branded as seditious.

The human rights guaranteed in national constitutions can only be meaningful when the institutions charged with their interpretation and application are able to act with a reasonable measure of independence from the executive branch and the legislature. There is increasing argument for a Bill of Rights, which legal minds agree would better protect everyone. Ben Nwabueze suggests that a Bill of Rights is the appropriate constitutional guarantee that will subject the government to the fundamental rights of the individual and protect the individual against governmental arbitrariness and autocracy. Nwabueze points out that "a Bill of Rights would enable the individual to maintain an action against the government for violations or threatened violations of his guaranteed rights, whether such violation is by legislative or executive act."[24]

Nwabueze states further that in a situation in which human rights violations have been part of the political culture for decades, the correct starting point is a Bill of Rights as a legal restraint. The aggrieved person should be able to enforce his rights as guaranteed in the Bill of Rights, and this is an adequate beginning in the transition from an authoritarian regime to a free and open society. Nwabueze notes that "there is no other legal mechanism known to us for ensuring that executive as well as legislative acts conform to the standards of liberty required by democracy."[25] He further underscores his argument by stating:

Without a Bill of Rights as an enforceable legal restraint, a government is inadequately limited, and is therefore, by definition, authoritarian unless the necessary restraint is supplied by firmly rooted tradition. . . . And no matter what other democratic institutions are created, e.g., elections, multi-partyism, etc., the rule of law cannot be an effective safeguard against the abuse of political power in the absence of a Bill of Rights.[26]

THE ROLE OF THE JUDICIARY

Under most military regimes the laws are designed to keep the population in check and thus are not democratic. An undemocratic leadership will not pass democratic laws. If democracy is to survive we need leaders with a different psychological orientation, and drastic changes in the judicial system. For the most part the judiciary are overworked and underpaid; the courts have no modern recording system, and there are shortages of judges. Members of the judiciary have extremely heavy workloads. Many also feel the brunt of poverty and the high cost of living that lures them to take bribes. For this reason the judiciary in Africa is accused of being corrupt and has lost some of its influence.

Apart from the problems mentioned heretofore, Osita Eze points out that there are some specific factors which decide whether citizens' constitutional rights are effectively protected. Among them are the nature of the rights protected, the access to courts, and the role of the bar.[27] We will now examine these issues one by one to find out whether they provide a basis for the protection of human rights and the sustenance of democracy in Africa.

The Nature of the Rights Protected

In most constitutions of African countries, political and civil rights are protected while economic rights are nonjusticiable, except for property rights. Eze argues that because the limited resources in most African countries tend to concentrate in the hands of a few, this will undermine the enjoyment of political and civil rights as well. As is often the case, only the rich would have the means to seek litigation when their rights have been violated. One would expect that in a democratic Africa the majority should be able to use the state machinery to secure justice. Economic justice must also be a preoccupation because poverty is the bane of Africa. If the masses are to live in dignity, they need to use the legal machinery to articulate demands for their economic rights.

Access to Courts

The poor rot away and die in prison unjustly; that is contrary to established law and the Constitution. Apparently that has hardly ever been the concern of the rich men in this country with very little exception. Because of the increasing corruptibility within the administration of justice system the opportunity of access to courts by the poor is diminishing rapidly.[28]

Those words by Justice Akinola Aguda echoed the frustrations of many who struggle to seek justice for the poor in rural African societies.[29] The problem has several faces, as expressed by participants at a seminar on "Paralegals in Rural Africa." Participants noted that most of the rural population are ignorant of their rights, lack formal education, have no access to legal services, are too poor to pay for them, and are liable to exploitation.[30] More often than not, human rights are alien to most victims of human rights violations. Not only that but, at times, those who are informed are afraid to assert their rights. In some cases, societal pressures can act as an impediment to attaining justice. Florence Butegwa explains that at times women are ostracized when they assert their rights. For instance, a woman who takes her husband to court for battering her would be shunned by her community, including women.[31]

In the case of Zimbabwe the problem of access to legal services for the poor has a somewhat different dimension. Because of the history of white domination under the Ian Smith regime, many blacks in Zimbabwe see the idea of asserting themselves as a foreign concept. They fear government harassment if they challenge the authority in court. One human rights lawyer put it this way: "Most blacks grew up thinking the law was the enemy. It never occurred to them to seek redress of their grievances in the courts. It was absurd. They knew it would be fruitless, that the deck was always stacked against them. Since then, the attitude toward the law has remained."[32]

Recourse to legal aid for the poor Zimbabwean remains a distant abstraction. Most Zimbabweans are unaware of legal rights, including the right to legal representation, even if they can afford it. The problem of access to the courts for most people in Africa can only be remedied if governments make legal aid available and educate the masses about their legal rights. However, this is a step that governments are unlikely to take. They are more likely to argue that there are limited economic resources. However, one needs to question their commitment to human rights for the poor. As Eze argues, justice is the domain of the ruling class. In the final analysis, the task of assisting the poor to seek justice through legal channels will remain the work of human rights NGOs and lawyers' organizations.

The Role of the Bar

As the African political scene evolves toward homegrown democracy, so too the role of the bar has begun to assume higher forms of activism. In the area of protecting and defending human rights, lawyers are creating new roles for the profession. Lawyers not only defend victims of human rights violations; the bar has a role to play in educating the masses about civic rights, pressuring government to make improvement in laws, and bringing legal services to people in rural communities.

Lawyers have now begun to see law as an instrument of development which should be used to improve the lives of the people. To this end, the African Bar Association at a conference in 1985 resolved that bar associations and law societies should encourage law schools to include the social sciences in their curricula so that lawyers would be better equipped to serve their countries. They also resolved that lawyers should play a leading role in popular education on human rights and responsibilities and that lawyers should not be deterred by political instability in their quest for social justice and the defense of human rights. In addition, they resolved that bar associations should work to ensure that free legal aid is made available to the poor in both civil and criminal matters.[33]

A recent groundbreaking achievement of the bar was the complete withdrawal of services by members of the Nigerian Bar Association (NBA) in Lagos in 1992 after the government refused to obey a judge's order to present four detained human rights activists in court. The NBA forced the government to comply with the order.

A number of lawyers' organizations aimed at human rights improvement have emerged, particularly dealing with improving women's lives. One such group is FIDA (Federation of Women's Lawyers) which comes under the broader umbrella organization, Women in Law and Development Africa (WiLDAF). Other organizations include the Legal Research and Resource Service in Nigeria and similar organizations in Zimbabwe and South Africa, whose main goal is to provide affordable, acceptable, and accessible legal services to the poor and disadvantaged in rural communities. The centers work to create in the rural poor the awareness of their fundamental rights, and to motivate them to seek their rights within the provisions of the national constitution. The centers also work toward the empowerment of rural dwellers so that they can participate fully in community and national development. A primary challenge of those who bring legal services to the rural poor is that of changing the psychological orientation of the average person toward the law.

Many rural dwellers are only acquainted with the traditional approach to handling disagreements among them. In this case, the chief or elder in the village decides the outcome of a case and the injured parties "kiss and make up." Even though legal services might be offered free of charge, many of the rural poor are still locked in the cultural pattern and shy away from legal services. Many also still hold firmly to traditional beliefs and can be manipulated and terrorized into desisting from court action against human rights violators. These are some of the challenges posed by merging traditional values with modern approaches. Changes will be slow, and education will be the vehicle to bridge the old with the new. The ultimate goal is to achieve justice.

Independence of the Judiciary

The proper performance of the judiciary is vital to the sustenance of democracy and the maintenance of a stable political climate. For this reason the judicial branch of government is expected to interpret the constitution with absolute integrity. Judges have the final say as to the powers and functions of the various branches of government; they also decide whether the fundamental rights of citizens have been infringed by government or its agencies. While this is the way the judiciary operates in the West, where liberal democracy is practiced, quite often judges in Africa cannot exercise their autonomy in decision making. Some of the factors that impede their work include:

1. Operating within a monolithic structure;
2. Erosion of their earnings by inflation, which causes them to be affected by economic hardship; and
3. Their vulnerability to bribery and corruption resulting from poverty.

Osita Eze explains that the independence of the judiciary might be jeopardized since the very function they are supposed to carry out could lead to conflict between the judiciary and the legislature. He supports this viewpoint quite well by making reference to an incident when the judiciary dismissed the sentences imposed on two Portuguese soldiers for illegally entering Zambian territory. The decision resulted in a dispute between Zambian President Kenneth Kaunda and the judiciary. Eze also informs readers that in socialist countries some leaders reject the notion of an independent judiciary. He points to the Algerian constitution of 1976, which states that the judge must obey the law exclusively, but at the same time insists that the judge is to contribute to the defense and protection of the socialist revolution.[34] This led Eze to assume that socialist-oriented African countries seemed to have a view of the independence of the judiciary which was not in accordance with the traditional practice of separation of powers. Socialist leaders in Africa appeared to consider the judiciary as an organ of the state that was expected to work in unison with other organs of the state to achieve the politico-economic aspirations of the state. Eze also points to the comments made by Sekou Toure of Guinea in 1963 concerning the independence of the judiciary. Sekou Toure had this to say:

While conforming to a particular system, it is worthwhile remembering that the service of justice is not a thing apart, that judges do not constitute a body independent of the other organs of State. The State of Guinea is an indivisible entity, and all its parts must work in unison towards the progress desired for the people . . . it is also necessary to remind magistrates that in order to harmonise the varying aspects of social justice, they must, prior to passing judgement, inform those responsible of any proceedings which, in the circumstances, are likely to have unfortunate repercussions on the political climate or public opinion.[35]

The government of Tanzania under President Julius Nyerere outlined in principle that the judiciary was independent and that the rule of law should prevail under socialism. Nonetheless, Eze points to the incident when the Chief Justice of Tanzania was confronted with a situation in which some village people brought litigation claiming compensation for land taken from them for the expansion of ujamaa (a form of socialism introduced by Nyerere in 1962). The Chief Justice refused to award compensation, noting that the judiciary could not be used as a tool to oppose ujamaa.[36] Eze hints that it was discernible that the judge's decision was influenced by the powers that be.

Up until recently, Nigeria enjoyed greater judicial independence than other countries in Africa. One reason for this is that the Nigerian Constitution consecrates the principle of the independence of the judiciary. The 1979 constitution recognizes the impartiality and integrity of the courts of law and stresses that this should be secured and maintained. The constitution also provides that human rights matters, including action brought by or against government or government authority, should be given fair hearing within a reasonable time by a court or other tribunal established by law and constituted in such manner as to secure independence and impartiality.[37]

The achievements of Justice Akinola Aguda are worthy of mention. Justice Akinola has performed in an exemplary manner in the defense of human rights. For example, in the case of *Agbaje v. Western State Commissioner of Police*, decided in June 1969, Justice Aguda ruled in favor of the victim, and these were his historic comments:

In a democracy like ours, even in spite of the national emergency in which we have been for the past three years, I hold the view that it is, to say the least, high-handed for the police to hold a citizen of this country in custody in various places for over ten days without showing him the authority under which he is being held or at least informing him verbally of such authority.[38]

Human rights have scored some legal victories despite the hostile political environment in which they operate. In 1986 Lagos State defied a court order and ejected Ojukwu (a human rights activist) and his family from the premises they were occupying. When the case of *The Governor of Lagos State v. Ojukwu* was heard in the Supreme Court, the judges ruled against the state. The Supreme Court ruled that "Once a dispute has arisen between a person and the government or authority and the dispute has been brought before the Court, thereby involving the judicial powers of the state, it is the duty of the government to allow the law to take its course or allow the legal and judicial process to run its full course."[39]

As recently as 1992, human rights activist Beko Ransome-Kuti brought action for damages against the Babangida administration for illegal arrest and detention. Justice Francis Owobiyi of the Lagos High Court ruled in favor of the victim, stating that "anything that derives its existence or emanates from illegal and un- lawful arrest or predicated thereon is, in itself, illegal and unlawful and therefore null and void and of no effect."[40] Justice Owobiyi further added that the arrest of Ransome-Kuti at his home at 4:15 A.M. (without a warrant) was illegal, unlawful, unconstitutional, and a violation of his fundamental human rights.[41]

Following the judgment in favor of Ransome-Kuti, the Babangida government failed to pay the N50,000 awarded in damages. In March 1993, court officials impounded the official vehicle of Justice Michael Ayoade in a bid to recover the N50,000 which had been awarded the plaintiff in 1992. When Justice Ayoade arrived at the court premises on that day, bailiffs who had apparently laid a well- rehearsed plan waited until the judge had gone upstairs. They then pounced on his driver, ordered him out of the car, and demanded the car keys. Court officials immediately deflated all the tires on the vehicle and proceeded to mark a bold "8" on the windshield, indicating that the vehicle was then in the custody of the court. When the shocked and embarrassed Justice Ayoade discovered what had happened, he then proceeded to the Chief Judge, Mr. Justice Ligoli Ayorinde. However, the Chief Justice refused to intervene, insisting that he would not ob- struct the execution of a valid and subsisting judgment of a court of competent jurisdiction.[42] This incident underscored a significant victory for human rights and for the supremacy of the rule of law. The actions of Justice Ayorinde and Justice Aguda demonstrate that Africa has leaders who offer hope for a future. Men of such high caliber should be consulted by international bodies (not governments) and assisted in their efforts to lay the right foundation for democracy and justice in Africa.

Although the majority of the Nigerian judiciary adhere to the independence of the judiciary, there have been some setbacks to the practice of law in recent times, notably the government's refusal to obey court orders to produce four human rights activists in court. The trial and condemnation of Zamani Lekwot and others in 1993 following the Zango Kataf riot has left even more disturbing signs for the judicial process in Nigeria.

In May 1992 there were two separate civil uprisings in Zango Kataf in northern Nigeria. The gravest incident was an ethnoreligious riot which resulted in heavy casualties. The federal government set up the Special and Communal Disturbance Judicial Tribunal, headed by retired Justice Benedict Okadigbo, to investigate the riots. The lawyer for the defense, G.O. Ajayi, was dismayed right from the beginning of the tribunal and expressed his dissatisfaction that the tribunal was comprised of a larger number of Muslims than Christians. The defense counsel's objections were ignored. During the conduct of the tribunal a retired major general, Zamani Lekwot, and the five others in his group were said to have been often embarrassed by Justice Okadigbo in the way he framed the questions put to the accused.[43] When the defense counsel expressed displeasure about the manner in which Justice Okadigbo was handling the case, he was accused of disrespecting the legal profession. The defense counsel therefore decided that he could not obtain a fair hearing for his clients and withdrew from the case. When the tribunal concluded its hearing, Justice Okadigbo condemned Lekwot and the five others to death for culpable homicide. There was a national outcry over the verdict, which many saw as a miscarriage of justice. Many felt that Justice Okadigbo had been used by the Babangida administration to do its dirty work. This incident was seen as a setback to the achievements made by honorable men in the legal profession in Nigeria.

Osita Eze underscores the need for the independence of the judiciary to check the excesses of government. He therefore proposes that the independence of the judiciary should be entrenched in the constitution. This would then give the courts full powers under the constitution to declare null and void any laws which are inconsistent with the provisions of the constitution. Until this is done, the principle of separation of powers will not work effectively. While one may entrench the independence of the judiciary in the constitutions, the vanguard of constitutional provisions must be the people themselves. That is why there is need for education and empowerment so that the people can check arbitrariness in their leaders.

Another disturbing aspect which affects the administration of justice is the harassment judges and lawyers face at the hands of government.[44] For instance, in 1982 three High Court judges in Ghana were abducted and murdered after handing down decisions that did not favor the Rawlings government. In Kenya, Gibson Kamau Kuria was detained in February 1987 and held until December 1987 without charge. In 1988, when he was awarded the Robert F. Kennedy Human Rights Award, Kuria was unable to travel to the United States to accept the award because the Moi government had previously confiscated his passport. Kuria was finally forced to seek refuge in the U.S. embassy when the Moi government embarked on a wave of repression against human rights lawyers and activists. In South Africa, lawyers who defended human rights were constantly harassed. For example, Raymond Suttner, a lecturer, was barred from entering any educational institution or participating in any activities of the United Democratic Front. Bulelan Ngcuka, a human rights lawyer, was arrested in 1989 because of his activities in the nationwide campaign of defiance against the exclusion of blacks in elections held in September 1989. Brian Currin, National Director of Lawyers for Human Rights, based in Pretoria, often received death threats and his family was frequently harassed. Seth Azhihangwisi Nthai, Regional Director of the Pretoria-based Lawyers for Human Rights, was also detained in 1989. At the time of his arrest, Nthai was providing legal advice to lawyers working on the case of Joyce Mabudafhasi, a member of the Detainees Support Committee (DESCOM).[45]

CONCLUSION

The protection of human rights in Africa is also an evolutionary process. The African Charter must be applied more effectively, and judges must be able to function independently. The current democratization exercise does not promise much hope for the short term. For one thing, many of the old sit-tight rulers are still hanging on to power. Majority Africans might have to wait for more than a decade for leadership with a new orientation to emerge. In the meantime, human rights NGOs in Africa must continue to lay the groundwork in educating the masses and providing leadership, because it is up to the people themselves to protect and defend their human rights.

NOTES

1. See The United Nations, International Bill of Human Rights (New York: United Nations, 1988), p. 30.

2. Egon Schwelb, *Human Rights in the International Community, The Roots and Growth of the Universal Declaration of Human Rights, 1948–1963* (Chicago: Quadrangle Books, 1964), p. 51.

3. Ibid.

4. Bayo Okunade, "An Introduction to African Human Rights Laws and Convention," paper delivered at the Human Rights Africa Training Institute, 1991, p. 11.

5. Osita Eze, *Human Rights in Africa: Some Selected Problems* (Lagos, Nigeria: Nigerian Institute of International Affairs, 1984), p. 196.

6. See Amnesty International, *Guide to the African Charter for Human and Peoples' Rights* (London: Amnesty International, 1993), p. 11.

7. Issa G. Shivji, *The Concept of Human Rights in Africa* (London: CODESRIA, 1989), p. 105.

8. Information gathered from a reliable source. This case was brought before the Africa Commission in Banjul for the October 1992 sitting. It could not be heard because the Cameroon government failed to file its report.

9. See *Human Rights Tribune* (Summer 1992): 22, 30.

10. International Commission of Jurists (ICJ), *Towards Universal Justice* (Geneva: ICJ, 1993), p. 9.

11. Ibid, p. 8.

12. Ibid., p. 85.

13. Ibid., p. 9.

14. Rhoda Howard, "Legitimacy and Class Rule in Commonwealth Africa: Constitutionalism and the Rule of Law," *Third World Quarterly* 7, no. 2 (April 1985): 323.

15. As quoted by Eze, *Human Rights in Africa*, p. 29.

16. Ibid., p. 34.

17. For detailed information on this, see Schwelb, *Human Rights in the International Community*.

18. Eze, *Human Rights in Africa*, p. 29.

19. Ibid.

20. Ibid.

21. Howard, "Legitimacy and Class Rule in Commonwealth Africa," p. 233.

22. Louis Henkin, *The Rights of Man Today* (New York: Columbia University, Center for Study of Human Rights, 1978), p. 83.

23. Ibid.

24. Ben Nwabueze, "Legal and Institutional Mechanism," in B. Caron, A. Gboyega, and E. Osaghoe, eds., *Democratic Transition in Africa* (Ibadan, Nigeria: Institute of African Studies, 1992), pp. 303–304.

25. Ibid., p. 304.

26. Ibid.

27. Eze, *Human Rights in Africa*.

28. Paper delivered by Hon. Justice Akinola Aguda in "Law and Human Rights in Democracy," report of Africa Leadership Forum, Farm House Dialogue No. 17.

29. For more detailed information see Adama Deng, ed., *Paralegals in Rural Africa*, seminars in Banjul, Gambia, 1989 and Harare, Zimbabwe, February 1990 (Geneva: International Commission of Jurists, 1991); *Justice Denied* (Lagos, Nigeria: CLO, 1992); *Zimbabwe Wages of War* (New York: Lawyers Committee for Human Rights, 1986); and Howard, "Legitimacy and Class Rule in Commonwealth Africa."

30. Deng, *Paralegals in Rural Africa*, p. 95.

31. See Florence Butegwa, "The Challenge of Promoting Women's Rights in African Countries," in Joanna Kerr, ed., *Ours By Right: Women's Rights as Human Rights* (Ottawa: ZED Books, in association with the North-South Institute, 1993), p. 40.

32. Lawyers Committee for Human Rights, *Zimbabwe: Wages of War*.

33. See Draft HRI African Directory, (Cambridge, Mass.: Human Rights Internet, Harvard Law School, 1989), p. 9.

34. Eze, *Human Rights in Africa,* p. 42.

35. Ibid.

36. Ibid., p. 43.

37. Ibid.

38. See Akin Ibidapo-Obe, "The Human Rights Philosophy of Honourable Dr. Akinola Aguda," *Journal of Human Rights Law and Practice* 2 (November 1991): 158.

39. See Awa Kalu, "Legal Process for Human Rights Enforcement: Review of Results," lecture delivered at Human Rights Africa Training Institute, August 20, 1991.

40. *Daily Times* (Lagos), July 2, 1992, p. 21.

41. Ibid.

42. *The Punch* (Lagos), March 2, 1993, p. 1.

43. See details of this case in the *The African Guardian* (Lagos), January 25, 1993, p. 19.

44. See Reed Brody, ed., *Attacks on Justice: The Harassment and Persecution of Judges and Lawyers—July 1989–June 1990* (Geneva: Centre for the Independence of Judges and Lawyers of the International Commission of Jurists). See in particular pp. 35–36, 50–53, and 80–83.

45. Ibid., p. 82.

Chapter 5

The Role of Human Rights NGOs
in Africa

Indigenous human rights NGOs in Africa do not have a very long history, and their beginnings have been rocky and tedious. One reason for this is that prior to their emergence, human rights violations in Africa were monitored by external organizations. Thus, human rights in Africa were viewed from an alien perspective. Among the earliest human rights NGOs in Africa was the International Service of the Red Cross and Crescent, which usually involved disaster relief efforts. Amnesty International has been on the scene in Africa for over thirty years; its main focus has been the release of prisoners of conscience, abolition of the death penalty, and an end to torture. A while later Africa Watch came on the scene. While Amnesty International and the International Red Cross have subregional offices in several African countries, the activities of Africa Watch are conducted from outside the continent. There was no consciousness of the African culture, tradition, and realities. As a result, the indigenous African NGOs did not have a realistic perspective from which to embark on human rights protection in Africa. Their efforts initially were ones of trial and error.

NGOs are mainly self-help organizations, and most of these sprung up as replacements for governments who increasingly failed to meet the needs of the masses. Most NGOs in Africa began to mushroom in the 1980s, and many of these were church-based. Those indigenous NGOs with stated objectives toward social justice and the rights of the individual include the CLO in Nigeria, the Legal Resource Centre in Tanzania, the Public Law Institute in Kenya, the Legal Advice Centres in Zimbabwe, and the Lawyers for Human Rights in South Africa, as well as the Law Societies and Catholic Peace and Justice Commissions of many African countries. As Africa moves toward democratization, human rights NGOs will have to assume a greater role. NGOs in Africa have a vital role to play in giving leadership to the masses as Africans struggle to transform the oppressive structures. There will be increasing need for NGO involvement in the following areas:

1. grassroots education and awareness programs;
2. police training;
3. taking measures to alleviate poverty; and
4. building democratic structures from the grassroots level.

In order to be able to enforce the fundamental rights guaranteed in the various international instruments, NGOs will need to pressure governments to ratify the various human rights instruments and also to review their laws to bring them in line with international standards. This means that to be effective, human rights NGOs must be autonomous of governments. While some NGOs might be genuinely committed to social justice and development, at the same time the emphasis on NGOs has created opportunities for some egocentric and fraudulent individuals to set up such organizations in order to access western funds. That will not benefit poor Africans. For this reason, there should be mechanisms to monitor and evaluate the performance and effectiveness of NGOs. Shivji argues that most of the present NGOs compromise themselves because they are connected to the authoritarian state. He also contends that "such organizations will have to move away from elitist orientation if they are to do genuine grass-root work among the people."[1]

The CLO in Nigeria has demonstrated the courage and leadership that sets the organization apart. The numerous arrests of its members bear witness to this. Apart from that, I have found the performance of some human rights NGOs to be disappointing and deserving of the sentiments shared by Shivji. The CLO for its part has shown that it can be relied upon to revive civil society and work toward empowerment of the masses. The following statement by its president, Olisa Agbakoba, demonstrates the foresight of the organization.

Non-governmental Organizations (NGOs) are the first stage in the evolution of the civil society. The willingness of individuals to organize in groups as NGOs at different levels of articulation enhances social ordering. . . . NGOs reflect societal concerns and differences at varying levels of resolution. Because of this, they are perhaps the most useful and vocal tools in the chemistry of the civil society.[2]

If democracy is to secure social justice, after elections are held NGOs will need to be at the forefront to press for respect of the fundamental liberties which are the hallmark of democracy. At the same time, in order to ensure economic justice, poverty must be tackled. Therefore, human rights NGOs are in a prime position to be the vanguard for political and economic evolution on the continent. In this section we will look at what ought to be the new perspective to enhance the role of NGOs in pursuing social justice on behalf of the African masses.

THE ROLE OF HUMAN RIGHTS NGOs IN POVERTY ALLEVIATION AND ERADICATION

The majority of Africans are victims of intellectual and material poverty, and often these are the people the police and others prey on. Such groups of people have no economic rights, and political rights for them are more a privilege than a right. Poverty and oppression go hand in hand. That is why it is expedient that poverty be tackled successfully. For this reason, all concerned groups in society must be part of the solution. For their part, human rights NGOs in Africa should:

1. Sensitize the public on the issue of poverty and poverty-alleviation measures.
2. Carry out studies when necessary on poverty-related issues.
3. Seek solutions to poverty by bringing relevant groups together for dialogue, informed discussion, and brainstorming.
4. Serve as a link between the grassroots and policymakers.
5. Initiate and assist in self-help projects at community and local levels.
6. Serve as advocates of the poor and ensure that their concerns are not ignored.

HUMAN RIGHTS MONITORING

According to Nigel Rodley, "monitoring is nothing more complicated than the assembling, presentation, and dissemination of pertinent data in a form that enables human rights performance to be assessed according to agreed-upon international standards."[3] Human rights NGOs have persistently monitored the state of fundamental liberties and basic freedoms and reported the misdeeds of states which do not conform to the standards set out in the Universal Declaration of Human Rights. There is, however, a lack of standards in monitoring and in approaches to human rights activism. This is an area that must be addressed in order to improve human rights in the future. By and large human rights monitoring bodies have not been able to establish a mechanism to allow the analysis, comparison, and integration of information pertaining to gross human rights violations. There is no formal consensus on approaches to monitoring. Gregg Beyer points to this vacuum. "Until now, none of these organizations focuses specifically on situations identified according to an agreed-upon typology, or systematically reports their findings to decision-making bodies which could ameliorate deteriorating situations."[4]

There is need to establish more efficient methods of human rights monitoring. There is no area where monitoring is needed more than in early warning. This would ensure that quick action is taken to prevent the agony of genocide, famine, environmental disasters, and so on. Helen Fein stresses the need to identify endangered peoples,[5] and she has been proven correct, particularly in recent times. Fein points out that such identification would prevent the slaughter of innocent victims. As the world becomes more xenophobic and racism intensifies, this is an area in which human rights monitoring should be even more vigilant. Given the tendency toward what warring factions refer to as "ethnic cleansing," human rights bodies will increasingly need to act expeditiously to avoid the type of carnage that is taking place in Bosnia in the 1990s and the threat of extermination for the Nubians in Sudan as they resist government efforts to Islamize their people. In addition, early warning could have prevented the slaughter of thousands of Issaks in Somalia in 1988.[6] The same applies for the recent slaughter of the Tutsis in Rwanda. This is a particular area in which human rights NGOs in Africa are rendered almost impotent.

There are various viewpoints on the subject of monitoring, particularly what to monitor and how. Both western and African scholars are unclear about this. Among African human rights NGOs there is disagreement as to the approaches to human rights. While some accuse others of "negative proclamations," at the same time they remain ambivalent as to which direction to take. Although I do not see how African human rights NGOs relying on foreign funding can adopt a posture of criticizing imperialism, since this is tantamount to biting the hand that feeds you, I do agree with Issa Shivji for accusing African Human Rights NGOs of "hyocricsy and opportunism."[7] My own observations prove Shivji correct when he says:

The so-called human rights activity in Africa has been largely dominated by lawyers. Thus even the developments of other social sciences have by-passed them. African NGOs that are set up, it would seem, are institutional mechanisms by which to obtain foreign funds: they are, what might be called, FFUNGOs (foreign funded NGOs) rather than grass-root organizations of the intellectuals and the people to struggle for rights.[8]

Shivji pointed out that other groups which could give effective input and leadership at the grassroots level have been ignored by mainstream human rights NGOs in Africa. He pointed to trade unions, church-based organizations, students and youth organizations, and women's groups. Much of his argument is correct, but so far, the CLO has been active with student organizations in Nigeria. For example, in 1992 and 1993 Olusegun Mayegun, President of the National Association of Nigerian Students (NANS), Femi Falana, and Gani Fawehinmi have been placed under arrest on several occasions as they collaborated to press for social justice in Nigeria.

If NGOs are to genuinely monitor human rights abuses, they should have an established mechanism for doing so. Michael Stohl suggests that the charting of human rights abuses as well as the different tactics regimes employ can be improved by measuring the severity, the frequency, and the range of human rights violations.[9] Stohl explains that in monitoring human rights one should be able to rank types of abuse from low to high, from the least abusive to the most abusive. As an example he points out that a regime which imprisons opponents would be ranked as a less egregious violator in comparison to one in which citizens are said to "disappear." Stohl also argues that the number of occurrences of each type of human rights violation should be measured as well. He notes that regimes often alter their strategies and vary the levels of both severity and frequency of violations. He suggests that at times a shift in emphasis may give the appearance that a human rights situation has improved. For instance, in a case of torture a government may engage in torture less often, but employ a more severe method. For this reason Stohl suggests that "at any given level of frequency, an increase in severity should be recognized as a deterioration of the human rights situation."[10]

Stohl suggests that if an adequate measure of human rights is to be achieved, it is necessary to measure how widespread is the repression and which segment of society is targeted. It actually focuses on whose rights are being threatened and how deeply it cuts into society.[11] By measuring the range it helps those monitoring human rights abuses to determine the differences between two regimes. For instance, one regime may employ frequent and severe repression against a large portion of the society while another might only focus on a minority group. Stohl feels that by disaggregating the severity, frequency, and range of human rights abuses, it would provide a clearer basis on which to determine the political peculiarities of individual cases, and in this way measurements of human rights violations might be more valid.

While approaches to monitoring are generating various theories among social scientists, a consensus on what to monitor is yet to be reached. If human rights monitoring is to be conducted effectively, there must be a mechanism that allows the measurement for the more than fifty human rights that are guaranteed in the International Bill of Human Rights. The problem is to bring monitoring down to manageable proportions—that is, to arrive at a workable number of rights and countries for effective monitoring.

Henry Shue argues that there is a duty not to eliminate a person's only means of subsistence (i.e., a duty to avoid deprivation). Also, there is the duty to provide subsistence for those unable to provide for their own.[12] While this approach emphasizes the right to subsistence, there are other broader sets of human rights that need to be covered.

Howard and Donnelly have suggested a short list of ten rights, which appear to be more comprehensive. They include:

1. Survival Rights, which guarantee rights to life, food, and health care.

2. Membership Rights, which include family rights and prohibition of discrimination.

3. Protection Rights, which guard the individual against abuse of state power by guaranteeing right to habeas corpus and the independence of the judiciary.

4. Empowerment Rights, which provide the individual control over the course of his life, which includes the right to education, freedom of association, and a free press.[13]

Howard and Donnelly argue that these ten rights could justifiably stand proxy for most of the rights guaranteed in the Universal Declaration and also make provision for economic rights, which are often not given the same priority as political rights. They claim that where a state protects these ten rights, it would be more likely that the state would protect most of the other human rights guaranteed the ordinary citizen, bearing in mind that human rights are interrelated.

PIOOM also suggests a mechanism for monitoring human rights. This approach is based on Articles 3, 5, and 9 of the Universal Declaration of Human Rights, which protects the rights to life, liberty, and security of person, protects the individual against torture or cruel, inhuman, or degrading treatment or punishment, and also protects against arbitrary arrest, detention, or exile.[14] Although there is strong international consensus on these rights, performance on these rights would not seem to be closely correlated with performance on other rights.[15] In addition, as Donnelly correctly points out, respect for human rights involves more than simply not killing, torturing, or arbitrarily detaining people. As such, there is no reason to believe that monitoring these rights will give an accurate picture of the whole human rights situation in a country.[16]

There is strong international consensus on PIOOM's short list of rights, and it is easier to acquire quantitative data on them,[17] but they are not comprehensive enough to give a global picture. Therefore, it might be a good idea to approach human rights monitoring using the short list of ten rights proposed by Howard and Donnelly. Until other practical ideas are proposed, this approach could be a step in the right direction.

Human Rights Education

Human rights education is defined as all those experiences, activist, artistic, and academic, which empower people everywhere to become aware of human rights as the fundamental principles of human and social relations.[18] Most people remain oblivious to the fact that they have fundamental human rights. If knowledge and awareness of human rights principles are to be improved, human rights education must be brought to the grassroots community—women's groups, artisans in the informal sector, peasants, and so on. The average person must be educated about his rights and conscientized to protect and defend those rights.

Human rights education must form part of the curriculum in primary and secondary schools. The main preoccupation of local and international human rights NGOs should be to find a workable vehicle to transmit knowledge of rights and duties to the wider population. The emphasis should be specifically on what should be taught and how. Efforts should be made to ensure that the process of learning involves the recipient of knowledge every step of the way. Human rights topics should be part of adult literacy classes. Important issues could be treated as a theme in a learning module. Human rights educators must persuade governments to include human rights education in police training, because the police are among the greatest abusers of citizens' rights. The police must cease being a law unto themselves; they should also learn to operate from the basis that criminals are entitled to fair treatment, even after being convicted.

Some NGOs such as the Legal Resources Foundation in Zimbabwe, the Legal Education Action Project (LEAP) in South Africa, and the Federation of Women's Lawyers in Gambia, Nigeria, and Ghana have been making remarkable strides toward training paralegals[19] who will educate the people in the rural communities in Africa on their legal and human rights. These are encouraging developments in Africa. At least Africans themselves have begun to build the relevant structures needed to affect change. These should be improved and expanded until African masses have attained a level of development and empowerment. There should be continued efforts to experiment and improve on methods of delivery. Also, emphasis should be placed on reaching communities through their local vernacular.

To my mind, the participatory learning method would be an excellent vehicle through which to teach human rights. For one thing it involves the people from the inception of the curriculum. It also allows those who design the curriculum and the training materials to begin from what the people do know and it allows the people to take charge. As Paulo Freire stressed in *Pedagogy of the Oppressed,* we must move from what he refers to as "the banking" method of teaching and adopt the problem-posing concept of education. According to Freire,

In problem-posing education, men develop their power to perceive critically the way they exist in the world with which and in which they find themselves; they come to see the world not as a static reality but as a reality in process, in transformation . . . hence, the teacher-student and students-teachers reflect simultaneously on themselves and the world without dichotomizing this reflection from action, and thus establishing an authentic form of action.[20]

Human rights education should be approached from reflection on a particular situation and making conscious decisions about actions one should take to change the situation. Nonformal educational programs should be conducted by local committees drawn from within the geographical area and versed in the local vernacular. What I propose is a method of "each one, teach one." Human rights NGOs should carve out areas where they will conduct human rights training. They should either form local human rights committees in the specific area or network with existing community groups and invite members from such groups to be part of the human rights training team. The human rights organization would then work with the local committee to find out the best approach to designing the training program. After designing the program, the human rights organization should train the members of the local committees. After they have received the training, they would then go to the grassroots communities and conduct training using the local vernacular. The training within the grassroots could be in the form of drama, storytelling, discussions, role plays, and so on. The facilitator's role should be to ensure that certain important tenets are brought out through the story or whatever medium, and emphasis should be on how to change such a situation. Traditional Africans were educated through fireside storytelling; let us revive this method to educate and empower civil society in Africa. At least it is cost-effective. Popular theatre would also be an extremely useful vehicle for education at the grassroots level. We must bear in mind that a greater percentage of learning takes place through visual modes.

The other section of society on which attention should be focused is the schools. Efforts should be made to ensure that governments include human rights education in primary and secondary schools' curricula. Children are usually the keenest and most capable individuals to interest parents in certain matters. We would like to see a situation in which members of human rights groups are invited to schools as guest speakers to give talks about civic rights and responsibilities. Human rights education is part of development, and if people are to participate in nation building, schools should be propagating social justice. It depends on the society the governments aim to build. If, in the face of democratization, they wish to build a repressive society, then they will hardly encourage human rights education. On the other hand, if the intention of government is to build a just society, there is nothing to fear, so they should collaborate with human rights groups on educating the citizenry.

If learning institutions are to effectively teach human rights and justice issues, adequate training materials should be designed. There is a serious lack of teaching aids such as textbooks, modules, and audiovisual materials. In fact, for the most part they appear to be almost nonexistent. African intellectuals on the continent should be called to task for this vacuum. They have not addressed the needs of the masses for empowerment through education. Many of these intellectuals have failed to undertake their roles and responsibilities in this area. There is need to develop modules focusing on various aspects of human rights, such as women's rights, the rights of the child, refugee rights, economic and social rights, cultural rights, political and civic rights, and the right to a clean environment. Where the schools lack teaching resources, the human rights organizations should be properly equipped and work with the schools so a lending system can be established. Teachers could borrow materials from the NGOs and return them. The problem in Africa is that financing for NGOs is usually a problem. Therefore, if such materials are to be developed, it would be with assistance from the international community and northern NGOs, which have greater expertise and access to financing.

Other approaches to human rights education might include community billboards, cartoons, and the media. Human rights principles can be propagated through radio interviews, weekly talk shows on radio and television, and so on. This would also require cooperation with the owners of the media houses and the government to avoid negative repercussions from the authorities.

One area that is currently debated is how to approach the teaching of economic and social rights. While much emphasis has been placed on political rights, especially in the curriculum of law schools, nothing has been done about the teaching of economic rights. For one thing, the United States does not recognize the provisions of the Covenant of Economic, Social and Cultural Rights as human rights, so little emphasis has been placed on this area in their policies, even though it affects the lives of Americans. The problem is, where countries have not ratified the Covenant on Economic Rights, the state cannot be held liable under international law.

At a 1989 retreat in Greece sponsored by the Harvard Law School Human Rights Program and Human Rights Internet,[21] representatives of human rights NGOs pointed out that one of the difficulties they face in designing curriculum for the teaching of economic rights is how to make concepts of economic indices and fiscal mismanagement comprehensible to illiterate citizens. In my experience in human rights training in Africa, I have taught the provisions of the constitutions and the Universal Declaration so that people can be informed that these provisions exist. When one realizes the extent of illiteracy at the grassroots level, it would be futile to introduce them to the lexicon of economics. The simple fact is that the constitution says their children should be given primary education, and government should direct its affairs to provide adequate health care. All that matters to those at the grassroots level is what touches their lives. They do not need to know economics to know they have no yams or gari (a staple of the West African diet), and that the prices keep increasing each time they go to the market (which we call inflation). That word might be Greek to the common man, but when his money cannot buy weekly food for himself and his family, he *does* understand. Then, when he sees his local government chairman driving a new Mercedes-Benz and other politicians have up to forty cars in their backyards, the common man knows that money is being misspent somewhere. That is how he will conceptualize fiscal mismanagement. All he needs to do is to be enlightened enough to know that the next time there are local government elections, he will not vote for those who did not provide basic amenities in his community. That is the language of economics that the common man relates to and practices.

Poverty is the greatest impediment to democracy in Africa, and the common man needs to know he has economic rights. We must therefore find a rudimentary approach to get the message across to him. He might not be able to take the government to court and use statistics to prove his right to food was violated, but the next election will be his "day in court." He does not have to be very literate to know that. The only thing that would prevent him from having his "day in court" is if he is so hungry that he is forced to accept a bribe to get something to eat. Africa is attempting democratization amidst abject poverty and a high rate of illiteracy; therefore, Africans need to devise their own unique approaches to solving their problems.

Strategy for Educating the Masses

The strategy for educating the masses which I present is relevant to empowerment and applies in a nonformal setting. However, it can evolve into a more formal training method. The level of illiteracy is so high that any attempt to teach the majority the concepts of social justice must be approached from where it hurts them most, not from theorizing.

1. It is important to begin by addressing the misery of the poor. The individual must be encouraged to reflect on his/her state of hunger, lack of shelter, or untreated ailments, and say, "Look at me." He must face the living hell he undergoes daily as if he is looking in a mirror. Then he must ask, "Why am I in this misery?"

2. He must be brought to the awareness that he lives in misery because someone has adopted bad policies or has neglected his obligations to the people.

3. If the state agent arrests their children unlawfully and detains them over a long period of time, how do people reflect on all this?

4. Now that they are conscious of the factors at work, the destitute masses must question their political leaders about the way their taxes are spent. Why haven't we been given facilities? What reason can you give for the increasing cost of food? Why is there no money to pay teachers? What are you doing to control the police and security agents?

This is how the average African must be conscientized to demand accountability from his elected representatives. Where responses are unsatisfactory or promises remain unkept, people will come together to voice their frustrations. Such situations will eventually galvanize communities into a collaborative effort to force changes to the status quo. Here one might ask about the problem of ethnicity, but it must be emphasized that ethnic disturbances are often engineered by unscrupulous leaders. The suffering masses bear the brunt of poverty and bad leadership with equanimity. They must therefore be conscientized to see the real culprit in their suffering.

Human Rights Advocacy

Governments in Africa most often do not respect the rule of law and the independence of the judiciary. In most cases governments in Africa are not accountable. Even though there might be "one man, one vote," that is where the buck stops. The people are not at a stage to place checks and balances on arbitrary leaders. We might have government by the people's vote, but not government *of* the people, *by* the people, and certainly not *for* the people, except for a few. There is no such thing as equal treatment for citizens, and victims of human rights abuse experience much frustration in obtaining redress. The law enforcement agencies are themselves the prime violators, and the courts do not function effectively and efficiently. If democracy in Africa is to deliver justice for the oppressed, there is need for advocacy on behalf of the downtrodden and ignorant.

Many African NGOs have investigated human rights violations and intensified efforts at civic awareness. They have adopted different approaches to human rights protection. For example, in Nigeria the CLO combines multiple activities in order to achieve its objectives. The organization issues press releases, holds press conferences, organizes public rallies and meetings, and pursues litigation on behalf of human rights victims. It also uses the direct mail approach to get action on urgent human rights matters. Amnesty International exposes the abuses of governments all over Africa by publishing press releases, letter-writing campaigns, and getting the international community to react to abuses. The All Africa Conference of Churches in Kenya is involved in matters relating to justice and unity, educational aid, self-help development and employment, and other areas of community service. Some groups criticize vocal human rights NGOs as being ineffective in halting human rights abuse in Africa. These human rights NGOs might not have been able to end human rights abuse, but were their voices not heard, governments would have treated the average citizen with even greater disregard.

Shivji argues that in order to terminate the oppression of the masses, human rights activism should take on a different dimension. He advocates that the human rights vocabulary be transformed. He feels it is not enough to sympathize with the victims of human rights violations and beg the violators to mend their ways by exposing violations in writing as is often the case. He advocates that "one joins the oppressed/exploited/dominated or ruled against the oppressors/exploiters/dominant and ruling to expose and resist, with a view ultimately to overcome, the situation which generates human rights violations."[22]

PROBLEMS OF HUMAN RIGHTS NGOs

Human rights NGOs in Africa face some major hurdles, among them (1) a hostile political environment, (2) financial constraints, and (3) undemocratic approaches to internal governance. If human rights efforts are to succeed in improving the material condition of the majority in Africa, governments must be willing to accept human rights activism as a tool in development. Until that happens, there will always be an atmosphere of hostility between governments and human rights groups. I would like to illustrate by referring to my own experience.

When I had newly arrived in Africa, the first time I met a person he/she often asked, "What are you doing in Africa?" I replied, "I came to work in human rights." On every occasion their reply was, "This is a sensitive area. How are you going to do it?" I said, "I am aware it is sensitive, but I do not think I will get into any trouble, because I believe that it is the individuals who must fight for their own rights and not me. I feel that if they are educated about what their rights are, they will not allow anyone to abuse their rights. Therefore, I will approach human rights work by linking with the communities, particularly the grassroots, as well as in the schools. In the communities, I would work within groups, such as women's groups, self-help groups, and so on, and offer enlightenment programs in human rights. To accommodate the local vernacular, I would work with individuals in the community who can communicate with the people. I would use nonformal methods of teaching such as role plays, drama, and pictures. I would try to get school teachers to allow me to come and give a talk about human rights to their class. In addition, I would encourage teachers to teach students about rights and duties, especially the provisions in the constitution. In fact, many human rights groups I have met are all advocating that civics should be taught in schools." Having said this, there was usually another question. "But the schools are owned by government, and if they hear that you are working in the communities, do you think they will let you?"

The recurring questions of whether or not the government would allow human rights education indicates that society is aware of the hostile manner in which governments view human rights. Just being aware of this type of relationship instills such fear in the citizenry that even educating the masses about rights needs much convincing. For instance, when one human rights organization proposed to offer a community education project on human rights and democratic values in Nigeria, the people were reluctant to attend the course, fearing that the government's security agents would harass them. They were so suspicious about the course at first that when they were told that everything would be free, including accommodations, meals, and transportation, the response of some of them was "there has got to be something wrong in this." That is the degree of fear instilled in the average person regarding his fundamental rights and freedoms. This is one of the many hurdles human rights NGOs will have to work to overcome.

The other, more serious problem is the continued harassment and detention of human rights activists by government. A look at a few of the problems of some human rights groups in Nigeria will give a clear picture. Most activists in Africa undergo similar travails. The problems of the executives of the CLO and the CDHR in Nigeria are worth mentioning. The human rights activists have been arbitrarily arrested and detained without prosecution, or their activities hampered on numerous occasions. For example, in November 1992 about 250 policemen and state security service agencies disrupted and dispersed a peaceful and non-sectarian vigil for democracy[23] which was organized by the CLO. State security service agents had earlier confiscated over ten thousand pages of documents relating to the activities of the Campaign for Democracy and the CDHR from the premises of Beko Ransome-Kuti.

When the Women's Rights Project (WRP), an organ of the CLO, organized a forum on "Women and Taxation in Nigeria" in December 1992, a combined team of police and state security service agencies disrupted the forum. Later, when the CLO attempted to hold a seminar in Benin City on "Human Rights and the Third Republic," government agents cordoned off the conference hall and aborted the seminar. The police subsequently detained CLO President Olisa Agbakaba, the Edo State chairman of the CLO, and others for three hours. All this time, close to one hundred heavily armed policemen were in place to prevent guests and organizers from entering the conference hall. Later on, police raided the CLO premises in Kaduna in northern Nigeria and carted away several documents. The executive director of the CLO alleged that "the government has placed the police and all security agencies on alert with instructions to disrupt, abort and subvert all human rights and pro-democracy groups and activities in Nigeria."[24] After this continued harassment, the CLO was so distraught that the director called on the people of Nigeria and the international community to prevail on the Babangida administration to "give human rights and fundamental liberties a chance."[25]

In its 1992 report, Amnesty International informs us that more than one hundred government opponents were detained and then released in 1991. Amnesty International also reports that a leading trade unionist in Zaire, Bikela Mafuila, who was arrested in June 1991, was reported to have died after being beaten by security forces. The Zaire Ministry of Rights and Freedom of the Citizen, which was established in 1980 to investigate allegations of human rights abuses, was abolished in April 1991, and its functions transferred to the Ministry of Justice. Amnesty International noted that there was no word of an inquiry into the death of Mafuila.[26]

Most of the human rights NGOs in Africa seek funding from external sources. The problem is that local businesses seldom support human rights work for fear of government reprisal. The problem with relying on external funding is that at times donors dictate how NGOs should function because of all the strings attached to their funding. Due to financial difficulties, many NGOs rely on voluntary staff, and there is generally a lack of commitment and continuity when using such workers. The major drawback regarding funding is that when no funding is forthcoming, some worthwhile projects might not be executed.

African human rights NGOs will need to be more creative and innovative, and find less costly means to deliver education or to protect the rights of the poor. I suggest the following: Where the NGO needs a vehicle for travel, organize chapters in various locations and get chapter representatives to use bicycles to travel to meet with community groups. Devise rudimentary and informal methods of teaching to reduce to a minimum the cost of producing teaching materials. Where hotel rooms are rented for conferences and fora, eliminate much of those activities and concentrate on grassroots activities. These are far less costly and far more effective. Oftentimes the only visible results of conferences and fora are piles of paper left to gather dust, presented in the form of communiques and reports.

In terms of leadership in African NGOs, there is often a problem of the NGO becoming a one-man show under the autocratic leadership of its founder. This is a recurring problem and has led to several fallouts among NGO groups throughout the continent. When the leadership is ego-centered, staff usually are unclear of their role. Consequently, the NGO fails to function efficiently. Communication is often lacking, and eventually workers become demoralized due to lack of motivation.

THE ROLE OF NORTHERN NGOS

Northern NGOs should reinforce the work of local NGOs in Africa. They could be vital in bringing local issues to the attention of the wider population in the international community. In addition, they are vital partners in fund-raising as well as important links for coalition building. They could offer technical expertise necessary for institution building; they could provide consultancy service for training, monitoring, and evaluating human rights projects and activities; and they could work to ensure the sustainability of the local NGOs. Northern NGOs must also forge links with all those interested in improving the human condition in Africa by doing the following:

1. Pressuring their governments and multinational corporations to bring an end to the selling of arms to African leaders.

2. Mounting pressure to get western banks to repatriate the monies that African leaders plundered from the continent and stashed in them.

3. Assisting in getting educational materials to distribute to schools and local communities in Africa.

4. Ensuring that the debt problem is resolved, and striving for a new international economic order.

5. Mobilizing support for crises, such as famine and natural disasters.

THE ROLE OF THE INTERNATIONAL COMMUNITY

The international community is entitled to interest itself and act upon the human rights situation in any country in the world. This is an essential aspect of the emerging international public order.[27]

That statement by B.G. Ramcharan suggests that the international community will take a more active role in protecting human rights in the future. This is an encouraging sign, but one also hopes that principles will be applied with consistency. Ramcharan suggests that the UN should have a mechanism which would enable the organization to act more expeditiously in areas of interstate intervention. This is an area in which the UN is increasingly being pushed to act and faces new challenges regarding state sovereignty. Now that the cold war has ended, the UN will need to adopt new and more effective strategies to deal with the root causes of ethnic, religious, and social conflicts, defending the independence of the judiciary, protecting the rights of refugees, and protecting minority rights.[28] What occurred in Somalia in 1993 is indicative of the complexities of the situation.

While the world expects the UN to ensure that humanitarian assistance reaches the needy, this is not so easy to do. The situation in Somalia in which the UN troops were drawn into battle with General Farah Aideed and his faction demonstrates the complexities of the problem. How the UN will balance the need to protect the suffering and restore peace against the notion of state interference is now a contentious issue. To intervene or not to intervene is increasingly becoming the question the UN must ask its lf. The recent situation in Bosnia is yet another example of the delicate problems the UN must address. In my view, there is need for the UN, as the supreme world body, to "police" those troubled spots of the world and take the best decision (regardless of criticisms) that will be for the good of the suffering, innocent victims. Either way, this sort of intervention will always be hotly debated among those with nationalist tendencies. On the other hand, when the UN refuses to intervene it is also accused of doing nothing.

The tensions all over Africa are calling for a more drastic and paternalistic relationship vis-à-vis the UN and OAU member states. While the OAU turns a blind eye to the atrocities of member states, the African Commision does not effectively protect citizens. Therefore, human rights NGOs and citizens alike need another umbrella of protection. If human suffering at the hands of tyrannical leaders in Africa is to be reduced, the UN should establish its own monitoring and policing body in Africa. There should be a UN regional body where citizens can take their governments or NGOs appeal on behalf of human rights victims. After thorough fact-finding missions, the UN should isolate those governments or ensure that external aid and loans no longer go to that administration. Not only that, but where a leader defies the movement for democracy, as in Zaire and Togo, the UN should assist the forces of opposition and civil society in removing that leader, even by force. Such leaders should be tried by the UN and made to return the country's stolen wealth and thrown into prison.

Ramcharan notes that the desire for people everywhere is to be able to live their lives in dignity and freedom under democracy without arbitrary deprivations of liberty. He feels that the future role of the UN should be propelled by these forces and suggests that the UN plot a strategy for supporting human rights in the development process. Ramcharan urges that survival requirements such as subsistence for every individual should be assured. This is of primary importance to Africa at the present moment, and if the international community is sincere about democratization in Africa, they would heed Ramcharan's advice. The UN can play a significant role in easing the problems NGOs face in dealing with governments by ensuring that human rights issues become a factor of development.

Ramcharan proposes that human rights projects should be designed on a country-by-country basis, bearing in mind that the legal institutional development of these countries may vary. This idea is a wise approach. Ramcharan suggests that the objectives for technical assistance for human rights in development should be the following:

1. Support the development and strengthening of laws, institutions, and programs that reinforce a democratic, economic, and social environment in which productivity is increased by the creative forces of free peoples;

2. Support the development and strengthening of a national human rights system in each country based on constitutional, legal, judicial, and administrative guarantees; educational, dissemination, and institutional arrangements; and specialized institutions for tackling the rights of vulnerable groups and the activities of human rights NGOs;

3. Help overcome human rights problems;

4. Train human rights-related personnel;

5. Support the ratification and application of international human rights norms;

6. Promote national and regional exchanges of experiences of human rights issues; and

7. Promote a culture of human rights in each country.[29]

Ramcharan also suggests that before a technical assistance project is initiated, a human rights profile of a country should be prepared to ensure that the project fits a rational strategy for strengthening respect for human rights in that country. I am in full accord with this idea; the people affected should be involved from the inception of the project. I trust that the profile will be prepared in consultation with the local human rights groups and governments, as well as civic leaders. Much of the development work in Africa must be done in the rural communities where most of the masses concentrate. Therefore, the local government bureaucrats and chiefs should be consulted so that they too can encourage the local people to participate in any project. In the case of a human rights project, be it educational or a food distribution outlet, the leaders in the local communities are vital to clearing up any anxieties the local people might have. For instance, when one human rights organization tried to offer free educational training in one of the local governments in Nigeria, the workers were reluctant to participate (as mentioned earlier). Even after they were told it was free, and they would be provided meals, lodging, and transportation costs, this did not help much. It is the chiefs and local government chairmen that these people look up to who can encourage and persuade them to appreciate the efforts of outside groups.

Ramcharan makes another suggestion—that perhaps an international institute of repute could be mandated to prepare and publish a global compendium of human rights and technical assistance needs of each country. Many Africans argue that external bodies always say what is good for Africa, and they object strongly to this attitude. Some Africans point out that in international fora there are usually many Africanists, but no Africans. When it comes to preparing this compendium of technical needs for Africa, the research could be done by indigenous Africans and then sent to the international institute. On the other hand, that body should work in close collaboration with African human rights NGOs.

The international community is criticized in other areas regarding its human rights performance. In fact, among many experts, there is the feeling that human rights protection within the international community is more rhetoric than reality. That is the thinking of Clarence Dias as he points to the inconsistencies in the performance of western governments, multinationals, and so on, and the impact of their actions on the lives of people in the Third World. He argues that "the process for international enforcement of human rights has tended to reek of hypocrisy with powerful countries adopting holier-than-thou attitudes in declaring, 'Do as I say and not as I do.' "[30] Dias points to three major flaws in the western liberal paradigm of human rights:

1. The idea of basic human needs and economic, social, and cultural rights is often translated as a conflict between bread and freedom and, with the liberal conceptions, freedom

usually wins. He recalls the words of Indian jurist Upendra Baxi, who stressed that "without bread, freedom of speech and assembly, of association of conscience and religion, of political participation . . . may be existentially meaningless for its victims."

2. Modern human rights thinking is excessively state-centered. Dias notes that the liberal discourse on rights is focused primarily on the rights of citizens against the state. However, an individual suffers the same degree of harm whether the violator is the state, a powerful landowner, an employer, or a multinational corporation. He points out that problems of securing relief and redress may be greater in pursuing nonstate actors than the state.

3. There is unwillingness to address issues relating to the use of violence in the claimed assertion of human rights. Dias notes that violence by nonstate actors purporting to exercise their rights is not a proscribed issue. He argues that the use of violence against any person must be brought under the regime of human rights laws. In his view, both the violence of the oppressed and the violence of the oppressor play a crucial role in the creation, promotion, and protection of human rights. He points out that violation of the rights of the elites is usually labelled as violence, while the violation of the rights of the impoverished to remain human is not labelled as violence.[31]

Dias is yet another voice challenging the universality of human rights norms. Human rights tenets are selectively applied and are definitely class-centered. The current process will not bring many changes to Africa's majority. Human rights will only be attained by civil society in Africa when they are enlightened to struggle for such rights.

Dias also dispels most of the western liberal notion of human rights as myths. He argues that the idea that harmony, which would exist in a situation where the haves would be forced to change their affluent style so that the have-nots could enjoy a humane existence, is a myth. He also argues that although the values enshrined in human rights instruments are said to be universal, it is a myth to believe that there is universal consensus about living up to these standards. On the question of equality, Dias agrees that the reality is that it is "all for the strong and none for the weak."[32]

Marc Bossuyt also finds weakness in the UN human rights machinery. He points to the politicization of human rights as the inherent weakness in the functioning of the UN Human Rights Commission. Bossuyt is concerned that governments, who are usually the main violators of human rights, are the ones who have voting rights with the Commission. He points out that it is NGOs who provide indispensible information on human rights violations, and it is through their efforts that governments are forced to take initiative.[33] Yet, NGOs are unable to table resolutions in the UN Commission on Human Rights. Bossuyt feels that human rights should be treated as an independent element of foreign policy. He states, "it is only when this is done that human rights stands a fair chance of being dealt with in an even-handed and credible manner."[34] Bossuyt also points to the lack of funding for the UN Centre for Human Rights, noting that the center is allocated less than 0.7 percent of the UN budget.[35] He laments that even this minimal amount is not made available, and if there is no immediate remedy, he fears the system could break down. In such an eventuality, progress made in the human rights field could be jeopardized.

Bossuyt shares a similar view to Ramcharan that human rights should be seen as an important aspect of development assistance. As he puts it,

For too long, development assistance has been seen as a purely technical matter without sufficient attention being given to the human rights dimension. Development assistance misses the point if it does not improve the living conditions and the human rights of the peoples of developing countries. Speeches lamenting deplorable human rights conditions in developing countries are empty if there is no willingness to respond effectively to the requests from the governments concerned for assistance to promote the minimum institutional machinery necessary for guaranteeing the rule of law.[36]

CONCLUSION

Human rights NGOs will be the catalyst for change in Africa as they seek political and economic justice on behalf of the oppressed. Some of the human rights NGOs have questionable agendas and are not making any significant contribution to the cause. However, there are others that are laying a solid foundation for grassroots education and the promotion of human rights. This augurs well for the future, since the appropriate structures are being laid. It is my belief that present governments will not take too keen an interest in efforts to promote human rights or to propagate human rights education. That is why I agree with Shivji that "human rights activity cannot be separated from the general struggle of the people against oppression. . . . Human rights struggles are an integral part of social movements and that is where human rights activity should be presently located."[37]

This would call for united efforts between human rights NGOs and the masses to confront poverty, violation of civic and political rights and, ultimately, to achieve a just society in Africa.

NOTES

1. Issa Shivji, *The Concept of Human Rights in Africa* (London: CODESRIA, 1991), p. 88.

2. See "NGOs and the Sustenance of Democracy in Africa," summary, conclusions, and papers presented at a conference of the Africa Leadership Forum in collaboration with the Friedrich Naumann Foundation, held in Ibadan, Nigeria on November 20–22, 1992, p. 28.

3. Alex P. Schmid and Albert J. Jorgman, eds., *Monitoring Human Rights Violations*, (Leiden University, The Netherlands: Centre for the Study of Social Conflicts, 1993), p. 1.

4. Ibid., p. 2.

5. Ibid., p. 4.

6. See details in Gregg A. Beyer, "Human Rights Monitoring and the Failure of Early Warning: a Practitioner's View—The Case of the Issaks of Somalia," in Schmid and Jorgman, *Monitoring Human Rights Violations*, pp. 111–114.

7. Shivji, *The Concept of Human Rights in Africa*, p. 61.

8. Ibid.

9. Schmid and Jorgman, *Monitoring Human Rights Violations*, p. 6.

10. Ibid., p. 66.

11. Ibid., pp. 66–67.

12. Henry Shue, *Basic Rights: Subsistence, Affluence and US Foreign Policy* (Princeton, N.J.: Princeton University Press, 1980), p. 53. Quoted in Richard Pierre Claude and Burns Weston, eds., *Human Rights in the World Community* (Philadelphia: University of Pennsylvania Press: USA, 1989), pp. 147–148.

13. Rhoda Howard and Jack Donnelly, "Assessing National Human Rights Performance: A Theoretical Framework," *Human Rights Quarterly* 10, no. 2 (1988): 214–248.

14. Schmid and Jorgman, *Monitoring Human Rights Violations*, p. 91. See also pp. 142–149.

15. Jack Donnelly, "Conceptual Issues in Monitoring Human Rights Violations," in Schmid and Jorgman, *Monitoring Human Rights Violations*, p. 92.

16. Ibid.

17. Ibid., pp. 91–92.

18. This is the definition adopted by the Decade for Human Rights Education in New York.

19. For more details see Adama Deng, ed., *Paralegals in Rural Africa*, seminars in Banjul, Gambia, 1989 and Harare, Zimbabwe, February 1990 (Geneva: International Commission of Jurists, 1991).

20. Paulo Freire, *Pedagogy of the Oppressed* (New York: Continuum Publishing Company, 1989), p. 70.

21. Henry J. Steiner, *Diverse Partners: Non-Governmental Organizations in the Human Rights Movement*. A report of a retreat of human rights activists (Boston: Harvard Law School Human Rights Program and Human Rights Internet, 1989).

22. Shivji, *The Concept of Human Rights in Africa*, p. 71.

23. *African Concord* (Lagos), December 28, 1992, p. 24.

24. Ibid.

25. Ibid.

26. See Amnesty International Annual Report, 1992, pp. 281–283.

27. B.G. Ramcharan, "Strategies for the International Protection of Human Rights in the 1990s," *Human Rights Quarterly* 13, no. 2 (May 1991): 165.

28. Ibid., p. 161.

29. Ibid., p. 168.

30. See Clarence Dias, "Rural Development, Grassroot Education and Human Rights: Some Asian Perspectives," in Kathleen Mahoney and Paul Mahoney, eds., *Human Rights in the Twenty-First Century: A Global Challenge* (Utrecht, The Netherlands: Kluwer Academic Publishers, 1993), p. 704.

31. Ibid., pp. 704–706.

32. Ibid., p. 703.

33. See Marc Bossuyt, "International Human Rights Systems: Strengths and Weaknesses," in Mahoney and Mahoney, *Human Rights in the Twenty-First Century*, p. 50.

34. Ibid., p. 51.
35. Ibid.
36. Ibid.
37. Shivji, *The Concept of Human Rights in Africa*, p. 89.

Chapter 6

Democratic Transition:
The Case of Nigeria

No nation can mumble throughout history.

Claude Ake[1]

Nigeria is the most populous country in Africa, with an estimated population of 88 million. The inhabitants are comprised of over 250 ethnic groups, the three main groups being the Hausa/Fulanis in the north, the Yorubas in the west, and the Igbos in the east. Each group has its own language and customs.

In the fourteenth century the Hausas converted to Islam and established a feudal system which was later solidified by the Fulani conquest in the nineteenth century. There was a centralized political system which allowed for separation of powers, and a reasonably independent judiciary. The Yorubas established the Oyo kingdom, which was generally headed by an oba. The political structure recognized lineage heads, chiefs, and the oba as paramount ruler. Although the oba wielded enormous power, there were checks and balances to ensure that the tendency toward authoritarianism would be curbed. There was also a machinery whereby vacant leadership positions were filled by the decisions of the chiefs. The Igbo community in the east established an egalitarian society whereby everyone had equal right to participate in the political process. People existed in small units and the clan heads represented the families.

At the end of the fifteenth century the European explorers began a lucrative slave trade with the Yorubas. By 1861 Britain outlawed the slave trade and later annexed the entire country into one colony in 1914. By this annexation an amalgam of peoples with different languages, customs, and orientations were brought under one head; this became the Republic of Nigeria when the country became independent in 1960. Not long after independence, tension exploded among the various ethnic groups, and led to the first coup in 1966. By 1967 the people of

Biafra, claiming to be unfairly treated within the Republic, declared their intention to secede. This action plunged the country into a traumatic civil war, which lasted for almost three years.

NIGERIA'S ECONOMY: FROM BOOM TO BUST

Nigeria is a country naturally endowed with oil, minerals, rubber, and cocoa, among other resources. In addition, Nigeria is blessed with a pool of the most highly educated individuals on the continent. The oil crisis in the early 1970s brought a boom to Nigeria's economy as oil exports increased to an estimated 2 million barrels per day. It is estimated that within a period of ten years the Nigerian economy saw a windfall yielding $100 billion dollars.[2] By 1985 Nigeria's economy had begun to decline, and the value of the naira began to slide. Nigeria had incurred a foreign debt of $12 billion,[3] and by 1986 the Babangida government introduced the Structural Adjustment Program (SAP). In implementing SAP, the government proceeded to deregulate the economy, remove government subsidies on important commodities, devalue the naira, and increase interest rates. Since then the inflation rate has skyrocketed, unemployment has increased, hunger and malnutrition have been the lot of many, and the health care system is near collapse as only the rich can afford to pay for medical care. Some diseases which were considered eradicated have even reemerged. After undergoing the brunt of SAP for three years, Nigerians finally took to the streets in May 1989 in an uprising that has been dubbed "The SAP Riot." When the dust settled and all the anger vented, some were dead, some thrown into prison, and the government distributed some relief packages. Such is the environment in which the Babangida administration has been attempting to steer Nigeria toward a Third Republic.

THE TRANSITION PROGRAM

Nigeria's attempts at democracy have been fraught with disappointment and uncertainty. After thirty-two years of independence, the country has experienced eight military coups and two failed attempts at civilian rule. In spite of these failures, Nigeria's hope for human development rests on the establishment of democratic governance. There is need to acknowledge that such a system will take time to evolve. Most importantly, it should adapt to Nigeria's peculiar needs and must benefit the majority of its citizens. With the largest population in the continent, Nigeria is seen as the torch-bearer for Africa; thus, achieving a lasting democracy in Nigeria would energize efforts at democratization in other parts of the continent.

The Babangida administration embarked on a timetable leading toward a democratic Third Republic in Nigeria in 1986 with the setting up of the Political Bureau. The bureau was mandated to draw up a comprehensive timetable for a transition from a military to a democratically elected government. The principle objective of the bureau was to ensure that a solid foundation was laid for a democratic culture in Nigeria. The report of the Political Bureau recommended, among other things, a two-party system and the empowerment of women and youths. Most of the recommendations were rejected outright. The government subsequently decided to clean the political terrain of corrupt practices by promulgating Decree 25 of 1987, which imposed a ban on those political aspirants who had served in the two previous civilian regimes.

In order to ensure that the transition program was successfully executed, the Babangida administration established the National Electoral Commission (NEC) and the Directorate for Social Mobilisation (MAMSER). During the last quarter of 1987, the government also held nationwide local government elections on a no-party basis. After partisan politics was deproscribed in 1989, thirteen political parties applied to the NEC for registration, but they all failed to meet the requirements imposed by the NEC. The government therefore disbanded political associations and later created two political parties—one a little to the left, the Social Democratic Party (SDP); the other a little to the right, the National Republican Convention (NRC).

Most Nigerians decried the action as arbitrary. They abhorred the fact that two parties were imposed upon the people of Nigeria and left them no choice but to join either one or the other party. Renowned economist and critic Sam Aluko forthrightly questioned this move by noting that the government had forced an assemblage of incompatibles to come together. He lamented that when a nation gives its rule to the military, that nation is finished.[4] Stressing the need to change the current political operations in the country, Claude Ake later remarked,

Our obsessive fear of allowing important social cleavage to be a basis of political parties and political pluralism has saddled us with two alienated political parties which are so similar that they offer no choice. Not knowing who they are and where they are coming from they cannot know where they are going.[5]

Amidst all the hue and cry of dissenting voices, the transition program was initiated. The transition timetable was set as follows:

July–September 1987: Establishment of
 The Directorate of Social Mobilisation
 The National Electoral Commission
 Constitution Drafting Committee
October–December 1987:
 Election of local government on a non-party basis
January–March 1988: Establishment of
 Population Commission
 Code of Conduct Bureau

Code of Conduct Tribunal

Constituent Assembly

Revenue Mobilisation Commission

April–June 1988:

Termination of Structural Adjustment Program (SAP)

July–December 1988:

Consolidation of gains of SAP

January–March 1989:

Promulgation of a new constitution

Release of new fiscal arrangements

April–June 1989:

Lift of ban on party politics

July–September 1989:

Announcement of two recognized and registered political parties

September–December 1989:

Local government election on party basis

January–June 1990:

Governorship and state legislature elections

July–September 1990:

Convening of state legislatures

October–December 1990:

Swearing in of state executives

January–December 1991:

Census

January–June 1992:

Election into federal legislatures and convening of National Assembly

July–December 1992:

Presidential Elections and final disengagement by the Armed Forces.[6]

As events unfolded over the years, there were frequent arbitrary changes and adjustments. The transition program foundered and wobbled, with the hand-over date changing from 1992 to January 1993 and later to August 1993.

The local government election was held in December 1990, a year behind schedule, while the gubernatorial and state legislative elections were postponed to December 1991. In addition, SAP, which was to have terminated in 1988, remained in place with even greater hardship. The naira continued to depreciate while the cost of living was at an all-time high, thus wiping out the middle class in Nigeria. The national debt, which stood at around $12 billion at the commencement of SAP, stood at about $33 billion by the end of 1992.[7] In May 1992, the people again took to the streets to vent their frustrations over the high cost of living as well as in reaction to a fuel shortage which saw transportation fares increase. Yet, there was no relief in sight for suffering Nigerians; things only got worse. The government justified the alterations in the transition program, claiming that there were urgent national problems to resolve before handing over.

The government embarked on a policy of states creation, which many argued would only weaken the basis for a stable Third Republic in Nigeria. Recognizing that new states need about three years to be properly organized before they participate effectively in any democratic transition program, it was suggested that the new state should have been created by 1987 to participate in 1990 elections. Nonetheless, the government continued to create new states during the transition program. The creation of new states adversely affected the activities of the two political parties and imposed unexpected financial strains on them. Another dilemma for both parties was that, like para-statals (state-owned enterprises), they had been funded by the government and never had financial independence. With the increased burden of new states, they were further dependent on the military regime for financing. Apart from the financial dilemma, the parties faced a constitutional crisis in adjusting to the sudden changes in the geographical configuration of the country as new states were created.

Money, Corruption, and Bribery

Apart from the problems of state creation, the government made the presidential campaign a race for the wealthy only. The NEC demanded a half million naira as registration fee for all presidential aspirants. This eliminated the women hopefuls from the presidential primary, as most of them were unable to raise such a huge sum of money. The campaign for president then became one for men only, in which all the "moneybags" vied to grasp the helm of the country. The conduct of elections and the bitter rivalry between both parties gave rise to corruption and vote rigging as never before witnessed in the country. Respected Nigerian hero Obafemi Awolowo had warned in 1980 that "Nigeria as a corporate entity would not survive another large scale and shameless election rigging as seen in the second republic or those who continue to rig the elections would only succeed in rigging Nigeria herself, as a country, out of existence."[8] His words would now seem to have been almost prophetic. The rigging of the October 1992 elections sent such seismic shocks throughout the country that, as Nigeria celebrated thirty-two years of independence, many began to question whether Nigeria could survive as one nation.

Corruption has become the bane of Nigerian society. Corruption poses a threat to democratization in Nigeria because state power has become the vehicle for personal enrichment and upward mobility. Politics in Nigeria is based on a winner-take-all system, and this incentive for riches drives ambitious people to resort to devious activities to get hold of power. Consequently, political rivals engage in rigging, bribery, and other misdeeds. This is what makes corruption treacherous to democracy in Nigeria. It bedevils the character of political competition, ruins the economy, and whittles away at the moral fabric of the society.

The political aspirants capitalized on the ignorance and want in which the majority of Nigerians are trapped. They merely resorted to buying votes but demonstrated no genuine interest in identifying the needs of the masses. During the time the politicians were jostling for the leadership of Nigeria, teachers were more often on strike than in the classroom because the government neglected to pay their salaries. In addition, the schools remained grossly overcrowded and ill-equipped, lacking teaching materials and modern laboratory equipment. Yet none of the politicians made any effort to improve education in Nigeria. For example, none of the politicians donated books or proposed to build a school from their personal finances. And some were reported to have spent close to a billion naira. The needs of the majority for basic sustenance such as food, proper health care, and education appeared to be no concern of theirs. None of them attempted to address the lack of basic infrastructure, such as reliable electricity, good roads, sewage disposal, potable water in rural communities, health care, and sanitation. Nigerian politicians spent enormous sums of money in their bid to gain power simply by buying votes or manipulating the machinery. Some were even said to have placed money in bread and passed it out to voters in the queues to lure them to change queues.

Nigerians have become so alienated from the government as an institution that they have no qualms about accepting bribes for their votes. There is no loyalty toward the state since people are generally of the view that politicians seek power in order to loot the treasury. For this reason, the masses see election time as an opportunity to get their share of the pie and are prepared to sell their votes to the highest bidder. SAP has also brought such untold hardship on the people that the destitute masses will do anything to survive. As Sam Apeh wrote in his letter to the *African Concord*, "Nigerians were forced to sell their consciences to survive the hard times accentuated by SAP. What is important to the common man today is democracy of the stomach."[9]

Larry Diamond had adequately analyzed the psychological orientation of Nigerians toward corruption in the following statement:

Both the elite and masses have schizophrenic mentalities: The politicians want to make democracy work to get rich doing so, even though their corrupt enrichment will quite likely bring down democracy. The masses, meanwhile, retain their profound cynicism regarding politics, but remain ready to join in whatever morsels can be had. Such schizophrenia produces all the intensity and passion of mass politics, but with none of the loyalty to democracy that would deter a military coup.[10]

To test the validity of Diamond's statement, I put the following proposition to a young Nigerian: "If one of these corrupt politicians offered you one million naira, would you take the money, or would you decry his corruption?" The individual replied that he had experienced such increasing hardship over the years that if a corrupt and unworthy aspirant made him such an offer, he would accept the money. Furthermore, he would never again speak one word in dissent against that aspirant. And if it became necessary, he would even revile anyone who dared to speak disparagingly about that politician. This is only one example, but one can safely say that many Africans would have made the same decision as this poor suffering individual.

In one particular community, individuals confided to me that on some days they drank gari for their three meals and, at times, if there was not enough gari to have three times, they would skip the portion they would have had for dinner and leave it for the next day. Would there be any way to convince such a person not to sell his vote or to be concerned about moral issues? Rousseau argued that none should be so poor as to be forced to sell himself, but the hardship experienced by many Nigerians has forced them to sell themselves without any reservations. The level of material lack has played a significant role in diminishing the chances of genuine democracy in Africa. There are other related problems as well. There is such a marked difference between the exploitative and ostentatious lifestyles of the rich in contrast to the degrading poverty of the poor that the situation has engendered bitterness and anger in the Nigerian society. Consequently the society is menaced by an increase in armed robbery and hosts of other social ills.

Women's Involvement in the Transition Program

Nigerian women are no longer prepared to sit back and surrender leadership of the Third Republic to men. As one articulate female politician asserted, "after we have given our men thirty years and we have ended up with an unsatisfactory state of affairs, women should now be given a chance to put things right."[11]

Despite their enthusiasm, Nigerian women who contested seats in the recent elections were unable to win enough support to get hold of the reigns of power. From among all the hopefuls who were initially in the race, only Ms. Kofo Bucknor-Akerele emerged as a senator-elect. Many women feel that religious and societal norms, lack of adequate education and exposure, and lack of financing militated against them. Most of the capable female aspirants were unable to raise the huge sums of money needed to compete against the so-called "moneybags" in the presidential primaries. The male-dominated bureaucracy had relegated the highest office of the land to those who could make the highest bid. In spite of a disappointing showing in the race for the Third Republic, the fact that Nigerian women have shown they are politically conscientized enough to jump into the political arena is a promising sign. Leadership in Africa will require the expertise of capable African women. Therefore, the political landscape will have to be altered, and soon. Nigerian women (Sarah Jibril, Rose Acholonu, Bolanle Awe, and others) have the intelligence and capability to steer their country out of its state of confusion. They must never relent. In fact, I have enough reason to believe that Africa's most populous country could one day be headed by a woman.

Nigeria's Human Rights Performance

Chapter four of the Nigerian constitution guarantees Nigerians the right to life, personal liberty, freedom of expression, and freedom to own property. Notwithstanding these provisions, the government has detained human rights crusaders unlawfully, continued attacks on students and academics, and has taken steps to muzzle the press. Within the community, Nigerians have been subjected to police persecution of innocent citizens, arbitrary killings by police, military harassment, and total disregard for their fundamental human rights.

While the Nigerian constitution states that citizens have fundamental rights, oftentimes one cannot get justice in courts. Reports in the *Constitutional Rights Journal* claim that the judiciary in Nigeria is far from independent. The human rights magazine explains that judges are appointed and dismissed by the Armed Forces Ruling Council (AFRC), and are thereafter sworn in by state governors. This being the case, a judge, being aware that he who hires also fires, would be loathe to decide cases against the hirer.

The right of Nigerians to choose their leaders has been usurped by the military. After staging a coup d'etat, these self-proclaimed messiahs immediately seek to entrench themselves in power by promulgating decrees. The Nigerian government passed a number of draconian laws which infringed on the rights of Nigerians. Noted among these decrees is the infamous (Detention of Persons) Decree No. 2 of 1984. This decree vests powers in appropriate officers to detain persons for acts prejudicial to state security without recourse to the courts. Decree 2 was a potent instrument for the violation of Nigerians' fundamental human rights, since it could be used indiscriminately by government functionaries to derogate the rights of social justice activists. Other obnoxious decrees included the Federal Military Government (Supremacy and Enforcement of Persons) Decree No. 13 of 1984. In addition, there were a number of other decrees which the government promulgated to keep the Nigerian polity in check. Such authoritarian measures only served to obstruct the transition to democracy as they not only negated the basic rights of the citizens, but at the same time they ousted the jurisdiction of the courts. The list included:

1. The Trade Union Decree No. 31 of 1973.
2. State Security (Detention of Persons) Decree No. 2 of 1984.
3. The Federal Military Government (Supremacy and Enforcement of Persons) Decree No. 13 of 1984.
4. Public Officers (Special Provisions) Decree No. 17 of 1984.
5. Transition to Civil Rule (Political Programme) Decree No. 19 of 1987.
6. Participation in Politics and Elections (Prohibition) Decree No. 25 of 1987.
7. National Electoral Commission (Amendment) Decree No. 8 of 1989.
8. Local Government (Basic Constitutional and Transitional Provisions) Decree No. 15 of 1989.

9. National Population Commission Decree No. 23 of 1989.

10. Student Union Activities (Control and Regulation) Decree No. 47 of 1989.[12]

In order to ensure that a culture of silence permeated Nigerian journalism, the government frequently raised its heavy hand against freedom of the press. When the *African Concord* published an in-depth analysis of the government's ineffective economic policies earlier in 1992, blaming the Babangida administration for the hardships inflicted on Nigerian people, the government's security agents immediately sealed off the newspaper's premises and closed down the publication. It was not until the chairman of Concord Publications, M.K.O. Abiola, relented and apologized to the government that the news organ was permitted to resume operations.

At the same time, Nigerians continued to languish in the memory of Dele Giwa, the Nigerian journalist who was killed by a letter bomb in 1986. The case remained unresolved, but Nigerians suspected that the state security service was responsible for the assassination. Following the death of Dele Giwa, Nigeria's generally outspoken press diluted their style of investigative reporting.

Open Ballot

Another feature of Nigeria's transition to democracy was the introduction of the open ballot system. Although authorities argued that the open ballot was intended to minimize electoral malpractices, there continued to be inflation of votes—technical rigging to the extent that in some constituencies the number of votes counted exceeded the census population figures for that particular area. It was reported that the rigging had become so pervasive that it was seen as heralding in a form of "new math" (an equation in which rigging on one side + rigging on the other side = 0 complaint). This was reported to be the argument that both parties made in defending themselves: "You rig and I rig, so what is there to complain about?"

The open ballot continued to disenfranchise a large portion of the electorate, many of whom feared recrimination from spouses, landlords, chiefs, elders, and employers. Money also became such a significant factor in elections in Nigeria that people were reported to have changed queues on the basis of which of the candidates made the highest offer for their votes. The use of the open ballot also contravened Article 21(3) of the UN Declaration of Human Rights, which states: "The will of the people shall be the basis of the authority of government; this shall be expressed in periodic and genuine elections which shall be by universal and equal suffrage and shall be held by secret vote."

Confrontation with Human Rights Groups

Many of the human rights organizations in Nigeria were skeptical of the conduct of the transition program, and they made this known to the government. In

November 1991 a coalition of major human rights groups in Nigeria formed an organization called the Campaign for Democracy (CD). The new organization was comprised of activists from students' associations, women's organizations, lawyers' associations, and other human rights bodies. The CD was conceived as a nonpartisan coalition to mobilize Nigerians to fight to protect human rights and to democratize the country through popular participation. Among the injustices which the new group deplored were the endemic violations of human rights committed by the Babangida regime, the open ballot system, the hardship of SAP, and the arbitrary changes to the transition program. In addition, the draconian decrees passed by the present administration banned many Nigerians from participating in the political process. The CD noted that elections under the present transition program failed to meet even the minimum constitutional and international standard for fairness. They lamented the poor voter turnout, which was said to be as low as 10 percent. The CD further decried the situation in which duly elected local government officials, elected for two terms, were dismissed after eight months in office as a result of the creation of new states. In addition, the two parties were created by the AFRC, which also wrote the parties' manifestos. In this case the CD contended that neither of the parties could be relied upon to resolve the problems facing the country. The CD also expressed concern over the outbreak of ethnic and religious violence in Nigeria, which resulted in alarmingly high casualties. The coalition traced these events to the government's tendency to mix religious issues with the affairs of the state.

By April 1992 members of the state security services seized the passport of Olisa Agbakoba of the CLO, thus preventing him from attending a conference in The Hague. In May 1992 the government arrested Beko Ransome-Kuti, Chairman of the CDHR, Olusegun Mayegun, President of National Association of Nigerian Students (NANS), Femi Falana, a noted human rights lawyer, and Gani Fawehinmi, a social justice crusader. They were all arrested and charged with treasonable felony after they had made calls for a national conference to address the myriad problems confronting the country. In spite of a judge's order that the detainees be presented in court, the government ignored the court order and continued to hold the activists incommunicado for almost a month.

Nigeria's democratic and human rights performance has been adequately summarized by the noted scholar Eme Awa:

In the Nigerian context, empirical evidence shows that there is gross deficiency in comprehension of equality and freedom. Equality of opportunity through the provision of education for all or even the lowest is regarded as some luxury which the government may take up at a convenient time. The great majority of our people are therefore not equal in the sense. . . . Our understanding of the concept of freedom is mostly superficial, for most people relate it to the opportunity to talk freely about all sorts of problems, but that the poor, the ignorant, the sick and the weak are being denied freedom by society is beyond appreciation of many, even among the intellectuals . . . the Nigerian brand of liberal democracy does result in the kind of inequality that dwarfs man and degrades general humanity.[13]

The Ethnic/Religious Rivalry

The persistent ethnic question and fermenting religious tension became a cause of worry for the march toward the Third Republic in Nigeria. In 1991 the religious hostility between Christians and Muslims erupted in a riot in Zango Kataf in Northern Nigeria (this incident is described more fully in Chapter 4).

The Zango Kataf incident brought Nigeria to the boiling point, but at the same time other ethnic frustrations continue to ferment. For one thing, the old wounds of Biafra still linger. Colonel Ojukwu (the former Biafran leader who was disqualified as a presidential aspirant for the Third Republic) found strong support among Igbos when he claimed that he was discriminated against because he is an Iboman. Many Ibos complain that they are discriminated in employment because of their tribe. At the same time, other ethnic groups have become more vocal. Ken Saro-Wiwa of the Ogonis, another minority tribe, has been unrelenting in his call for an equitable share of the resources of their state. The Ogonis claim that while the oil and other resources are found on their soil, they enjoy very little in terms of improved amenities and decent living standards. The Ogonis sought international support in order to draw attention to their plight and to ensure their demands were not ignored. Still other groups, such as the residents in Benue State, remain disgruntled about how they have been treated. They continue to immortalize Gideon Okar, who was executed after leading a coup in 1990. Okar was attempting to ensure that the people of his state had a fair share as well; thus, his fellow tribesmen see him as a hero. One problem in Nigeria that has been overlooked for a long time is that the three major ethnic groups have conducted the affairs of the country as though the more than 250 other groups were nonexistent. This has brought another dimension to the problem of governance in Nigeria, as minority groups have begun to demand their fair share of the nation's pie and assert their right to participate.

The ethnic/religious rivalry has always been featured in Nigerian politics. It was the interethnic conflict that led to the civil war in 1960, and the situation has not changed much since then. There is resentment among southerners who feel that the northerners are not prepared to give up their hold on power. The tension between the Hausa-Fulanis in the north and the rest, being the Igbos and the Yorubas, characterized the march to the Third Republic, so much so that the question of whether the leader should be a northerner or southerner were all deciding factors among the citizenry. Ethnicity and religion became such important features in Nigerian politics that some experts advised the flagbearers to ensure a mixture of Muslim president and Christian vice president to appease both groups. Some strategic moves were also made to select vice presidents from certain ethnic groups which would guarantee the votes of the residents in those states.

Both parties exploited and manipulated the ethnic/religious factor to ensure their party's victory. Yet, only two weeks before the June 12 elections in 1993, I heard an official on the radio imploring Nigerians to refrain from voting along ethnic or religious lines. I thought the statement was ludicrous, because it is precisely the way most of the people vote. Those who thirst for power want it badly enough to exploit any means to get it, especially in Nigerian politics, where there is no such thing as a graceful loser.

Botched Primary

As the transition to democracy continued to wobble along, the political scenario in Nigeria degenerated into a theatrical spectacle of rigging, bribery, and cheating. The entire public was so disgusted with the turn of events that the Babangida administration was inundated with pleas from patriotic Nigerians to put an end to the necrotic ailment that had become endemic within the Nigerian polity. Most critics placed the blame on the NEC for its conduct of the elections. The NEC had sweeping powers to disqualify aspirants without giving reasons, and often did so after the aspirant had already won the nomination. As part of its mandate, the NEC was to supervise the two parties, monitor their activities, and screen their candidates. The NEC also made the decisions as to who should be the leader of each of the two parties, and laid down the ground rules as to how the contest was to take place. Although the NEC had such wide powers, the Commission refused to conduct the presidential primaries for the two parties, even after the first attempt was botched.

After the shameful display of presidential aspirants in October 1992, the CLO called on the Babangida government to dissolve the AFRC and inaugurate the National Assembly to handle the country's affairs. The human rights organization pointed out that the transition to democracy had failed under the Babangida administration and therefore the government should resign. Beko Ransome-Kuti, Chairman of the Campaign for Democracy, lamented that the march to progress in Nigeria was in reverse and, in spite of the country's enormous resources, Nigeria was thrown down the ladder of prosperity to the "thirteenth poorest nation in the world" (according to World Bank 1992 statistics). The human rights crusader called for a national conference to address the country's problems. In sheer exasperation, Ransome-Kuti lamented, "Never in the history of the country has pent-up frustration grown so high! Never has the future become so bleak for the young and upcoming generation of Nigerians! Never has pessimism on the continuity of Nigeria as a corporate existence risen so high."[14]

Calling on Babangida to hand over the government by January 1993 as planned, former head of state General Olusegun Obasanjo lamented that all the values Nigerians held dear were being assaulted, and the nation was wracked by tension and despair. He further added that hope had become a scarce commodity in the country, while fear was a constant companion. Obasanjo pointed out that the crisis was preventable. He felt that a lack of honest purpose and diligence in implementation of the program were responsible for the rugged trudge in which Nigerians were marching toward democratic rule. The retired general further lamented that

In the name of political engineering, the country has been converted to a political laboratory for trying out all kinds of silly experiments and gimmicks. Principle has been abandoned for expediency. All kinds of booby-traps were instituted into the transition process. The result is the crisis we now face.[15]

Babangida ignored all calls for his resignation. However, as a consequence of the barrage of complaints and public outcry, the government promulgated Decree 37, which stipulates penalties for erring aspirants. The Babangida administration then assured Nigerians that those aspirants found guilty of electoral malpractices would be dealt with in accordance with the decree. By the time the dust settled over the bungled presidential primaries, the AFRC cancelled the primaries and set up caretaker committees for both the SDP and NRC. By November 1992, as Nigerians waited to learn the fate of the transition program, the Babangida administration disqualified all the presidential aspirants and introduced a new transition timetable, which Babangida explained was in accordance with Option A4, as recommended by the NEC. He then extended the transition program to August 27, 1993.

Option A4 was a process of elimination which operated in four stages: the ward, the local government, the state level, and the national level. The winning aspirant for a political party would proceed from one stage to the next until one individual emerged as the winner. Option A4 introduced an entirely new approach to the transition program. The initial selection of candidates was done by wards at the local government level. Following this selection, the presidential aspirants who had been endorsed were presented to a special delegates' state congress of the party. The state congress totalled nearly 1,400 delegates, selected from the various wards and local government areas of the state. Each member of the congress voted for one of the presidential aspirants of the party from the state. The flagbearer emerged from the aspirant who received the highest number of votes. In a situation in which there was only one presidential aspirant from a state, the aspirant would have been endorsed or rejected by a majority "Yes" or "No" vote. By the end of this exercise there was expected to be thirty-one aspirants for each party. Three days later, a special delegates' national convention was convened to elect the party's flagbearer. Under Option A4, on Day 1, members of the special convention were accredited. The first ballot took place on the second day, and each member voted for three persons. The first three aspirants to obtain the highest vote proceeded to the second ballot. The second ballot was held on the third day, and each member of the special convention voted for one of the three aspirants. The aspirant who obtained the highest vote eventually emerged as the party's flagbearer.

Initially, the newly introduced Option A4 raised skepticism among Nigerians. The general view was that Option A4 was a recipe for greater confusion than before. Of particular concern was the fact that the process would produce sixty-two candidates. Nigerians pointed out that the NEC could not properly handle thirty candidates before. Therefore, now that the number was doubled, there would be greater confusion. This would then give Babangida another reason to further extend the transition program. In the final outcome, Option A4 surprised the skeptics, and the process successfully produced two presidential candidates. For the National Republican Convention, the candidate was Bashir Othman Tofa, and Moshood K.O. Abiola was the candidate for the Social Democratic Party.

My view at this stage was that whoever won the leadership would face a daunting challenge in attempting to rectify the myriad problems confronting Nigeria at the time. As Claude Ake said,

the rot is deeper and more pervasive than it appears and much of what is offered by way of remedy does not even begin to address it. For the transition process in particular, it has succumbed to its own confusion and irrelevance to the necessities of democratization. . . . It may well be that we may soon have a civilian government. Even so, the real problems will remain unsolved, a veritable time-bomb. . . . We may be lucky to struggle to safety before it blows. Then again, we may not.[16]

Conclusion

Nigeria's transition to a democratic Third Republic was dogged by the deep-rooted problems of ethnicity, inequality, corruption, and political repression, as well as a lack of goodwill on the part of the government. Consequently, the seven-year-long democratization process became the longest transition in recent history anywhere in the world. When the transition program is examined in light of political participation, the majority were excluded when the NEC stipulated the half million naira registration fee for presidential aspirants. In addition, the open ballot disenfranchised many from the voting process. (The Open Ballot was later changed to the Modified Open Ballot System).[17] As Claude Ake stated when the aggrieved presidential aspirants lamented Babangida's outright banning, "Ordinary people had already been banned."[18]

In conducting the transition program, the Babangida administration committed serious and persistent human rights violations which gravely undermined the government's credibility and popular support. In addition, Babangida himself at no time demonstrated goodwill and sincerity toward establishing a democratic Nigeria. When he embarked on the transition program in 1986, Babangida set in place certain structures (MAMSER and the NEC in particular) to assist in social mobilization of the Nigerian society and prepare the population for democracy through public enlightenment programs. Most of these failed to bring about the expected results, yet Babangida did not move to correct these problems. The NEC, which was to be in charge of the transition program, failed to assume responsibility for the selection of candidates and left it in the hands of the two parties. Consequently, the infighting and corruption that ensued gave Babangida reason to continually alter the transition timetable.

There were reasons to question Babangida's sincerity each time he maintained his desire to hand over the helm of the country. For example, Babangida was not absent from Nigeria for any extended period during the transition program. He and the other government bureaucrats were watching all these developments. Why did the administration fail to make sure that the structures work by fine tuning them and making changes that would bring desired results? The only changes Babangida continually made had been in the handover date. Right up to the June 12, 1993 elections, it appeared that Babangida did not want to go. That being the case, he should have resigned from the military and declared his candidacy instead of misleading Nigerians.

Finally, this is a juncture in Nigeria's history packed with tension resulting from the hardship of SAP and the brazen inequity of lifestyles between the rich and the depraved. For these reasons, whoever wins the leadership of the Third Republic will have to perform a delicate balancing act. Democratization for Africans means a change in living conditions, and for that reason Nigerians are expecting a new leader to improve the value of the naira, lower the price of beans and gari, and deliver them from the misery they are currently undergoing. For the majority of Nigerians, "democracy of the stomach" is their concern at present, and nothing else matters. The question is: Will the new leader deliver, and how soon?

The problems in Nigeria are so severe that it will be a miracle if any improvements are made over the next few years. In the meantime, Nigerians will continue to suffer and the masses will become increasingly disgruntled. The military, who are only lurking in the barracks, will be ready to regain control. If things do not improve, the people might even be willing to accept the military when they move in again. This is an undesirable scenario, but it is a very likely one.

I made this analysis prior to the June 12 elections. The confusion that followed the annulment of the election results made way for another coup by November 1993.

Annulment of the Elections

Presidential elections were held in Nigeria on June 12, 1993. For the first time in Nigeria's history, the elections were considered to be free, fair, and orderly by both national and international observers. The SDP flagbearer, M.K.O. Abiola, carried the majority vote as president elect. However, in an unprecedented move, Babangida stunned the nation and the international community by ordering the cancellation of the election results. If anyone doubted whether or not Babangida was sincere about handing over the helm of Nigeria, they now had their answer. The reasons Babangida gave for the cancellation had no basis of support and were seen as flimsy and unacceptable. Following this unexpected turn of events, Nigeria was thrown into further chaos and uncertainty as anxiety heightened among its citizens. There was a mass exodus of foreigners, while nationals fled the city to return to what they considered the safe haven of their villages. The impasse dragged on for weeks while a flurry of dialogue between the international community, concerned Nigerians, and Babangida took place in an effort to find a successful solution to the impasse. Meanwhile, several newspapers were shut down and a number of journalists arrested. Many human rights activists were arrested, among them Femi Falana, Beko Ransome-Kuti, and Gani Fawehinmi. When a judge ordered their release, the government ignored the order by invoking the (Detention of Persons) Decree No. 2 of 1984, continuing to hold the activists in detention.

The cancellation of the first-ever fairly conducted democratic election in Nigeria damaged the country's image in the international community. Many began to question Nigeria's boast as being the giant of Africa. It also dashed the hopes of those who saw Nigeria assuming a leadership role on the continent in the twenty-first century. While the world watched with anxiety and nervous anticipation, General Babangida finally left office and handed over leadership to Ernest Shonekan (governor of the Central Bank of Nigeria) before August 27. A few months later, Nigerians faced yet another coup led by Sani Abacha. The problem of Nigeria's leadership is yet to be resolved, and Nigeria's future and the future of democracy in that country still remains doubtful.

NOTES

1. Claude Ake, "The Feasibility of Democracy in Africa," *Daily Times* (Lagos), October 12, 1992.

2. As quoted by Blaine Harden, *Africa, Dispatches from a Fragile Continent* (New York: W.W. Norton & Company, 1990), p. 288.

3. "Will Nigeria Survive?" *The African Guardian*, October 5, 1992.

4. *Tell*, April 15, 1987, p. 52.

5. *Daily Times* (Lagos), October 19, 1992, p. 7.

6. See Campaign for Democracy, Bulletin Number 2, "An Endangered Transition" (Lagos, Nigeria: CLO, n.d.), pp. 2–3.

7. See "Will Nigeria Survive?"

8. Obafemi Awolowo, *Path to Nigerian Greatness* (Enugu, Nigeria: Fourth Dimension Publishers, 1981), p. 176.

9. *African Concord*, October 26, 1992, p. 5.

10. See Larry Diamond, "Political Corruption: Nigeria's Perennial Struggle," *Journal of Democracy* 2, no. 4 (Fall 1991): 79–80.

11. Dupe Desioye, "Women Fight for Power as Third Republic Draws Near," *Poise* 2, no. 5 (July 1991): 8–11.

12. Olusegun Obasanjo and Akin Mobogunje, eds., *Elements of Democracy* (Ota, Ogun State, Nigeria: ALF Publications, 1992), p. 9.

13. Eme Awa, "Democracy in Nigeria: A Political Scientist's View," unpublished paper delivered to the Association of Political Scientists, Lagos, Nigeria, 1991.

14. See comments made by Beko Ransome-Kuti in "Nigeria Which Way Forward," *Liberty* (April–June 1992), p. 7.

15. *The Guardian*, November 16, 1992, p. 28.

16. *African Concord*, January 4, 1993, p. 12.

17. In this system all voters queue in one line, making it impossible to identify the

choice of a voter through the queue he/she joins. The accredited voter uses the voting card and chooses his/her candidate in secret, but casts the vote openly. Votes for each polling station are counted at the venue and results announced on the spot.

18. *African Concord,* January 4, 1993.

Democratization via National Conferences

Democratization in Africa was given added impetus following developments in Benin Republic at the end of the 1980s. The beginning of 1990 saw months of strikes and demonstrations as political activists pressed for democratic reforms in that country. Military leader Mathieu Kerekou, who had held power for over twenty years, convened a national conference which was intended to discuss the political and economic destiny of Benin Republic. The concept of a national conference originated in France over two hundred years ago. In this process the Estates-General of prerevolutionary France convened a gathering to discuss festering economic grievances. In contemporary Africa, a national conference brings together most of the important groups in civil society, such as church leaders, academics, trade unions, business groups, women's groups, and peasants to air their views and express their dissatisfaction with the leadership of their country. Such a move should enable citizens to release frustrations and foster healing.

The conference in Benin Republic was comprised of representatives from banned opposition groups and other political leaders. The gathering was mandated to discuss the country's problems and make recommendations to the government. The council which was set up to oversee the recommendations of the national conference approved, among other things, the formal establishment of a 42-member National Human Rights Commission. A new constitution was prepared which included important human rights safeguards prohibiting arbitrary detention and making torture a criminal offense. President Kerekou remained head of state while an interim government, headed by Nicephore Soglo, was to steer the country to democracy. When democratic elections were held in March 1991, the military regime of Kerekou was voted out of office. Thus, for the first time in the history of Africa, a military government was democratically voted out of power. Soglo became the first democratically elected leader of Benin Republic and was given the mandate to improve the economic performance of the country and to ensure that the fundamental liberties enshrined in the country's constitution would be upheld.

Buoyed by the results in Benin Republic, social justice crusaders in other parts of the continent have called for national conferences to address the political, economic, and social problems facing their countries. Noting that the UN Declaration of Human Rights guarantees citizens the right to self-determination, activists argue that a national conference offers all citizens the opportunity to proffer ideas as to what type of leader should govern them. Proponents point out that a national conference allows the society to reflect on the past, appraise the present, and contemplate the future as a collective body. This becomes even more necessary when the society is at odds with its fundamental constituents and the national survival is threatened. It is imperative that the community come together, identify the forces at work, combat the divisive ones, and promote the unifying ones. The end of such a process should be a regenerated society, buoyed with fresh hopes and new ideas geared toward collective advancement. Another argument is that a national conference would empower working groups of women and youths to undertake positive participation in nation building, which democracy is all about.

While such ideas may sound like the panacea for the end of authoritarianism in Africa, there are a number of factors that should be considered. For instance, when political activists pressed for a national conference in Nigeria after the botched elections of October 1992, renowned political scholar Claude Ake cautioned that national conferences were events of exceptional complexity which could degenerate into confusion, or worse.[1] Ake had this to say: "Going by the present state of our politics, there is just a chance that a National Conference could deteriorate into bitter contestation of parochial concerns with the result that instead of understanding our differences in order to manage them better, we may absolutize them to our grief."[2]

While pointing out one important consideration, Ake himself overlooked the need to have the backing of the military and other important factors. With some foresight, Ake could have undertaken research on this new experiment in democracy. Other scholars made some contribution. Zahui Gama Feidnad and Maitu Weneeslas De Saiza (1993) point out that for a national conference to succeed, the following are some of the factors that are necessary:

1. The present ruler must be generally interested in the process. Where that is the case the national conference succeeds in transforming the society. . . . If the present leader remains obdurate, disregards the democratic process and is determined to put self-interest first, the national conference will be doomed to fail.

2. External pressure tied to assistance conditionalities.[3]

These have been proven correct, but other factors have proven an impediment to the national conference experiment. These include the level of conscientization of the masses and the need to have the military on the side of the people. During the interim period leading up to elections, it is also neccessary to establish clearly who is really in charge. I will examine the national conference by discussing (1) the lack of commitment on the part of incumbent leaders and (2) the role of the military.

LACK OF COMMITMENT ON THE PART OF INCUMBENT LEADERS

While incumbent leaders appeared to cooperate with the national conference, they had no intention of giving up power. They simply intended to use this type of forum to ensure that their hold on power was legitimized by a democratic process. Even in Benin Republic the end result was not what Kerekou expected. If he was not lulled into a false sense of security, he would not have ordered his loyal soldiers to remain in the barracks. The main objective of the national conference in Africa is to unseat the long-standing tyrannical leader with a new, democratically elected leader. Therefore, key players such as Bishop Laurent Mosengo in Zaire and Kokou Koffigoh in Togo were mistaken to think that the incumbent military dictator would be willing to cooperate. Interim leaders were naive to embark on the exercise without the backing of the military, or without broad-based community support. (We will develop this argument later on.)

With the exception of a few cases, the national conference became victim of the whims and fancies of Africa's tyrants. While a few leaders acceded to public pressure to convene a national conference, others refused to capitulate. Both Blaise Compoare in Burkina Faso and Paul Biya in Cameroon have not acceded to calls for a national conference. Instead, Compoare opened a Forum for Reconciliation in February 1992, but this immediately stalled when no decision could be reached as to its mandate. Paul Biya ignored demands by opposition leaders and other groups for convening a national conference and extended his hold on power in the last election in Cameroon.

After a national conference was convened in the Congo, President Dennis Sassod Nguesso was stripped of power and Andre Milongo replaced him as interim leader. Following a national conference in Niger Republic in 1991, a new constitution was adopted and an interim government headed by Amadou Cheffou, working alongside President Ali Saibou, took over the helm of the country. While there was a ray of hope in some countries, in Gabon, Togo, and Zaire the national conference was frustrated by leaders who were determined to ignore the will of the people.

In Gabon, President Omar Bongo convened a national conference in 1990, but instead of releasing power to an interim leader, he moved to consolidate his stronghold on the people.

In 1991, President Gnassingbe Eyadema of Togo formed a transitional government headed by Prime Minister Kokou Koffigoh to steer the country to multiparty elections. The national conference in that country degenerated into a bitter power struggle between its supporters and the Togolese army. Interim Prime Minister Koffigoh had no power to make political or economic decisions regarding the running of the country. At one point, when he dismissed two ministers, Eyadema promptly reinstated them. In August 1992, Eyadema called off the referendum which was to ratify the constitution and the electoral laws, claiming that the draft law insisted that a presidential candidate must be at least forty-five years old and must not be a serving soldier. Clearly, Eyadema saw the law as preventing him and his faithful henchmen from attempting to seek power in future democratic elections. The national conference turned into a protracted standoff between Eyadema and Koffigoh while the country's economy ground to a halt. Meanwhile, the Togolese people lived in constant fear and uncertainty from day to day. Events began to reach a climax by late November 1992. The Togolese Trade Union called for a national strike to support democratization in the country and mobilize civil society to bring an end to the stalemate. As these events unfolded, Prime Minister Koffigoh was forced to call on outside intervention to help avert a full-scale civil war in that country. Despite such a reign of terror, Eyadema manipulated his way back into the running of Togo. When elections were held in 1993, he frustrated the leading opposition contender and wound his way back into power.

Similarly, when political elites demanded change in Zaire, President Mobutu Sese Seko reluctantly agreed to a national conference, which began in 1990. Mobutu did not give up his authority over the Zairean treasury and only embarked on a few modest reforms, such as releasing prisoners of conscience and allowing political opposition. The national conference was a victim of Mobutu's manipulations.[4] He constantly replaced interim leaders in an arbitrary manner to ensure he had his own way. At one point, Mobutu replaced Prime Minister Etienne Tshisekedi with Mungul Diaks, a former member of the UPDS (Union pour la Democratie et le Progres Social) who had lost credibility with the Zairean people. Tshisekedi was replaced on the pretext that he failed to swear fidelity to the constitution and the president. However, it was revealed that the real reason for his replacement was because he gave orders to block Mobutu's control of the currency. The conference was stalled in September 1991 and reopened three months later. This time the more than two thousand conference participants included political parties, public institutions, professional bodies, individual representatives from each region of the country, and NGOs. As soon as the conference organized itself into a well-directed working group, Prime Minister Nguz announced that it was suspended. The general suspicion was that the orders came from Mobutu himself. A deadlock followed in which Zaireans demonstrated their determination to continue the national conference. When the exercise reconvened, Tshisekedi was reappointed interim leader.

The Central Bank in Zaire was thrown into crisis in 1992 when Mobutu continued to release false currency. Interim Prime Minister Etienne Tshisekedi moved to assert his leadership and fired the governor of the Central Bank, Mr. Nyembo. The governor refused to leave and argued that only Mobutu who appointed him could fire him. Mobutu then reappointed Nyembo and went as far as to provide his Special President Divisions troops to surround the bank to ensure that Nyembo could have access to the bank. This was not only an embarrassment for the leaders of the national conference, but it demonstrated how powerless the key players were. When the experiment was initiated, the most serious oversight on the part of the key players was failing to establish clearly who was really in charge of the affairs of the country.

Transition to democracy in Zaire was hijacked by Mobutu's manipulations. He promised and cancelled elections, replaced interim leaders at will, and allowed disgruntled soldiers to unleash their fury on the Zairean people. Mobutu rejected any authority by the national conference to alter the provisional constitution or to appoint a transition government. He informed Zaireans that he alone could exercise the sovereign power of the people. Mobutu arrogantly announced that the national conference had no authority over him and that any legitimate government would have to be appointed by him. In 1993, Mobutu dismissed Tshisekedi and appointed his own crony, Faustin Birindwa, as interim Prime Minister. The national conference in Zaire remains stalled, and no elections have been held.

THE ROLE OF THE MILITARY

The military is a significant factor in the democratization movement in Africa. The military in Togo was in full support of Eyadema, and in Zaire the loyalty of the military continued to undergird Mobutu's bid to cling to power. Interim leaders did not have the backing of the military when they convened the national conferences, and that was largely the reason for the disappointment and humiliation they suffered.

From the time the national conference divested most of the leadership power to Prime Minister Koffigoh in 1991, Togo was destabilized by the army. When the Rally of the Togolese People (RPT) was outlawed in November 1991, fighting immediately broke out in which two people were killed and an estimated one hundred were injured. In that same month, the army surrounded the government headquarters and locked the prime minister inside. They then announced to the Togolese people that the transitional government had been ousted. This impasse resulted in the death of more than twenty people and left many more injured.

In the months that followed, soldiers loyal to Eyadema refused to release their hold on power. Instead, they unleashed a reign of violence and held the Togolese people hostage for almost two years. In the trail of events, the leader of the opposition, Gilchrist Olympio, was shot and wounded in May 1992 while four of his supporters were killed. An inquiry conducted by the Paris-based International Federation of Human Rights linked the attack to forces loyal to Eyadema, including his son, Ernest Eyadema. In June, another opposition leader was captured, beaten, and detained. In July, another opposition leader, Tavio Amorin, was gunned down and later died in Paris. When Togolese women organized a march in support of the transition program in August 1992, they were greeted with gunshots at early dawn, forcing them to disperse and cancel the march. By September, Togolese soldiers gave Prime Minister Koffigoh an ultimatum to announce his cabinet or they would announce their own. The outcome of the impasse was the formation of a new cabinet which included a number of former Eyadema cabinet members.

By October 1992, the Togolese army stormed the parliament and took forty deputies, three ministers, and other officials hostage. The soldiers, who besieged the Lome Congress Building throughout the night, demanded repayment of compulsory subscriptions they and other Togolese wage earners had paid to the former ruling party (the RPT) over a period of ten years (1980–1990). The money, estimated to be at 6.5 billion CFA,[5] was frozen when the national conference was convened in 1991. Ever since then both General Eyadema and members of the armed forces have demanded that they be reimbursed for their subscriptions in the RPT funds. The soldiers threatened to dissolve the national assembly and replace it with a provisional assembly unless the High Council of the republic passed a law within forty-eight hours ordering that they be given the money. The soldiers continued to intimidate the Togolese population by setting off a bomb at the French Co-operation Mission, not too far from the seat of parliament. Following these incidents, Prime Minister Kokou Koffigoh agreed to unfreeze the funds of the RPT, thus acceeding to the soldiers' demand.

The national conference in Zaire was also characterized by terror. Soldiers loyal to Mobutu harassed opposition groups, students, and human rights activists and intimidated the Zairean population. In May 1990 it is alleged that soldiers, dressed in civilian clothes, attacked students at the Lumbashi University campus, killing approximately twelve students. Although a parliamentary inquiry accused government and security officials of committing this atrocity, no one was brought to trial. By the end of that year, about thirty students were still under arrest after a demonstration in which several students were killed. When Prime Minister Nguz cancelled the newly reopened national conference in December 1991, workers went on strike and the people demonstrated in protest. Soldiers loyal to Mobutu harassed and intimidated the people and prevented them from exercising their civil rights. Following one of the marches, the director of the Zairean Human Rights League was detained by police while his home and office were ransacked. Harassment, torture, and the disappearance of opponents, including university students, followed. In 1993, Mobutu's loyal soldiers went on a rampage, killing an estimated one thousand innocent people, including the French Ambassador to Zaire.

Interim leaders were naive to embark on the exercise without any commitment from the army. They should have made overtures to woo the army to their side. From the start, a number of important details needed to be worked out. The idea of such a national forum looked promising on paper, and the key players left themselves open to be taken off guard. All that resulted during the period was a tug of war between forces loyal to Mobutu and Eyadema and those intellectuals (backed by a portion of civil society) who were aiming for political leadership of the country. Interim leaders lacked the power to wield influence. In Africa power flows from the barrel of a gun, and since the interim leaders had no guns, the leader who controlled the guns won out.

CONCLUSION

In both Zaire and Togo, leaders remained obdurate because they knew that material lack among the masses was a preoccupation. They also took advantage of the lack of political enlightenment among the majority. This allowed both Mobutu and Eyadema to resort to the usual ethnic loyalty to sway their tribesfolk and drag the country into a standoff between leaders. The national conference itself was another situation in which the intellectual elites were attempting to wrest power from their sit-tight leaders. Even though people of various strata of society participated in the forum, one needs to examine how they were selected. It was easy for participants to be corrupted because they received a per diem for attending, and for many this amounted to more than their usual earnings. Therefore, many people saw the gathering as a source of income. When all is said and done, the urban intellectuals were the ones who really had the last say. The role of a national conference should be that of a forum which makes decisions for the future direction of the country, and then dissolves. But in Zaire and Togo it became a partisan group with political ambitions and agendas. If the national conference is to succeed in Africa, the interim leader should be a neutral individual with no plans to contest the elections.

The international community did not do much to help the cause of the masses. Up until the French ambassador was killed in Zaire, the West was largely indifferent. If greater external pressure had come from western countries, the outcome might have been different, and the human suffering in those countries would have been significantly mitigated.

What could the West have done? For one thing, freeze all the assets these leaders stashed in western banks, thus leaving them without the means to support the army and their supporters among the comprador elite. Also, their elaborate lifestyles would have been affected over time if they could not get their hands on their wealth. The international community could have joined with the NGOs who were at the forefront of the struggle, such as the trade unions, the student groups, the academic unions, and the opposition groups, and supported them both locally and internationally. A number of students were killed in the Lumbashi attack in Zaire in 1990, but no penalty was imposed on Mobutu at the time. Unless international human rights NGOs do more than merely report human rights violations by African dictators, they will continue to ignore human rights tenets. It is disheartening that after all the suffering and killings Eyadema and his cronies inflicted on the Togolese people, he could deny the real opposition leader the right to stand for elections and maneuver his way back into power in

1993. One wonders how legitimate could such a regime be considered. Where are the international human rights norms that should be applied in this case?

The national conference itself is a good process to promote lasting democracy in Africa. However, those who convene such a forum should prepare the grass-roots community before embarking on the exercise. The only national conference in Africa that has resulted in democratic elections was the one in Benin Republic, where the discussion started at the grassroots level and then grew in popularity. It is important for the national conference to gain momentum from the grassroots level because the soldiers whom the selfish leaders use to thwart the exercise have family members themselves. If their mothers, sisters, wives, and so on were con-vinced of the importance of the national conference, these people could persuade the soldiers to take a position. In this case, interim leaders would have some support among the military, because a cross-section of the military would be forced to align themselves with the people. Outside such an eventuality, the ex-ercise becomes a class struggle. Even where an interim leader might not have the full support of the army, some soldiers would give support to the movement for change, and it is likely that there could be a split in the army. All this, coupled with mass popular support, could result in the sort of people power that drove Marcos out of power in the Philippines. Although that did not happen, these are errors from which one can learn. Existing democracies evolved over hundreds of years. Efforts to democratize Africa will involve experiments that must be tried and tested. No genuine change in Africa will be affected overnight.

NOTES

1. *African Concord,* January 4, 1993, p. 13.

2. Ibid.

3. See Zahui Gana Feidinad and Maitu Weneslas De Saiza, "Democratic Transition and Good Governance in Africa: Methods of Sharing Positive Experience Among African Countries," in Africa Leadership Forum, Conclusions and Papers Presented at Confer-ences of The Africa Leadership Forum on Sustainment of Democratization and Good Governance in Africa, Cotonou, Benin Republic, October 5–6, 1992; and "Challenges of Leadership in Democracy and Good Governance in Africa," Nairobi, Kenya, March 10–12, 1993 (Ogun State, Nigeria: ALF Publications, 1993), pp. 32–33.

4. For some details on this see "Zaire Two Years Without A Transition," *Africa Watch* (July 1992).

5. *African Concord,* November 9, 1992, p. 15.

Chapter 8

Challenges to Democracy and Human Rights in Africa

Africans have pursued a path to democratization out of sheer frustration over their dire need and the injustices that have been the fate of the majority. For oppressed and starving people, democratization means more than voting. When the voting is over, citizens look to their governments for improvement in their material condition. That is the problem that Boris Yeltsin faced in the newly formed Commonwealth of Independent States of the former USSR. People want immediate deliverance, and they demand it with all the force of the newfound liberty which they are allowed in the name of democracy. Alexis de Tocqueville in *Democracy in America* made a wise observation over a century ago, which is just as valid today.

General prosperity is favourable to the stability of all governments, but more particularly of a democratic one, which depends upon the will of the majority, and especially upon the will of that portion of the community which is most exposed to want. When the people rule, they must be rendered happy, or they will overturn the state: and misery stimulates them to those excesses to which ambition rouses kings.[1]

Poverty remains the greatest threat to the survival of democracy in Africa. The majority in Africa are victims of material and intellectual poverty. If democracy is to take hold in any meaningful way in Africa, there must be economic democratization. The economic structure must be altered to allow for a mixed economy with built-in mechanisms for equity, empowerment, and capacity building along with free, equal, and open access to the system. This means access for the majority, not just access for a few masters while the majority share the crumbs of the nation's pie. Such demands will be best articulated by enlightened masses.

Corruption and instability pose serious challenges to the establishment and sustenance of democracy on the continent and must be addressed with as much urgency as the poverty question.

Civil wars are disruptive to economic development in a number of ways. Not only is there a toll on human lives, but the resultant instability discourages foreign investment. More importantly, the huge sums spent on the military are needed to improve health and education, which are prerequisites for human development on the continent. In this chapter we will examine the extent of poverty in Africa and how it affects the ongoing democratization process. We will also discuss the causes of poverty in Africa and proffer solutions to poverty and underdevelopment on the continent. The impact of structural adjustment programs on the lives of the poor will also be discussed. We will discuss the problem of corruption in Africa and suggest ways to fight it. We will also examine the root cause of ethnic disputes in Africa and show how ethnicity threatens the establishment and sustenance of democracy in Africa.

THE EXTENT OF POVERTY IN AFRICA

The majority of Africans presently find themselves in a state of material and intellectual poverty. About two-thirds of the 420 million people in Sub-Saharan Africa live in absolute poverty.[2] Reginald Green of the Institute of Development Studies in England paints an apt picture of the plight of the poor in Africa.

The average human conditions of Africans—women and men, the young and aged, peasants and urban slum dwellers, the ill and the crippled, displaced victims of drought and of war—is appalling. Worse, it is not improving. . . . The rips in the social fabrics are lengthening, the cracks in the pots are widening.

These facts are statistically known from a wide range of indicators: infant mortality and life expectancy, malnutrition and food supplies, access to pure water and to sanitation, illiteracy and access to education, income per household and environmental degradation. The stark reality is that the fabrics of many African societies—national, regional and local—have been rent. The cooking pots of millions have been broken. To pretend otherwise is to deceive ourselves and to betray the poor and vulnerable people.[3]

Green's summation is backed by the UN Programme of Action for African Economic Recovery and Development (UN–PAAERD) in its review of the economic situation on the continent for the period 1986–1990. UN–PAAERD revealed that human condition worsened considerably during this period. It noted that the percentage of total government expenditure devoted to health in 1985 was nearly 6 percent, and to education 15 percent. By 1990, the share of health and education in total government expenditure had declined to 5 and 11 percent respectively.[4] UN–PAAERD also disclosed that the illiteracy rate had increased and primary school enrollment rates fell from 77 percent in 1980 to 70 percent in 1990.[5] The report added that due to cuts in health expenditures, progress in reducing infant and maternal mortality rates were slow. This resulted in an increase in the number of severely undernourished people, particularly children.

In voicing his concern over Africa's continued underdevelopment, Oxfam Director David Bryer called for a Marshall Plan for Africa and lamented that

After a decade which has seen hard-won gains in health and education eradicated, economic infrastructure disintegrate, and average living standards (which already are the lowest in the world) plummet to the levels of two decades ago, Africa is now the only Third World region where poverty is on the increase.[6]

We will now look at how poverty affects education, health, and economic development in Africa, and ways in which material and intellectual poverty thwart the establishment and consolidation of democracy on the continent.

Education

Education has been on the decline in Africa, both in terms of enrollment as well as physical infrastructure, material, and equipment. There has been little advancement in technology. For that matter, the information age has bypassed Africa. Democracy grows from the confidence and faith of a people in their own abilities to attend to their own needs. It is therefore totally dependent upon an educated and informed electorate who have access to ideas and opportunity to express and experiment with those ideas.

In order for democracy to be effective, civil society must be in a condition that enables it to follow the basic principles of democracy. At present, illiteracy and ignorance are impediments. The adult literacy rate is under 50 percent in Angola, Benin, Burkina Faso, Burundi, Chad, Guinea, Liberia, Mali, Mauritius, Namibia, Senegal, Sierra Leone, and Sudan, and under 20 percent in Somalia. Nigeria, the most populous African country, has a male literacy rate of a mere 54 percent, while the female literacy rate is 31 percent.[7] Only twelve of the fifty-one countries in Africa have a male literacy rate over 70 percent, and in all countries female literacy rates are significantly lower than males. Africa Recovery reported that "women predominate among 60 per cent of Africa's population that is illiterate."[8] It added that African children would have greater chances of survival if more African women were literate.

Illiteracy affects the sustenance of democracy because uneducated people cannot make informed political decisions. At the same time, poverty negates the citizens' human right guaranteed in Article 26 of the Universal Declaration, which states:

Everyone has the right to Education. Education shall be free, at least in the elementary and fundamental states. Elementary education shall be compulsory. Technical professional education shall be made generally available and higher education shall be equally accessible to all on the basis of merit.

The impact of poverty on democracy is profound. Lack of education impedes participation in government. In order to participate in government, a person must understand the principles of government and the nature of political operations. If the majority remain uneducated and unaware of the principles of majority rule, democratization in Africa will not be sustained.

Education is vital for human resource development, and that in turn builds a foundation for the establishment of a stable democracy. If adults are equipped with basic education as far as level 8 (the equivalent of two years of secondary school), the result would have tremendous impact on economic improvement. The benefits include:

1. increase in productivity;
2. improved opportunity to escape poverty;
3. improved ability to handle innovative tools and use fertilizers, thus increasing farming yields; and
4. improvement in health and nutrition in women and their families since literate women care better for their children, place greater emphasis on educating their own children, and usually have fewer pregnancies.

Education is an effective weapon against poverty and authoritarianism. But since the exploitative rulers in Africa have no intention of changing the social inequity, it is no oversight that education is given little priority.

Health

Africa's statistics on health care are grim. Statistics in 1990 showed that life expectancy in many African countries ranged between 41 and 69. Infant mortality ranged between 23 and 169 per 1,000 live births. Up to 1988 less than 40 percent of the population in eighteen African countries had access to safe water.[9] By the beginning of the 1990s Africa had regressed to the extent that some diseases that previously were eradicated had reemerged. Most of the diseases are caused by poor sanitation, lack of access to medical care, insufficiency of hospital beds, and all the other problems related to poverty. While malaria afflicts about 90 million Africans annually,[10] another more serious threat to the African population is AIDS. By the end of 1991, an estimated six million[11] African adults were HIV positive. Africans make up about 78 percent of the three million[12] people in the world afflicted with AIDS and tuberculosis. (The validity of these data on AIDS in Africa might be disputed in some medical circles.) Added to these more alarming diseases are frequent outbreaks of cholera and meningitis. Other ailments that plague the people on the continent include elephantiasis, which is estimated to afflict 28 million[13] Africans; river blindness, which afflicts another 17 million;[14] and guinea worm, leprosy, and sleeping sickness.

Lack of proper health care impedes democratic development because a sickly and malnourished population will not be productive. Undernourished children do not learn well in school, and that is a disturbing omen for the Africa of tomorrow. The quality of human resources necessary for nation building and economic advancement in Africa is seriously threatened with such disappointing health statistics.

Health, like education, simply cannot compete with military priority in Africa, and that has contributed to the woeful specter of the continent today. While African leaders argue that there is no money to pay teachers' salaries or purchase health care supplies, there is never any such problem when it comes to buying guns.

The Economy

The picture of the African economy since the beginning of the 1980s has been one of constant decline. By 1989 the gross national product (GNP) per capita in Sub-Saharan Africa was only $340.[15] Between 1980 and 1989 the GNP per capita in Sub-Saharan Africa had a negative growth rate of 1.2%.[16] In 1988 alone the GNP per capita of the forty-seven Sub-Saharan countries, with the exception of South Africa, declined by 3.1%,[17] and in 1989 there was no change in the GNP per capita. With an estimated growth in population of 3.2%, this would result in a negative growth rate of GNP per capita of 3.2.[18] The IMF also projected a drop of 3% in real growth rate of gross domestic product (GDP) in 1992, taking into account the growth in population.[19]

Who Comprise the Poor in Africa?

The destitute in Africa are found among peasants, female-headed households with little access to land, war victims, children with no support, people in the informal sector, the urban unemployed or underemployed who languish in the inner cities, and those affected by ecological degradation.

Causes of Poverty in Africa

Several factors contribute to poverty and underdevelopment in Africa:

1. Lack of accountability, which makes it easy for leaders to plunder Africa's wealth and stash it in foreign banks and corporations;

2. Poor economic management;

3. Decision making by a top-down bureaucracy whereby policies and programs are imposed on the people without involving those who are affected by such decisions; and

4. The intellectual brain drain which results when the educated are forced to flee for fear of their lives.

Both the loss of the educated and the activities of the kleptomaniac leaders have deprived the continent of the human and capital resources needed for development and to combat poverty. The political and economic policies of those western powers that are opposed to development in Africa serve to maintain their hegemony over Africa. This is also a significant factor.

In the World Bank report (1991), Chief Economist Lawrence Summers gave two major explanations for development failure. First, national development failure is the fault of national policies. Summers feels that these cannot be blamed on a hostile international environment or any kind of physical limits to growth. Second, national policies fail when governments thwart progress by supplanting markets rather than supporting them.[20] Others, such as renowned economist Pius Okigbo, point to drought, worsening external environment, declining terms of trade, shortfalls in capital inflows, domestic mismanagement, and the crushing debt burden as reasons for development failure.[21]

Whatever the causes suggested for the scourge of poverty, the social and political impact are astounding. The repercussions from massive inequality and human deprivation include riots, strikes, corruption in every strata of society, noncooperation of employers and officials, and much more. In addition, poverty and lack of education have a negative impact on the individual's ability to exercise his civil rights. Poverty and freedom are strange bedfellows. A poor illiterate individual cannot enjoy the values of democracy. Therefore, poverty alleviation must occupy priority on the agenda for democracy and development in Africa. While efforts must come from Africans themselves, the debt burden continues to strangle governments in Africa.

The Impact of Structural Adjustment

Economist Susan George has outlined in detail the impact of the outflow of currency from debtor nations in the south to northern lending institutions. George discloses that

Every single month, from the outset of the debt crisis in 1982 until the end of 1990, debtor countries in the South remitted to their creditors in the North an average six-and-a half billion dollars in interest payments alone. If payments of the principle are included, then debtor countries have paid creditors at a rate of almost twelve-and-a half billion dollars per month—as much as the entire Third World spends each month on health and education.[22]

Africa's debt burden, which was $203 billion in 1986, increased to $271.7 billion in 1990.[23] Although Africa paid $23 billion in debt servicing in 1990, this was only 60 percent[24] of the debt service due. In light of this situation, former UN Secretary General Javier Perez de Cuellar urged that debt reduction must be a major priority because "it is simply not possible for African countries to develop with their current debt burden exceeding $270 billion."[25] Despite this outflow,

George points out that the debtor countries as a whole began 1990 a full 61 percent more in debt than they were in 1982, adding that Sub-Saharan Africa's debt increased by 113 percent during this period.[26] George quite correctly points out that "the top layers of Third World societies remain largely insulated from debt distress, while ordinary people in the South sacrifice to pay loans they never asked for."[27]

Statements coming from a number of African trade unionists substantiate George's argument. For example, the Zimbabwe Congress of Trade Unions criticized the Harare government for removing the subsidy on the price of bread, causing it to double, while at the same time promulgating a law to finance political parties which benefit the ruling ZANU (Zimbabwe African National Union).[28] At the same time, the Secretary-General of Benin's Centrale des Syndicats Autonomes (Center for Independent Trade Unions) complained that sacrifices are not shared as they should be in Benin. He argued that "the government has recently increased the Ministers' and MPs' wages while subjecting the salaries of all other civil servants to a 10 percent cut."[29] The suffering of workers is also discussed in the 1989 report of the International Confederation of Free Trade Unions (ICFTU). The report points out that "in most of Africa the drop in wages has been so great that the urban wage can no longer support an average family. Real wages in Sierra Leone in 1986 were 74% the level of 1976, and the average monthly after-tax income is now below the cost of a basic food basket for a household." It further adds that, "since people cannot afford minimum nutritional intake, Sierra Leone now has one of the lowest life expectancy rates and the highest infant mortality rates in the world."[30]

The ICFTU report also points out that since 1979 the share of national budgets allocated to social services has been reduced substantially in several countries. It notes that changes in welfare spending result in basic health and education indicators. It notes that by 1983 per capita intake of food declined to 1,400–1,600 calories per day in Ghana, Mali, Chad, and Mozambique.[31] It adds that in Ghana, child mortality rose from 100 to 115 per thousand from 1980 to 1984 and in Ethiopia from 155 to 172. In Nigeria, real per capita GNP fell from $760 in 1985 to below $400 in 1987. In Lesotho, research undertaken by the Lesotho Confederation of Free Trade Unions found that the average real urban wage fell by 4.3% over the period from 1982 to 1985 and that of low-income households fell by 6.1%.[32]

At the International Conference on the Human Dimension of Africa's Economic Recovery Development, held in Sudan in 1988, participants issued the Khartoum Declaration, which criticized structural programs as "incomplete, mechanistic and of too short a time perspective," which are "rending the fabric of African society, aggravating rather than improving the human condition."[33]

The current African debt is a nightmare for leaders. The debt burden should not be imposed on democratic leaders in Africa. As George justifiably argues, "democratically elected governments should not be expected to assume the debt burdens of dictatorial predecessors."[34]

Canada's Joe Clark has pointed out that the insistence of the West on structural adjustment, if crudely designed, can erode the roots of democracy and human rights. He urges financial institutions to act in partnership with developing countries "to ensure that SAP preserves the social foundations for future growth."[35] This advice appears to have been largely ignored.

If the West is serious about democratization in Africa, consideration must be given to debt cancellation for most African countries, or else development will be nearly impossible. It does not seem to be fair for newly elected leaders to be strangled by the debt burden, while at the same time western banks continue to hold Africa's billions of dollars stolen by its autocratic predecessors.

Solutions to Poverty in Africa

Reginald Green suggests that the following four-point strategy, backed by substantial policy, institutional, personnel, and resource allocations, is needed to resolve the problem of poverty.

1. Provide asset, ongoing extension and other productivity raising measures to enable poor people to produce and to earn more.

2. Provide physical infrastructure (such as vehicles, working capital to competitive traders) which will allow for market expansion.

3. Rehabilitate and expand basic services/human investment, by concentrating on basic health services (educational and preventive as well as curative), accessible household water, primary and continuing (adult) education and basic sanitation.

4. Provide and promote [a] safety net including calamity relief, old age and disabled pensions, transfer payments (especially in urban and peri urban areas) to temporarily and permanently unempowerable households and persons, such as orphans and victims of drought.[36]

These suggestions do sound like the logical approach to the problem, but they are more likely to be implemented by governments that are committed to the needs of the masses. Most African governments, up to now, have not demonstrated genuine commitment to the plight of the poor. Therefore, it is the people who must be empowered to demand change. At the same time, the West must also be prepared to change the way it does business with Africa. One of the causes of development failure in Africa was that she rushed to industrialize without educating the people. For instance, new machineries were quickly sold to African governments, but the people had little knowledge of how to use and maintain them. Also, many of the actions which the West regards as efforts to solve Africa's problems are in reality opportunities for multinationals to go into Africa and take more out of Africa, leaving the continent worse off. For such reasons the masses must be educated to detect the capricious actions of their leaders and to question western methods. I propose the following approach to poverty alleviation: (1)

educate the masses; (2) improve health services; (3) support community initiated projects; and (4) encourage individual entrepreneurship.

Africans themselves have been seeking ways to tackle poverty and underdevelopment on the continent. To this end, a number of Africans met in Kampala in 1991 to chart a course for the future peace, stability, and development of the continent. This group of eminent leaders and scholars drafted the Kampala Document, which outlines measures that must be taken to move Africa forward into the twenty-first century. To ensure development takes place in Africa, the Conference on Peace, Security, Stability, Development and Cooperation in Africa (CSSDCA) made a number of recommendations. Among them it called for the restructuring of the African economy through diversification in agriculture along with industrialization.[37] One important recommendation that needs to be reinforced was that "specific policies such as an international reporting system on capital flight aimed at the repatriation back to Africa of the continent's human and financial resources be put in place."[38] This is an area that should be actively pursued.

While it is essential that Africans take measures to salvage the continent, the imbalance in trading practices and the operations of the international markets must be addressed. A new economic world order is now urgent if developing countries, especially Sub-Saharan Africa, are to survive.

A New International Economic Order

The economic picture of the developing countries reveals an increasing gap between the North and the South. Helmut Schmid, in his report on ways and means of encouraging flow of financial resources to the developing countries, titled "Facing One World," discloses that

Over the last 20 years the gap between industrialized and developing countries has widened enormously. Between 1965 and 1987, the real per capita GNP (calculated on the basis of 1987 dollars) increased from $140 to $270 for low income countries, from $980 to $1,680 for middle income countries and from $8,820 to $14,550 for industrialised market economies.[39]

The report notes that special attention should be given to Sub-Saharan Africa since average per capita GNP is declining while population is increasing. It points out that "while 70 per cent of the population is dependent on the land for its living, land erosion is widespread and increasing at the rate of 8 million hectares per year."[40] The report states that Africa is a continent in crisis. It points out that Sub-Saharan Africa depends largely on a single commodity or a narrow range of commodities and thus they are more vulnerable to commodity price fluctuations and deteriorating terms of trade.

In calling attention to the unfairness of the international trading structure, Michael Barrat Brown and Pauline Tiffen argue in *Short-Changed: Africa and*

World Trade that an examination of the markets for twenty-two African exports including cocoa, coffee, timber, tea, diamonds, and oil revealed that export-oriented policies are nothing short of a veiled form of exploitation.[41] Kenneth Bauzon reinforces their argument. He explains that international lending institutions and transnational corporations erode sovereignty in a number of Third World countries through (1) the use of manufacturing technology that displaces human labor, despite the argument that transnational corporations provide employment; (2) the inability of primary products from the Third World to penetrate western markets, despite numerous attempts to break down barriers through North-South meetings under the auspices of the United Nations Conference on Trade and Development (UNCTAD); and (3) persistent protectionism of industrialized countries' own industries, despite their loud rhetoric about free trade.[42] Bauzon worries that such imperfections will eventually reverse democratization in the Third World.

It was in an effort "to correct such inequalities and redress existing injustices, (and) to eliminate the widening gap between developed and the developing countries"[43] that the world was called upon in 1974 to create a new International Economic Order. This change was to have come about by encouraging commodity producer cartels, discouraging development of synthetic substitutes for commodities, and indexing commodity prices so they would rise and fall along with the prices of manufactured goods. More significantly, the developed countries were to lower tariffs which discriminated against goods produced in underdeveloped countries. The international monetary system was to be reformed and there was to be debt forgiveness or rescheduling. There was also a call for increases in aid.[44]

Since the UN passed Resolution 3201 declaring the establishment of a New International Economic Order in 1974, there has been constant bickering between the North and the South as the North resisted changes. In fact, aid flow has decreased while most of the industrialized countries have become increasingly more protectionist. By 1992, British Labour Party leader Neil Kinnock warned the industrialized world that "if common sense does not make the security-seeking countries of the industrialised world put the insecurities of the developing countries high on their agenda of political and economic businesses now, greater tragedy will compel attention soon."[45] He further appealed to the relatively wealthy and relatively free countries of the world to combine among themselves and with the poor to promote the spread of wealth and freedom.[46]

It is extremely difficult for freedom, respect for human rights, or a vibrant democratic culture to be a reality in the South unless there is a willingness on the part of the North to share wealth, technology, skills, and knowledge. As Rajni Kothari notes,

An end to authoritarianism without a concerted effort to eliminate the worst form of human misery will not make sense in a large number of countries. The right to human dignity includes both political and economic rights. While an open polity is an essential prerequisite for carrying on the struggle for social justice by the deprived sections of the people, it is necessary also to recognize that the existence of democratic institutions does not by itself guarantee that the poor and the dispossessed will be able to fight for their basic economic and social rights.[47]

Economic disparities have devastating impact on human rights and fundamental freedoms of the poor in the South. Kinnock makes a contribution toward resolving this problem in his suggestion that a Strategic Development Initiative (SDI) aimed at bringing about global security be put in place. The initiative should promote:

—coordinated international action to restore and sustain growth in the global economy on which developing countries' prospects depend;

—debt reduction measures that provide incentives to debt-distressed developing countries;

—the freeing of world trade from its dangerous path towards protectionism in the richer countries;

—policies to protect the global environment which links northern energy use to southern poverty;

—growth in the flow of aid and its effectiveness.[48]

Kinnock further warns that failure to take such an approach and to build a new world order would result in world disorder. Richard Sklar also points out that "Retarded development and the related growth of massive physical misery pose a challenge to scholars and scientists comparable to the continuing menace of nuclear weaponry. Both dangers have genocidal implications."[49] Such appeals have been largely ignored. Africa is now more marginalized than ever before, with its problems worsening daily. Aid flow to Africa has almost dried up, while attention turns to Eastern Europe or to countries where aid is expected to bring the donor economic returns.

In his criticism of the liberal concept of human rights, Dias dismisses the notion of equality of rights for all human beings. He labelled the idea a myth. As he sees it, the have-nots cannot begin to enjoy a decent living unless the haves give up some of their affluent lifestyle. He points out that many of the human rights violations in Asia can be traced to the "causal relationship that exists between need in the Third World and greed in the First World."[50] From all evidence, the notion of a level playing field in the international community appears to be a myth. What is evident is that, as in George Orwell's *Animal Farm*, some are in fact more equal than others.

Article 28 of the Universal Declaration of Human Rights states, "Everyone is entitled to a social and international order to which the rights and freedoms set forth in this Declaration can be fully realized." The international community, which has set standards for human rights, has an obligation to ensure that conditions are created which will allow the attainment of these standards. The UN

Under Secretary General for Human Rights, Jan Martenson, stresses that these conditions are universal, and they are major tenets of human rights. Enjoyment of the right to life, food, shelter, freedom from torture, and so on are universal to all human beings no matter on which side of the globe they find themselves. Martenson makes a compelling statement when he says, "There are no second class citizens for human rights, and no people should be made to sit in the back of the human rights bus."[51]

If the planet is to be saved and humanity is to survive in peace, moves to restructure the world's trading pattern and usher in a New International Economic Order will ultimately become inevitable.

INSTABILITY

In order for Africa to achieve sustainable development, which is vital for the sustenance of democracy, it is essential that the continent be a stable and secure place. Africa is devastated by civil wars and ethnic tensions from one corner to the next. Most of the tensions that were fueled by the Cold War have been brought to an end. However, ethnicity, religious fundamentalism, and border disputes are the causes of present instability. Africa remains in crisis and in desperate need of a solution. In the following poem, Kenneth Kaunda[52] has captured the dimensions of the problem as he muses about the situation on the continent.

No Sleep for Africa

Oh God, my God:
How dare I sleep?
Africa, my Africa, knows no sleep.
The bleeding of Somalia is deep!
Lord, it is Somali killing Somali
Lord, it is Islam killing Islam—
Oh God, my God what of 'Djibouti?
How dare I sleep even if there be hope for Ethiopia!

Lord, how dare I sleep?
Africa, my Africa, knows no sleep.
The bleeding of the Sudan is deep!
I see Lord, Arab killing African—
I see Lord, African killing Arab—
Lord, hear my humble cry!
It is Allah's man killing God's man!
Yes, Lord, it is God's man killing Allah's man!
Oh God, my God—All this is in thine Holy name—
How dare I sleep!

Lord, how dare I sleep?
Burundi and Rwanda refuse to sleep.
For they only want to identify

Who in Rwanda and Burundi should live and sleep
—Muhutu or Mututsi?
Oh, Lord God Almighty
Teach me, the Muhutu, to learn the Mututsi also
comes from thy holy hand!
Yes, Lord, teach me, the Mututsi to learn the
Mututu also comes from thy holy hand!

Oh God, my God—
How dare I sleep?
In the only Begotten Son's name there Christian
kills Christian—
Keen to know which tribes are more Christian and,
therefore, better!
Yes, Lord, they are keen to know which tribes shall
inherit Thy Kingdom in Monrovia by killing the
other tribes!

Oh God, my God—
How dare I sleep?
Africa, my Africa knows no sleep.
Morocco and Saharawi await Allah's inspired UN
decision.
Blood continues to flow!

Lord the fundamentalist calls his own tune of
self-destruction in Algeria—
Yes Lord, the fundamentalist calls his own tune of
self-destruction in Tunisia.
How dare I sleep, Lord!

Oh God, my God—
Burkina Faso, Mali, Tchad and Togo are set,
Lord, towards self-destruction!
Here tribe rises against tribe—
Lord God, here Christian rises against Moslem.
Yes, Lord, here Moslem rises against Christian.
Lord God, how dare I sleep! Africa bleeds, I can't sleep!

Oh God, my God—
The continent is wide and long!
Yes, Lord—so are the problems wide and long!
My little legs need a rest that is long!

Yes, Lord my Africa bleeds.
How dare I sleep Lord!

Lord my beloved population giant sleeps!
She is uncomfortably in a giant sleep!
Her heartbeat is weak and tired!
Unable to decide whether she:

Is going Moslem or Christian—
is going North or South—
is going civilian or military!

Oh God, my God—
How dare I sleep.
Ghana in the shadow of her giant neighbour
Stands still unable to decide whether to go
forward or backward or just wait until . . . !

Oh God, my God—
How dare I sleep, Lord, for I know not,
Lord, whether Senegal and Mauritania will call on the
name of Allah, the Compassionate, Allah the
Merciful,
to be compassionate, to be merciful upon them—
Or they will resume their war even after the healing
Islamic Summit!

Oh God, my God—
The giant in decay is my neighbour.
How dare I sleep Lord?
How do I know Lord that someone will not need my
neighbour's services?
Lord, only Thee knoweth where I stand with my giant neighbour!

But, Lord, how dare I sleep?
Africa, my Africa bleeds—
Which way, Lord, is my beloved Zambia whose hour
for self-destortion, for self-destruction has indeed
come,
going?

Lord God, my God—
Look with mercy at Angola and Mozambique—
Long independent and for that long dependent!
Why Lord; Yes, Lord—why should many more
thousands perish; many more homeless and maimed?

Lord God—hold for us together our hope in new
Uganda,
Kenya, Malawi, Swaziland, Mauritius, Seychelles,
Tanzania, Zimbabwe and two most hopefuls Botswana
and Namibia!
Lord wilt thou bring back to sanity our Lesotho!

Oh God, my God—
This continent bleeds for thine children in
South Africa! Lord, please teach them to see only
Thee, Lord:
    In every colour—

In every race—
In every tribe—
In every religion
In every human!

Oh God, my God—
Thou hast taught every human being is made
in thy image, Lord.
Teach us all on this continent
to love thee, Lord, our Creator
To love our neighbours as we love ourselves, Lord—
To do unto others as we would they did unto us.
When this is fulfilled, Lord,
Thy servant, Lord, will enjoy a giant and eternal
sleep in peace.
Oh, God, my Creator, hear my humble prayer!!!!!

Instability in Africa drains the continent of well-needed resources that go into military buildup rather than education and human development. Also, the millions of lives that are lost robs the continent of well-needed manpower. The destruction of homes and property causes refugee flight and its attendant human misery. For all these reasons, instability poses a dangerous threat to democracy. One of the major causes of tensions and wars is ethnic rivalry. Ethnic conflicts are often a result of the squabble to share scarce national resources. There is often discontent as to how national revenue is allocated and which groups benefit the most. Political opportunists at times fan the flame of ethnicity by ensuring that certain groups benefit from their largesse to secure their constant hold on power. There is the feeling that politicians exacerbate ethnic rivalries in their countries to detract citizens' attention from their inefficient performance in the administration of their duties. Scholars such as Gordon posit that "ethnicity is mostly an elite or bourgeois or privileged class strategy which involves the exploitation and manipulation of the non-elite to serve their own interests.[53]

In the following statement Rabuskha and Shepsle explain how politicians ferment ethnic discord to suit their own ends.

Politicians are office seekers. For whatever reasons—prestige, power, material prerequisites—they are in the business of winning elections. And in order to win elections, they must assemble electoral organizations. . . . The natural cleavages that divide men in the community provide the obvious and perhaps strongest nuclei around which coalitions are built. The astute politician latches on an issue precisely because of the groups he believes it will activate.[54]

African politicians have consistently fanned the flames of ethnicity to hold on to power. Such was the case of Eyadema as he stalled the national conference in Togo, backed by his Lamakara tribesmen. Paul Biya continues his grip on the Cameroon people with the backing of his Ewondo supporters, while exacerbating tension between them and the Bamilekes who support the opposition Fru Ndi. In Kenya, it is the Kikuyus against arap Moi, who hails from the minority Turgen tribe. In Burundi the struggle is between the majority Hutus and the long-ruling minority Tutsis. When the first Hutu president was elected in July 1993, he was killed in October that same year. Democracy has continued to be derailed in that country. The recent slaughter in Rwanda between the Hutus and the Tutsis was a most horrifying and devastating blow to humanity, and has set back the clock of democratization perhaps for another generation in that country.

The ethnic rivalry persists in Africa because of a lack of education and political enlightenment among the masses. In reality, people of all ethnic groups bear the brunt of the high cost of living, lack of basic infrastructure, and so on when those in power adopt bad policies. The masses have lulled themselves into a false sense of security on the subject of ethnicity. What people lack is the ability to see through the caprice of their leaders. In his discourse in *Perpetual Peace,* Immanuel Kant noted that "where the ruler is not a fellow citizen, but the nation's owner and war does not affect his table, his hunt, his places of pleasure, his court festivities . . . he can decide to go to war for the most meaningless of reasons."[55] That is the problem in Africa. The politicians think they are the owners of the country, and war does not disrupt their exotic lifestyles. Therefore, they refuse to give up no matter the human cost. While leaders order war, there has been no record of any contemporary leader in Africa taking a gun and going to war. It is others who die for them. For example, after all the slaughter in Liberia, Charles Taylor, leader of the main warring faction, is still alive. Many died in Zaire and Togo, but Mobutu and Eyadema are both enjoying the pleasure of living. In Angola, despite the numbers killed during sixteen years of civil war, Jonas Savimbi (another faction leader) lived to reignite the fighting after democratic elections were held in 1992.

Unless the structures are built from the bottom up and people are empowered to dictate the political direction, Africa will remain a hotbed of crisis. Politicians disregard social justice and merely fan ethnic and religious fervor to perpetuate themselves in power. It is only the victims themselves who will transform the continent through their collective struggles.

Africans Search for Stability and Security

When a group of eminent Africans drew up the Kampala Document in 1991, they sought a blueprint to ensure peace and stability on the continent. Participants stressed that "The security of the African people, their land and property and their states as a whole is an absolute necessity for stability, development and cooperation in Africa."[56] They emphasize that participating member states should pay greater attention to measures to prevent or contain crisis before it erupted into violent confrontation. They note that while military security is important, food security is equally important.

The document underscores the need for African governments "to initiate, design and implement policy measures and strengthen institutions which adjudicate disputes, resolve conflicts and attenuate the possibility of violence."[57] To ensure intracountry stability and cohesion, the document calls for the entrenchment of a bill of rights in the constitution of every member state, the separation of the party from the state, a limit to the tenure of office for political leaders, the guarantee of security for the judiciary provided for in the constitution, an independent civil service, and the establishment of institutions that promote accountability in public service.[58] If bureaucrats are to be held accountable, the masses must be educated and conscientized to question the decisions bureaucrats make. The people need to know why the bureaucrats made the decision and express their views on the impact of such decisions. That is the type of accountability needed.

The Kampala Document also recommends the establishment of an African Court of Justice, which would adjudicate between government and peoples' rights. Stressing the need to foster stability and to protect and promote human rights of individual citizens, the document requests every participating state "to sign, ratify and implement African and other relevant international legal instruments in the field of human rights."[59]

While the member states of the OAU should take steps to ensure stability and resolve conflicts, it is the people who must say when enough is enough. This can only happen when people are educated and speak from their collective strengths. At the same time, the international community also has a role to play in the area of stability and protecting the rights of African citizens. Africans cannot operate in a vacuum.

The Role of the UN

The UN should take a more active role in ensuring respect for human rights for African citizens. The organization should also have a mechanism that enables it to intervene directly to mediate conflicts in Africa. In the area of human rights, the UN needs to work as a broker between governments and local human rights groups. Until governments can be persuaded to work together with human rights groups, the working class individual will continue to be afraid to accept as much as a training program from a human rights NGO. That is because the masses witness the constant harassment and imprisonment that some human rights activists undergo.

The UN should be increasingly watchful and ready to act in situations of internal crisis. Africa has become such a hotbed of internal strife that, for my part, the UN needs to police Africa to ensure that human rights are respected. For instance, the situation in Liberia was allowed to drag on too long, with its attendant toll of human suffering. Yet another case in point is the imbroglio in Togo and Zaire. Ramcharan states that

The legitimacy of governments is now determined by whether or not governments have been formed and behave in accordance with the precepts of human rights. Thus a government has come under the reign of international human rights norms. Second, an increasing number of international conventions on human rights have been enlarging the area of international concern that governments have accepted of their own volition. Third, evidence is increasing that if the international community considers a human rights issue to be of such a nature as to affect the international public order, it will feel entitled to act on the issue.[60]

Africans watched in amazement and frustration as their fellow Africans in Zaire and Togo lived daily in the misery of tension and killing, while Mobutu and Eyadema defied popular will for democratic governance. What is disheartening is that these atrocities were allowed to continue for almost two years. The question here is whether such leaders were considered legitimate, based on Ramcharan's statement. The human rights of these citizens were violated daily, and even though the UN might not have considered it appropriate to intervene, other steps could have been taken. The West did not freeze the money that these leaders had stashed in their banks. This would have dried up some of the finances that are used to fuel the fighting and keep the military happy.

An even more disappointing scenario was the plight of the people of Angola. After democratic elections were conducted with the supervision of the UN itself, Savimbi and his cronies in UNITA (a rebel group) renewed fighting and continued to inflict even greater misery on the people of Angola. One report pointed out that the situation in Angola in 1993 was worse than ever before. It stated:

Not only has UNITA not laid down its arms, it has grown immensely stronger with the help of its friends in South Africa, the USA, Zaire, Ivory Coast and Morocco. With the aid of the sophisticated weapons and mercenaries supplied by its friends, UNITA continues to hold the ten million people of Angola to ransom. Fifteen thousand have died in Huambo alone since its latest offensive, and three million are faced with starvation in areas where its massacres have driven the inhabitants into the bush. The diamonds it steals in the areas it has captured, are openly sold in Zaire to the De Beers Organisation which has a contract with the legitimate government of Angola.

But despite the viciousness of its agression, UNITA has not been condemned. . . . The UN, which was supposed to broker peace and organise elections, refuses to condemn UNITA as a rebel for breaking the peace and rejecting the results of the elections. And while the situation in Central Angola is a hundred times worse than in Bosnia the UN has not given one hundredth the assistance it has given to the former Yugoslav Republic. The USA, the sole remaining superpower, has condemned UNITA only when it threatened to kill and capture US oilmen in the Angolan enclave of Cabinda from its bases in Zaire.[61]

In light of these circumstances, there is need to question the following statement made by Ramcharan:

International protection emanates from the international community as a whole, which is under a responsibility and a duty to ensure the enjoyment of human rights by every human being by guaranteeing the inviolability of internationally recognized norms of human rights. . . . Every state is under a duty to respect the human rights and fundamental freedoms of every human being and to subject itself to legitimate measures of international scrutiny that the international community is entitled to utilize to ensure protection of human rights and fundamental freedoms.[62]

One must ask whether the international community needed any more evidence than the world saw in Togo and Zaire throughout 1992 and in 1993. The situation in Angola also raised questions. The UN itself monitored the election, yet Savimbi rejected the results and continued to inflict misery on innocent people. How long is the waiting period before the international community investigates and takes decisive action? One is also forced to ask: to which groups of human beings does the international community have a duty to ensure the enjoyment of human rights? It is necessary to be reminded of the words of Louis Henkin— that all human beings are guaranteed human rights regardless of where they are placed geographically and regardless of race, color, or creed.[63]

With that said, we must turn our attention to the inertia in the OAU. The hypocrisy of the OAU has been frustrating to many Africans. If the OAU had lodged a complaint to the UN requesting its intervention in Zaire and Togo, the international community would have been forced to act. Much of the blame, therefore, rests squarely on the OAU. Even though there is significant evolutionary progress regarding the sanctity of state sovereignty in international law, the machinery is not yet in place to permit the UN to remove a brutal head of state without being asked. If that action had been taken, there would certainly have been an outcry from many countries. Since there is no such procedure established in international law, it is the OAU that should have first acted and invited the UN into Zaire and Togo. The complacency among member states of the OAU is due largely to the fact that most of the governments are not much better. There are factions among them ranging from the radicals to the conservatives and from the senile to the more liberal—and they do not want to hurt their old, established allies. It is therefore a question of who will bell the cat. One difference is that they knew how to speak vociferously against apartheid in South Africa.

The OAU has failed to serve the human development needs of the peoples of Africa, and most people express disappointment in the organization. Mostly they are noted for elaborate parties and grand ceremonies in which huge sums are spent on saloon cars, glamorous costumes, and dining on the most exotic dishes flown in from abroad. That being the case, the other option the UN could have adopted is to follow its mandate, to protect the life and liberty of every human being, and therefore work with the human rights organizations in Zaire and Togo. Based on complaints and substantive evidence, the UN could still have intervened.

We will now discuss yet another menacing threat to the sustenance of democracy in Africa, the threat posed by endemic corruption on the continent.

Corruption

While the misuse of office for private ends is not unique to any system of government, the problem it poses for democratization in Africa is that it has reached endemic proportions. As Robert Klitgaard stresses, "widespread corruption stunts economic growth, undermines political legitimacy, and demoralizes public officials and ordinary citizens."[64]

There are reports of the brazen display of wealth by former leader Hastings Kamuza Banda in Malawi. Zaire is said to operate as a kleptocracy, and the Kenyatta family in Kenya has been accused of accumulating massive wealth during the reign of Jomo Kenyatta. However, of all the countries in Africa, corruption has been woven most deeply into the fabric of Nigerian society and has become a threat to the survival of democracy in that country. This is how one Nigerian expresses his frustration. "In Nigeria everybody's middle name is corruption. Perhaps even the breast milk our mothers fed us with contained some viruses of corruption. Otherwise why is it that as soon as a child is able to talk, walk and eat his speech, movement and diet exude corruption?"[65]

Corruption is endemic in Nigeria because there is corruption of the leadership as well as the led. The problem has two distinct faces; one of them lies in the military. For this reason, the expressed purpose of many university graduates who join the military is to grab hold of power to enrich themselves. The other dimension of the problem is that when a person aspires to political power his family, friends, and kinfolk think it is their turn to loot the treasury. The winner-take-all system allows a low-risk path to easy riches. Most of the political aspirants are men who have enriched themselves through corrupt means. They then use that money to gain political power, an avenue which allows them to get more money. There is a cycle in which money begets power, and power begets more money. Larry Diamond aptly summarizes the situation in the following statement:

At work is a crude process of class formation. For 40 years, Nigerian officials of every rank have systematically misappropriated public wealth. For 40 years, the gulf has widened between an impoverished general populace and the dominant class . . . riven by ethnic, regional, and religious cleavages, by shifting partisan and factional divisions, and by continual civil-military tensions. Nigeria's dominant groups nevertheless constitute a class bound together by a shared taste for extravagant consumption and acquisition financed by access to state power. . . . Indeed, they are best designated a "political class" precisely because their wealth flows from control over relations of power, not production.[66]

How can a nation socialized to enrich itself without emphasizing the utilization of entrepreneurial skills and creative talents be expected to rise above poverty? Nigerian leadership has failed to lay any sound fiscal basis for the development of Africa's most populous nation. Most of the factors of production have either been ignored, underutilized, or misused. Fertile agricultural lands lie dormant while unemployment and crime rates soar. The windfall during the oil boom was badly misspent, and much of it stolen. What is even more distressing is that there is no maintenance culture. The lavish buildings erected during the boom days are presently crumbling, and that includes universities and leading hospitals. This is a time that all Nigerians need to seriously turn the searchlight inward.

The situation is ominous for the Third Republic in Nigeria because the military sees control of government as their avenue to riches. Therefore, they are not prepared to allow democracy to go through "growing pains." They will be ready to use the slightest opportunity to take control again. The threat of a failed coup attempt, with its resulting bullet at the back of the head, is not enough to stop them; that has been made clear. In addition, the "moneybags" who are struggling to get hold of the reins of the country are spending such huge sums that it is seen as an investment which will yield huge returns once they get into office. Diamond has correctly analyzed the mentality of Nigeria's power seekers in the following statement:

The "new breed" in Nigeria—both civilian and military—is a hungry breed. No appeal to values or principles is likely to deter them, any more than it deterred the "new breed" politicians of the Second Republic or the new generation of military politicians that succeeded them. . . . There is an entrenched culture of corruption in Nigeria. . . . Corruption has flourished in Nigeria because of perverse incentives that only structural change can remedy.[67]

Corruption is so pervasive in Nigeria that some have even suggested legalizing it. It seems that the idea is "if you can't beat it, legalize it," which sounds similar to the war on drugs. When a person is elected into political office, he is indebted to those who financed his campaign—relatives, friends, and in-laws, among others. When a person wins an election, the friends and relations throw a huge party to celebrate the "windfall" that is about to come to the family. Such a person is naturally expected to hand out contracts to undeserving (but financially supportive) cronies. Other jobs are given to relatives, while applicants who merit those positions remain unemployed. A more unfortunate aspect of corruption is that when a person who is honest and has a sense of morals tries to shy away from corrupt practices, he is considered a fool. He therefore feels he has no choice but to join in the looting.

As Diamond observes, Nigerian attitudes toward corruption are schizophrenic; the entire populace cries out against corruption, yet they are the same ones committing it. The same society knowingly awards chieftaincy titles to fraudulent individuals. Universities, which should be leading the rest of society in morals and respect for excellence, confer honorary doctorates on undeserving, corrupt individuals, as long as the price is right. Likewise, media attitudes are schizophrenic. Day after day newspaper headlines balk at corruption and reiterate the need to attack the cancer that has eaten into the society; yet, some of those same media personnel are frequently bought off. They are often paid not to print a story, or vice versa. Corruption has reached a stage where people are a law unto themselves. Immigration officials can be paid to deport victims who have been duped out of their finances while they are seeking justice in court, and public servants misappropriate funds without being investigated, creating a situation in which a public servant who earns 27,000 naira annually is able to send three children to a private school in Switzerland at a cost of $57,000 each annually.

There have been efforts to curb corruption in Nigeria. The Second Republic administration set up the Code of Conduct Bureau to impose penalties, seize assets, or disqualify individuals from office for ten years if found guilty of corrupt practices. However, this was not very successful. More recently, the Centre for Advanced Social Sciences, headed by reputed scholar Claude Ake, has made it its primary goal to fight corruption in Nigeria. In a charter on corruption, Ake suggests that public officials should be suspended for corrupt practices and calls for the empowerment of the legislative arm of government to appoint "a special prosecutor to collect evidence and prosecute any public official for corrupt practices" to enhance accountability.[68] Ake points out that corruption thrives in Nigeria because there is a limited sense of Nigerian identity. He laments that for most of its history, the Nigerian state has been generally intimidating, uncaring, inefficient, and partial in its treatment of the disparate groups which it rules. Therefore, many Nigerians have no qualms about ignoring their responsibilities and appropriating resources through corrupt practices.[69] Ake feels that accountability has suffered because the general public has not insisted on monitoring corruption. He reiterates that the fight against corruption can only be won when "the Nigerian state wins the loyalty of its citizens."[70] That can only come about from a Nigerian leadership that is established from a bottom-up structure with input and cooperation of people at all levels.

Robert Klitgaard is of the view that many leaders wish to reduce corruption, but despite the best intentions corruption cannot be eradicated overnight.[71] To address corruption, Klitgaard suggests that one should first identify the various types of corruption. Among the types of corruption Klitgaard lists are the misuse of important policy instruments, such as tariffs and credit; irrigation systems and housing policies; the enforcement of laws and rules regarding public safety; the observance of contracts; and the repayment of loans.[72] One could also include the misuse of procedures. Klitgaard notes that corruption can become systematic when it infects the daily operations of government such as tax collection, contracting services, police work, passing items through customs, and so on. He adds that another form of corruption involves the manner in which political parties raise funds. This could be done legally or through influence peddling, bribery, or extortion.

Klitgaard proposes that corruption be attacked from the root, and that is in monopoly power. He suggests the following steps be taken:

1. Analyze the organization to assess where and how corruption occurs.
2. Evaluate the costs and benefits the various kinds of corrupt activities entail, and to whom.

3. Assess the various policies through which one can affect the calculations of potentially corrupt officials and citizens.

4. Choose the appropriate type of corruption to attack and appropriate types, levels, and sequences of anti-corruption policies to employ.[73]

Klitgaard cautions that an anti-corruption campaign should not be pushed so far that its costs outweigh the benefits of cost reduction. He correctly stresses that the main goal should be to prevent the practice. Klitgaard suggests that the methods used to fight corruption should be information and incentives. I also believe that when people are empowered they will demand accountability. In addition, poverty and want encourage corruption. For example, why wouldn't a hungry man sell his vote? Or why would a civil servant who makes 500 naira per month and has three children to feed not drag his feet in processing the papers of a rich businessman until he is given a bribe to speed up the job? After all, the cost of beans and gari has escalated while his salary remains static. Therefore, one effective incentive would be improved material condition.

In using information and incentive, Klitgaard proposes the following approach:

1. Select people of honesty and integrity within the organization and get them to work with a team of outside auditors to examine a few cases, offices, or decisions to find evidence of corruption or inefficiency.

2. Conduct an inquiry.

3. Use undercover agents.

4. Devise new or indirect measures of corrupt behavior, such as the wealth or spending habits of corrupt officials, that would be abetted by official corruption.

5. Involve the public through hot lines, or by conducting random sampling of clients.[74]

The problem with these ideas is like setting a thief to catch a thief, because corruption in Africa is almost a way of life (and in Nigeria in particular). It is an evil that is aggravated by want in many instances. In addition, ethnic cleavage plays a significant role because each person looks out for his own tribe. As Klitgaard correctly notes, anti-corruption campaigns must go beyond party politics. He adds that the sources of corruption must be eliminated, and steps taken to prevent a recurrence of the problem. He also adds that both the bureaucrats and ordinary citizens must participate.

Conclusion

With the democratization movement underway on the continent, Africans are relentless in their demands for social justice. For one thing, the masses have had enough of the rich getting richer and the poor languishing in penury. Therefore, they are ready to take on the establishment. Concerned scholars, such as Ake, and working-class Africans are increasingly vocal about tackling corruption. If the effects of poverty were to be mitigated the masses would be less inclined to collude with dishonest leaders and bureaucrats.

At such time as African communities are allowed to decide their objectives, identify their needs, and bring these needs to leaders who will listen, the type of development needed in Africa will take place. When leaders can be truly held accountable, such an arrangement will give little rise to the type of corruption that exists at present.

NOTES

1. Alexis de Tocqueville, *Democracy in America* (1835), ed. and abr. Richard D. Heffner, 1956 (New York: Penguin Books, 1984), pp. 129–130.

2. Akin L. Mobogunje, "Eradication of Poverty in Africa," paper delivered at Conference on The Eradication of Poverty in Africa, organized by Africa Leadership Forum, Ota, Nigeria, July 27–29, 1992, p. 1.

3. Reginald Green, "Pluralism, Participation and Decentralization in Sub-Saharan Africa," *Third World Legal Studies, 1989:* 32.

4. *Africa Recovery* 5, no. 2–3 (September 1991): 15.

5. Ibid.

6. "Oxfam Calls for a Marshall Plan for Africa," *African Business* (June 1993): 13. Oxfam is a leading international NGO.

7. *Africa Recovery* (September 1991): 29.

8. Ibid., p. 34.

9. Ibid., p. 29.

10. Ibid., pp. 32–33.

11. Ibid.

12. Ibid.

13. Ibid.

14. Ibid.

15. "Africa in the 90s," *Management International* (September 1992): 37.

16. Ibid.

17. Ibid.

18. Ibid.

19. Ibid.

20. Ibid., p. 38.

21. Ibid.

22. Susan George, "The Debt Boomerang," *New Internationalist* (May 1993): 26.

23. *Africa Recovery* (September 1991): 16.

24. Ibid.

25. Ibid.

26. *New Internationalist* (May 1993): 27.

27. Ibid.

28. *Africa Business* (June 1993): 11.

29. Ibid.

30. ICFTU, *The African Development Challenge*, Pan-African Conference sponsored by Central Organization of Trade Unions (COTU) of Kenya and International Confederation

of Free Trade Unions (ICFTU) in cooperation with the Organization of African Trade Union Unity (OATUU), Nairobi, Kenya, October 25–27, 1989, p. 31.

31. Ibid.

32. Ibid.

33. Ibid., p. 27.

34. *New Internationalist* (May 1993): 28.

35. Joe Clark, "Human Rights and Democratic Development," in Paul Mahoney and Kathleen Mahoney, eds., *Human Rights in the Twenty-First Century* (Utrecht, The Netherlands: Kluwer Academic Publishers, 1993), p. 685.

36. Reginald Green, "Toward Livelihoods, Services and Infrastructures: The Struggle to Overcome Absolute Poverty," paper delivered at a Conference on the Eradication of Poverty in Africa organized by Africa Leadership Forum, Ota, Ogun State, Nigeria, July 27–29, 1992, p. iii.

37. Africa Leadership Forum, *The Kampala Document* (New York: ALF, 1991), pp. 20–21.

38. Ibid.

39. Helmut Schmidt, *Facing One World*, report by an Independent Group for Financial Flows to Developing Countries, 1989, pp. 4–5.

40. Ibid., p. 9.

41. Quoted in "Trade Most Unfair," *African Guardian*, June 28, 1993.

42. Kenneth E. Bauzon, ed., *Development and Democratization in the Third World: Myths, Hopes and Realities* (Washington, D.C.: Krane Russak, 1992), p. 12.

43. General Assembly Resolution 3201 (S-V1) (May 1, 1974): "Declaration on the Establishment of a New International Economic Order," in United Nations Resolution (1972–74) Vol. 14, pp. 527–29, preamble, para. 3. As quoted in Rhoda Howard, *Human Rights in Commonwealth Africa* (Totowa, NJ: Rowman and Littlefield, 1986), p. 79. See also "Shaping a New World Order," *World Goodwill Newsletter*, no. 3 (1991): 2.

44. Ibid.

45. Neil Kinnock, "New World Order Now," *Africa Forum* 2, no. 1 (1992): 22–24.

46. Ibid. p. 22.

47. Rajni Kothari, "Human Rights as a North-South Issue," in Pierre Claude Richards and Burns H. Weston, eds., *Human Rights in the World Community: Issues and Action* (Philadelphia: University of Pennsylvania Press, 1989), p. 137.

48. Kinnock, "New World Order Now," p. 22.

49. Richard L. Sklar, "Developmental Democracy," in Richard L. Sklar and C. S. Whitaker, *African Politics and Problems in Development* (Boulder, Colo.: Lynne Rienner Publishing, 1991), p. 286.

50. Clarence Dias, "Rural Development, Grassroot Education and Human Rights: Some Asian Perspectives," in Mahoney and Mahoney, eds., *Human Rights in the Twenty-First Century*, p. 703.

51. Jan Martenson, "The UN and Human Rights Today and Tomorrow," in Mahoney and Mahoney, eds., *Human Rights in the Twenty-First Century*, p. 926.

52. *Africa Forum* 2, no. 1 (1992): 15–16.

53. M. Gordon, 1964, quoted by Eghosa E. Osaghae in "Ethnicity and Democracy," in Ayo Fasoro et al., eds., *Understanding Democracy*, proceedings of a conference organized by African Democratic Heritage Foundation (ADHERE), Ibadan, Nigeria, August 19–20, 1991 (published by ADHERE), pp. 45–46.

54. Ibid., p. 46.

55. Immanuel Kant, *Perpetual Peace and Other Essays*, trans. Ted Humphrey (1983) p. 113, as quoted by Thomas Axworthy in "Democracy and Development: Luxury or Necessity," in Mahoney and Mahoney, eds., *Human Rights in the Twenty-First Century*, p. 723.

56. ALF, *Kampala Document*, p. 10.

57. Ibid., p. 15.

58. Ibid., pp. 15–16.

59. Ibid., p. 17.

60. B.G. Ramcharan, "Strategies for the International Protection of Human Rights in the 1990s," *Human Rights Quarterly* 13, no. 2 (May 1991): 161–162.

61. Ahmed Abdullah, "The Bleeding of Angola," *African Concord*, March 22, 1993, p. 8.

62. Ramcharan, "Strategies for the International Protection of Human Rights in the 1990s," p. 162.

63. Louis Henkin, *The Age of Rights* (New York: Columbia University Press, 1990), pp. 3–5.

64. Robert Klitgaard, "Political Corruption: Strategies for Reform," *Journal of Democracy* 2, no. 4 (Fall 1991): 86–100.

65. "Corruption," *Satellite* (Lagos), January 23, 1993, p. 9.

66. Richard Sklar, "Contradictions in Nigerian Political System," as quoted by Larry Diamond in "Corruption, Nigeria's Perennial Struggle," *Journal of Democracy* (Fall 1991): 79.

67. Ibid., pp. 80–81.

68. See "Caging the Monster," *African Concord*, November 9, 1992, p. 34.

69. Ibid.

70. Ibid.

71. Klitgaard, "Political Corruption," p. 90.

72. Ibid.

73. Ibid., pp. 86–90.

74. Ibid., pp. 95–96.

Chapter 9 _____

Prospects for the Future

From the foregoing discussion, we can conclude that democratization has not been democratizing Africa. In the area of human rights, there have been continued arrests and harassment of human rights activists, and there is every indication that things could get worse as the old sit-tight leaders who have used their powers of incumbency to hold on to power continue to suppress the peoples' voice for democratic governance. Even those countries where new leaders were elected have seen little real change. For instance, the Chiluba government in Zambia, which was democratically elected less than two years ago, has already declared a state of emergency in that country. The Moi administration (one of the old guard), elected in Kenya only December 1992, started off by suspending Kenya's new multiparty parliament after it had sat for only one day.[1] Not only that, but in choosing his cabinet, Moi selected only staunch KANU (Kenya African National Union) supporters, making a mockery of the results of the election, where the opposition secured eighty-eight seats in his 200-seat chamber. Less than six months after the election victory, the Moi government also embarked on the prosecution of journalists and arrested the editor of a church magazine for producing a publication the administration deemed unfavorable. All this makes it difficult to dismiss Shivji's argument when he states firmly that "the first important building-block of the new perspective on human rights in Africa . . . must be thoroughly anti-imperialistic, thoroughly democratic and unreservedly in the interest of the people."[2]

The process of change must begin with the grassroots peasants and others in the villages throughout Africa. This group of people must be conscientized to demand from their community leaders the services for which they pay taxes. They must know how to initiate collective actions on matters pertaining to civic and economic justice that impact their lives directly. If long-promised medical facilities are not provided, what should be done? If the police beats one of the village youths to death, what action should be taken without resorting to violence? The battle for human liberty is won only when the people themselves feel convinced of it and are prepared to wage it.[3] Such a direction is inevitable if the African masses are to survive. Nonetheless, it will be a long and tiresome process because of the level of underdevelopment in Africa.

The unexpected outcome of elections and disappointing human rights performance of African leaders are directly linked to the high degree of illiteracy, ignorance, and material lack on the continent. How else could one explain the reelection of Eyadema in Togo in elections held in August 1993, after his loyal troops killed and maimed opposition figures and unleashed a reign of terror on the Togolese for almost two years? Even Mobutu in Zaire boasted that if multiparty elections were to be held in Zaire he would win. Mobutu could only make such statements because he realizes he is dealing with a docile and ignorant population. General Babangida in Nigeria was only able to "dribble" (a term Nigerians coined for his actions) the entire population for over seven years of transition because the struggle is a class struggle waged by a few who are equally aiming at the public purse while the vast majority of the Nigerian population remains oblivious to what is really going on. For instance, all Babangida had to do to "get away with murder" was to hand out huge and generous sums to union leaders, academicians, and other demagogues who spoke out against his wrongdoings, and there was immediate silence. The seven-year-long transition to democracy and Babangida's final cancellation of the election results was largely due to the proddings of the parasitic comprador elite who benefitted from Bagangida's being in power and who were urging him to stay on.

The present scenario is disappointing and perplexing. One concerned young African lawyer expressed this very mood in response to my comment that the road ahead for Africa is a rough one. His reply was, "We do not even have a road as yet; the bushes have not even been cleared to make a path for the road. We first must clear the bushes, grade the road, and after that we will need to pave the road. That is how much work we have to do." Though metaphorically expressed, he nonetheless summed up the magnitude of the task ahead. And it is only pertinent to ask: Is there any hope for Africa? My answer is yes, but Africans must map out a different strategy. The entire exercise in Africa must take on a new dimension. Why so? Because events have shown clearly that democratization and human rights protection in Africa can only come from a bottom-up movement waged by civil society, and that foundation is yet to be laid. The change will only come when the masses are conscientized enough to be responsible for charting a democratic course anchored in respect of human rights. And the African majority are too hungry, illiterate, and indifferent at present to undertake the task. Presently, democratization and human rights concerns are the domain of the intellectual imperialistic elite. And what do we have? Voting which simply replaces the old with the new, or for the most part, the old with the old.

Democratization and human rights is an exercise that will not amount to much under the current brand of African leaders. That has been clearly established. And there is no guarantee that those who hope to wrest power from the current leadership via the ballot box will do much better. That is why Shivji makes so much sense in the following statement:

In Europe, democracy was the battle-cry of the rising bourgeoisie. In Africa today, by and large, such a bourgeoisie virtually does not exist. The African bourgeoisie is strategically compromised with imperialism to the extent that it cannot head even a democratic revolution. Hence the task of an anti-imperialist, democratic revolution falls largely on the shoulders of the working people. (This is what is new or national in the new or national democracy.)[4]

In this type of fundamental societal evolution, popular participation will play a pivotal role. We will now examine the role of this new phenomenon in revolutionizing African society toward achieving social justice and sustaining democracy. In addition, we will examine ways in which Africans in the diaspora can join hands with Africans on the continent in efforts to save the continent from extinction. Things might not improve much in the short run, but there is reason to be optimistic about the future, though cognizant of the long journey ahead.

While the task of educating and conscientizing the masses should occupy the agenda of transformation, economic integration in Africa is equally paramount. With the increasing economic trading blocs being formed throughout the globe, Africans need to be united in managing and controlling the resources on the continent. As things stand, there has been frequent dialogue aimed at African economic integration, but the process often gets sidetracked by language problems, currency debate, interregional trade barriers, and so on. African leaders must recognize that nothing will be achieved without the political will on the part of all involved. In addition, there will be greater stability on the continent if communities govern themselves in an African federation which allows decentralized power for ethnic and minority groups within each country. The new agenda for development, human rights, and democracy in Africa should aim to successfully undertake the following: (1) popular participation; (2) empowerment of the masses through education; and (3) collaboration with Africans in the diaspora.

POPULAR PARTICIPATION

It is manifestly unacceptable that development and transformation in Africa can proceed without the full participation of its people. It is manifestly unacceptable that the people and their organizations be excluded from the decision-making process. It is manifestly unacceptable that popular participation be seen as anything less than the centerpiece in the struggle to achieve economic and social justice for all.[5]

This statement is the affirmation of the African Charter for Popular Participation in Development and Transformation, and it is without doubt the only way out of the crisis of democracy and development in Africa. If the continent is to be truly democratized, the majority of the people must be able to assert and protect their human rights and play a role in decision making. The rural population in Africa constitutes the majority; therefore, the emphasis will be placed on how to empower this segment of the population to ensure their effective participation in democratization. The lot of the rural farmer has been one of continued pauperization. According to James C.N. Paul, during the period from 1978 to 1986, agriculture deteriorated and per capita food production declined. He states, "It is estimated that at least 20 per cent of rural people in most countries are undernourished."[6] Lamenting the decline in food production in Africa, Paul reiterates the need for policies to address the problem of the small farmer. He wisely argues that "the problems of the small farmer can never be properly defined, let alone addressed, without his—and, today, her—participation in the effort."[7] The rural dweller faces problems of lack of infrastructure, such as transportation, lack of access to markets and consumer goods, inability to communicate by telephone, lack of access to medical facilities, and so on. The powers that be must be pushed to improve such conditions, and the agitation must come from the people themselves. Paul makes a statement that is instructive.

The empowerment of the people with capacities to identify, assert, and protect their vital interests requires recognition of many component rights, such as access to information; freedom to form and finance different kinds of self-managed organizations and use them as vehicles for many different kinds of collective action; freedom of communication and access to the media; access to officials, government agencies, the courts and other forums; and often freedom to form organizations to provide assistance, including legal assistance to help others realize their rights.[8]

Rural people must be able to articulate their interests to their local government representatives and be heard. This can only happen when they are enlightened through education (particularly using the strategies suggested in Chapter 5). Paul[9] suggests that in order to ensure participation of the rural community, there must be a mechanism for generating and sharing knowledge. He points out that for development projects to address the widely shared community needs, the concerns of the various groups must be discussed and fair consensus established. Such concerns as the impact of a project on women, the understanding of social structures or labor cycles are matters to be addressed. Paul argues that neither outside experts nor any one person within the community may be aware of or fully informed about all the relevant matters. This point needs to be underscored. The rural population might have different needs or concerns about projects than the bureaucrats who administer development projects using the top-down approach without consulting the targeted beneficiaries. This is all the more reason why people must be fully informed and encouraged to organize themselves to protect and promote their interests. The rural population must have access to all relevant information, including information controlled by development agencies.[10] Paul sees a role for NGOs in catalyzing group discussions, helping to organize collective decision-making, and mediating between different groups and between groups and officials. He urges that the process must be free of state control.

The rural population will need to adopt strategies to ensure that local governments are accountable and responsive. To this end, there is need for mobilizing, organizing, demanding, protesting, and electioneering.[11] More importantly, there must be freedom to engage in such activities. If rural people are to create autonomous, self-managed enterprises, there should be laws to allow groups to become legal entities. It is important that community be involved in and accept local laws regulating overgrazing, deforestation, and so on, as well as laws governing the setting up of group-organized credit systems.

The rural population should also be in a position to use the law or the media to publicize their demands for accountability of local government officials or during their negotiations for better prices or other benefits. The rural population should also use the courts to seek protection from projects that pose risks or incur harm to them. Rural people need to prepare the basis for active participation in politics by forming coalitions or unions and developing the capacity to wield power in regional and national fora. They should organize NGOs to supply external catalysts, support, and advocacy to local grassroots organizations. They should also be involved in fund-raising activities. Specifically, attention must be given to empowering women as actors in all these functions.[12] In order for these initiatives to be undertaken, rural dwellers must be accorded empowerment rights. The African Charter for Popular Participation in Development and Transformation, which offers a blueprint for popular participation, is a ray of hope for the destitute majority. However, one must caution that while African leaders draw up elaborate plans, they often fail to actualize them.

The African Charter notes that "popular participation is, in essence, the empowerment of the people to effectively involve themselves in creating the structures and in designing policies and programmes that serve the interests of all as well as to effectively contribute to the development process and share equitably in its benefits."[13] The Charter particularly points to the critical contribution made by women to African societies and economies and the extreme subordination and discrimination suffered by women in Africa. For this reason, the Charter affirms, "It is the consensus of the participants that the attainment of equal rights by women in social, economic and political spheres must become a central feature of a democratic and participatory pattern of development."[14]

The Charter emphasizes that the role of people and their popular organizations is central to the realization of popular participation. It stresses that people must be fully involved and committed, and must seize the initiative. The Charter notes that it is essential that independent people's organizations be established at various levels that are genuinely grassroots, voluntary, democratically administered, and self-reliant.[15]

The Charter calls upon African governments "to yield space to the people, without which popular participation will be difficult to achieve."[16] The Charter also acknowledges that "too often, the social base of power and decision-making are too narrow." It calls upon governments to broaden these; to galvanize and tap the people's energy and commitment; and to promote political accountability by the State to the people.[17] All of this is sweet-sounding and offers hope, but only if taken seriously. Unfortunately, the current brand of leaders in Africa have proven themselves to be lavish on declarations but short on performance. The Charter presents a basis for the type of fundamental change that Shivji advocates. This can only come from the struggle and sacrifice of the popular working class in Africa.

The Charter points to the fact that if people are to participate meaningfully in their self-development, they must be free to express themselves without freedom from fear. To this end, the Charter urges all governments to "vigorously implement the African Charter on Human and Peoples' Rights and the Universal Declaration of Human Rights, the Convention on the Rights of the Child, the ILO Convention No. 87 concerning Freedom of Association and Protection of the Right to Organize and the Convention on the Elimination of all Forms of Discrimination Against Women."[18] The Charter also urges governments and all parties to African conflicts, domestic and external, to seek peaceful means of resolving their differences and to establish peace throughout Africa.[19] The Charter notes that there would be a positive multiplier effect on social welfare in Africa if savings could be made in defense spending as a result of the elimination of strife or intercountry conflicts. All these recommendations point in the right direction, but it appears such discourses have consistently fallen on the deaf ears of Africa's sit-tight leaders. Consequently, the onus is on the oppressed majority to effect such changes. Now more than ever the liberalizing education espoused by Paulo Freire becomes more relevant to the African working class in the struggle for a different type of political dispensation in Africa.

EMPOWERMENT OF THE MASSES THROUGH EDUCATION

In *Pedagogy of the Oppressed*, Freire argues that the only effective instrument to rehumanization is a humanizing pedagogy in which revolutionary leadership establishes a permanent relationship of dialogue with the oppressed.[20] Education must take on a dimension of educating both leaders and people or teachers and students. Both parties must be involved in the task of unveiling the reality, and must come to know it critically in the task of recreating that knowledge. It is when they attain this knowledge through common reflection that they discover themselves as permanent recreators. Freire makes a point that is instructive. "Freedom to create and to construct, to wonder and to venture. Such freedom requires that the individual be active and esponsible, not a slave or a well-fed cog in the machine."[21] The rural population in Africa needs to move away from this position of docility and passivity and become active participants.

Clarence Dias posits that "human rights are a means of empowerment of vic-

tims through resisting exploitation, debt bondage, pauperization and marginali-
zation."[22] He stresses that "the essence of any human right is the power to
command the protections promised by the right."[23] Dias emphasizes the need for
a participatory human rights–empowerment approach which in his view is based
on four underlying propositions:

1. Law is a resource which can be used both defensively and assertively by the rural poor
   in their struggles against conditions which produce impoverishment, deprivation and
   oppression.

2. Human rights are very important "legal resources" because they empower the rural poor
   to participate in these struggles and demand protection of their basic interests.

3. Non-governmental organizations (NGO's) of various kinds (from grass roots to international groups) have vital roles to play in these struggles.

4. Human rights must help bring about the structural changes needed to ensure the dignity
   and worth of all human persons, especially the "have nots." In the words of Theo Van
   Boven, the "have nots" regard human rights as a means of change, as tools in a process
   towards emancipation and liberation. Human rights are arms in their struggles for
   liberation.[24]

Education which empowers Africans must also be geared toward productive
work. Too many Africans graduate from institutions of higher learning to join
the ranks of the unemployed. There is need to train the human resources in Africa
to meet the needs of development on the continent. Food self-sufficiency is in
dire need, and yet not enough people are trained in agriculture. Engineering and
other areas of technology are also seriously deficient. Participation of the rural
poor will be minimal unless literacy programs are successfully brought to them in
their local vernacular.

People need to build a sound basis before they can appreciate the responsibility
that comes with making political decisions. In this regard, there is much work to
do in achieving a liberalizing education on the continent. As stated in Chapter
5, African intellectuals have fallen short on educating the masses toward achieving
empowerment. A number of African scholars do intellectual work, but their au-
dience is seldom ever the masses who really need to know what is going on and
to be encouraged to act. Sadly, many African intellectuals who access power also
engage in corrupt practices and commit human rights abuses against the masses.
Such intellectuals form part of the 10 to 15 percent among the comprador parasitic
group of Africans who continue to inflict wounds on the continent. Empowerment of the masses should be undertaken by various groups: local and international NGOs, African scholars, community groups, health professionals who meet
the sick daily, and paraprofessionals. While Africans on the continent must come
to grips with the problems and endeavor to surmount them, Africans in the
diaspora can offer much-needed assistance.

AN APPEAL TO AFRICANS IN THE DIASPORA

Without doubt, many Africans in the diaspora must be concerned about the state of the African continent. Africa's problems have many faces, but they can be tackled with goodwill. Africans in the diaspora can make a positive contribution toward improving the human condition in Africa. The continent is marginalized in the global sphere, but it presents the opportunity for Africans to evolve and dictate their political and economic direction in the process of rebuilding. The Japanese were demolished in the Second World War, and Japan is now a force to reckon with globally. There is no point in continuing to repine that Africa is increasingly being marginalized. That is not going to help; *only action will help.* What is needed to save Africa is a mixture of technological expertise, commitment to hard work by Africans themselves, and selflessness on the part of the ruling class. Those leaders who have ravaged and plundered their country's wealth must be made to repatriate the money. I refer to Mobutu, Eyadema, Banda, and all those Nigerians among the list. I appeal to Africans in the diaspora to come together in a group called Project Motherland. The group should strive (1) to improve the technological deficiencies in Africa through the infusion of foreign expertise and (2) to recover the wealth which duly belongs to the African masses and has been plundered by African leaders.

In order to realize such objectives, I call upon the wealthy and influential Africans in the diaspora (Bill Cosby, Oprah Winfrey, Michael Jackson, Harry Belafonte, Diana Ross, and others) and social justice crusaders in the diaspora, such as the Reverend Jesse Jackson, Mrs. Coretta Scott King, and Maya Angelou to come together and establish a foundation, similar to the Aga Khan Foundation in Asia, to assist Africa. The foundation should recruit technical expertise from among Africans in the diaspora in the United States, Canada, or elsewhere to work in Africa. Particular areas of urgent need are engineering, communication, health, sewage disposal management, research and development, mining, education, and transportation. There are numerous Africans in the diaspora as well as indigenous Africans in the West who are highly trained. Such people must be encouraged to work in Africa by offering them proper incentives to do so. Another primary undertaking for the agency would be to supply books, journals, periodicals, and equipment for chemistry and physics laboratories in universities and schools in Africa. This group should encourage schools in the United States to begin exchange programs between African schools and American schools so that African youth in the diaspora can learn about Africa. In this way they will take an interest in the continent when they grow up, rather than harbor negative images currently portrayed in the western media.

In an effort to recover the stolen billions, the group should lobby their congressmen and women to bring the matter before the UN. They should have a thorough modality worked out and present their case before the UN General Assembly. They should keep the pressure on so that those banks that are holding money are forced to release the funds, regardless of whether they were deposited using a mere number or whether or not the depositor has met his demise. Those banks know the countries where the money came from. All they need is to return the money either to the country or to the UN, who will decide how it should be handled. There is need for thorough investigation to find out exactly who has how much and where the money has been hidden (i.e., in a Swiss bank, a U.S. bank, or a dummy corporation). They should get the facts and then act upon them. Having collected the facts, they should then garner public opinion. The American public should be disgusted with this injustice enough to lend their support to any effort to correct the problem. For one thing, Africans can count on the support of Congressman Robert Doran.[25]

CONCLUSION

If Africa is to be salvaged from its current quagmire, Africans and non-Africans who empathize with Africa must garner the will to act. There are too many preachers and too few doers. As Claude Ake said, everyone is looking for a leader, instead of being a leader himself. The African working class will need to form democratic alliances and aspire toward the betterment of themselves and their country. The more privileged Africans should endeavor to become their brother's keeper and give leadership to the grassroots struggle. Those among the parasitic ruling class would be wise to eschew selfish greed and curb their penchant for huge excesses, because even the most ignorant individual is aggravated by such inequities. Sympathetic Africans in the diaspora can contribute to Africa's struggle for development in a positive way. Non-Africans in the international community can lend support to improving the human condition in Africa by influencing government policies on Africa and through their assistance to indigenous NGOs in Africa. As Maya Angelou said in an interview after rendering her beautiful words of hope in the poem titled "On the Pulse of the Morning," during the inauguration of President Clinton, "If we don't begin to look at each other and admit what we see and admit that we are not just our brother's and sister's keepers but in fact are brothers and sisters ourselves, unless we do that, we can become like the mastodon and the dinosaurs."[26]

This book was written primarily to stir a united effort among three particular groups of actors: Africans on the continent, Africans in the diaspora, and non-Africans in the international community. If Africa is to be saved from becoming a dinosaur in the annals of history, those words of Maya Angelou must be taken seriously. If those concerned about the human condition in Africa could personally take the initial step in a spirit of goodwill, the book will have accomplished its mission. Despite the present state of the continent, I have not given up on Africa.

Long live Africa!

NOTES

1. See "Out With Them," *The Economist,* February 6, 1993, p. 46.

2. Issa Shivji, *The Concept of Human Rights in Africa* (London: CODESRIA, 1989), p. 70.

3. Rajni Kothari, "Human Rights as a North-South Issue," in Richard Pierre Claude and Burns H. Weston, eds., *Human Rights in the World Community: Issues and Action* (Philadelphia: University of Pennsylvania Press: USA, 1989), p. 137.

4. Shivji, *The Concept of Human Rights in Africa,* p. 70.

5. International Conference on Popular Participation in the Recovery and Development Process in Africa, *African Charter for Popular Participation in Development and Transformation* (Arusha, Kenya, 1990), p. 33.

6. James C.N. Paul, "Participatory Approaches to Human Rights in Sub-Saharan Africa," in Abdullahi Ahmed An-Na'im and Francis M. Deng, eds., *Human Rights in Africa: Cross Cultural Perspectives* (Washington, D.C.: The Brookings Institute, 1990), p. 226.

7. Ibid.

8. Ibid., pp. 217–218.

9. James C.N. Paul, "Rural Development, Human Rights and Constitutional Orders in Sub-Saharan Africa," in Jack A. Hiller, Mary G. Persyn, and Paul H. Brietzke, eds., *Third World Legal Studies—1989* (Valparaiso, Ind.: Internationational Third World Legal Studies Association and the Valparaiso University School of Law, 1989), p. 65.

10. Ibid.

11. Ibid., p. 66.

12. Ibid., pp. 66–67.

13. African Charter for Popular Participation in Development and Transformation (Arusha, Kenya, 1990), p. 19.

14. Ibid.

15. Ibid., p. 20.

16. Ibid., p. 21.

17. Ibid.

18. Ibid.

19. Ibid.

20. Paulo Freire, *Pedagogy of the Oppressed* (New York: Continuum Publishing Company, 1989), pp. 55–56.

21. Ibid.

22. See Clarence Dias, "Rural Development, Grassroots Education and Human Rights: Some Asian Perspectives," in Kathleen Mahoney and Paul Mahoney, eds., *Human Rights in the Twenty-First Century* (Utrecht, The Netherlands: Kluwer Academic Publishers, 1993), p. 707.

23. Ibid.

24. Ibid.

25. Congressman Doran expressed his frustrations with the situation in an article titled "Greedy African Dictators Stealing $Billions We Give to Feed Starving People," *The National Enquirer,* February 2, 1993, p. 31.

26. Quoted in *The Art Magazine,* January 28, 1993, p. B2.

The African Charter on Human and Peoples' Rights

PREAMBLE

The African States members of the Organization of African Unity, parties to the present convention entitled "African Charter on Human and Peoples Rights";

Recalling Decision 115 (XVI) of the Assembly of Heads of State and Government at its Sixteenth Ordinary Session held in Monrovia, Liberia, from 17 to 20 July 1979 on the preparation of "a preliminary draft on an African Charter on Human and Peoples' Rights providing inter alia for the establishment of bodies to promote and protect human and peoples' rights";

Considering the Charter of the Organization of African Unity, which stipulates that "freedom, equality, justice and dignity are essential objectives for the achievement of the legitimate aspirations of the African peoples";

Reaffirming the pledge they solemnly made in Article 2 of the said Charter to eradicate all forms of colonialism from Africa, to coordinate and intensify their cooperation and efforts to achieve a better life for the peoples of Africa and to promote international co-operation, having due regard to the Charter of the United Nations and the Universal Declaration of Human Rights;

Taking into consideration the virtues of their historical tradition and the values of African civilization which should inspire and characterize their reflection on the concept of human and peoples' rights;

Recognizing on the one hand, that fundamental human rights stem from the attributes of human beings, which justifies their international protection and on the other hand, that the reality and respect of peoples' rights should necessarily guarantee human rights;

Considering that the enjoyment of rights and freedoms also implies the performance of duties on the part of everyone;

Convinced that it is henceforth essential to pay particular attention to the right to development and that civil and political rights cannot be dissociated from economic, social and cultural rights in their conception as well as universality and that the satisfaction of economic, social and cultural rights is a guarantee for the enjoyment of civil and political rights;

Conscious of their duty to achieve the total liberation of Africa, the peoples of which are still struggling for their dignity and genuine independence, and undertaking to eliminate colonialism, neo-colonialism, apartheid, zionism, and to dismantle aggressive foreign military bases and all forms of discrimination, particularly those based on race, ethnic group, colour, sex, language, religion or political opinion;

Reaffirming their adherence to the principles of human and peoples' rights and freedoms contained in the declarations, conventions and other instruments adopted by the Organization of African Unity, the Movement of Non-Aligned Countries and the United Nations;

Firmly convinced of their duty to promote and protect human and peoples' rights and freedoms taking into account the importance traditionally attached to these rights and freedoms in Africa;

HAVE AGREED AS FOLLOWS:

PART I. RIGHTS AND DUTIES

Chapter I. Human and Peoples' Rights

Article 1

The Member States of the Organization of African Unity parties to the present Charter shall recognize the rights, duties and freedoms enshrined in this Charter and shall undertake to adopt legislative or other measures to give effect to them.

Article 2

Every individual shall be entitled to the enjoyment of the rights and freedoms recognized and guaranteed in the present Charter without distinction of any kind such as race, ethnic group, colour, sex, language, religion, political or any other opinion, national and social origin, fortune, birth or other status.

Article 3

1. Every individual shall be equal before the law.
2. Every individual shall be entitled to equal protection of the law.

Article 4

Human beings are inviolable. Every human being shall be entitled to respect for his life and the integrity of his person. No one may be arbitrarily deprived of this right.

Article 5

Every individual shall have the right to the respect of the dignity inherent in a human being and to the recognition of his legal status. All forms of exploitation, and degradation of man particularly slavery, slave trade, torture, cruel, inhuman or degrading punishment and treatment shall be prohibited.

Article 6

Every individual shall have the right to liberty and to the security of his person. No one may be deprived of his freedom except for reasons and conditions previously laid down by law. In particular, no one may be arbitrarily arrested or detained.

Article 7

1. Every individual shall have the right to have his cause heard. This comprises:

a) The right to an appeal to competent national organs against acts violating his fundamental rights as recognized and guaranteed by conventions, laws, regulations and customs in force;

b) the right to be presumed innocent until proved guilty by a competent court or tribunal;

c) the right to defence, including the right to be defended by counsel of his choice;

d) the right to be tried within a reasonable time by an impartial court or tribunal.

2. No one may be condemned for an act or omission which did not constitute a legally punishable offence at the time it was committed. No penalty may be inflicted for an offence for which no provision was made at the time it was committed. Punishment is personal and can be imposed only on the offender.

Article 8

Freedom of conscience, the profession and free practice of religion shall be guaranteed. No one may, subject to law and order, be submitted to measures restricting the exercise of these freedoms.

Article 9

1. Every individual shall have the right to receive information.

2. Every individual shall have the right to express and disseminate his opinions within the law.

Article 10

1. Every individual shall have the right to free association provided that he abides by the law.

2. Subject to the obligation of solidarity provided for in Article 29 no one may be compelled to join an association.

Article 11

Every individual shall have the right to assemble freely with others. The exercise of this right shall be subject only to necessary restrictions provided for by law in particular those enacted in the interest of national security, the safety, health, ethics and rights and freedoms of others.

Article 12

1. Every individual shall have the right to freedom of movement and residence within the borders of a State provided he abides by the law.

2. Every individual shall have the right to leave any country including his own, and to

return to his country. This right may only be subject to restrictions, provided for by law for the protection of national security, law and order, public health or morality.

3. Every individual shall have the right, when persecuted, to seek and obtain asylum in other countries in accordance with the laws of those countries and international conventions.

4. A non-national legally admitted in a territory of a State party to this present Charter, may only be expelled from it by virtue of a decision taken in accordance with the law.

5. The mass expulsion of non-nationals shall be prohibited. Mass expulsions shall be that which is aimed at national, racial, ethnic or religious groups.

Article 13

1. Every citizen shall have the right to participate freely in the government of his country, either directly or through freely chosen representatives in accordance with the provisions of the law.

2. Every citizen shall have the right of equal access to the public service of his country.

3. Every individual shall have the right of access to public property and services in strict equality of all persons before the law.

Article 14

The right to property shall be guaranteed. It may only be encroached upon in the interest of public need or in the general interest of the community and in accordance with the provisions of appropriate laws.

Article 15

Every individual shall have the right to work under equitable and satisfactory conditions, and shall receive equal pay for equal work.

Article 16

1. Every individual shall have the right to enjoy the best attainable state of physical and mental health.

2. States parties to the present Charter shall take the necessary measures to protect the health of their people and to ensure that they receive medical attention when they are sick.

Article 17

1. Every individual shall have the right to education.

2. Every individual may freely take part in the cultural life of his community.

3. The promotion and protection of morals and traditional values recognized by the community shall be the duty of the State.

Article 18

1. The family shall be the natural unit and basis of society. It shall be protected by the State which shall take care of its physical and moral health.

2. The State shall have the duty to assist the family which is the custodian of morals and traditional values recognized by the community.

3. The State shall ensure the elimination of every discrimination against women and also ensure the protection of the rights of the woman and the child as stipulated in international declarations and conventions.

4. The aged and the disabled shall also have the right to special measures of protection in keeping with their physical or moral needs.

Article 19

All peoples shall be equal; they shall enjoy the same respect and shall have the same rights. Nothing shall justify the domination of a people by another.

Article 20

1. All peoples shall have right to existence. They shall have the unquestionable and inalienable right to self determination. They shall freely determine their political status and shall pursue their economic and social development according to the policy they have freely chosen.

2. Colonized or oppressed peoples shall have the right to free themselves from the bonds of domination by resorting to any means recognized by the international community.

3. All peoples shall have the right to the assistance of the States parties to the present Charter in their liberation struggle against foreign domination, be it political, economic or cultural.

Article 21

1. All peoples shall freely dispose of their wealth and natural resources. This right shall be exercised in the exclusive interest of the people. In no case shall a people be deprived of it.

2. In case of spoliation the dispossessed people shall have the right to the lawful recovery of its property as well as to an adequate compensation.

3. The free disposal of wealth and natural resources shall be exercised without prejudice to the obligation of promoting international economic co-operation based on mutual respect, equitable exchange and the principles of international law.

4. States parties to the present Charter shall individually and collectively exercise the right to free disposal of their wealth and natural resources with a view to strengthening African unity and solidarity.

5. States parties to the present Charter shall undertake to eliminate all forms of foreign economic exploitation particularly that practised by international monopolies so as to enable their peoples to fully benefit from the advantages derived from their national resources.

Article 22

1. All peoples shall have the right to their economic, social and cultural development with due regard to their freedom and identity and in the equal enjoyment of the common heritage of mankind.

2. States shall have the duty, individually or collectively, to ensure the exercise of the right to development.

Article 23

1. All peoples shall have the right to national and international peace and security. The principles of solidarity and friendly relations implicitly affirmed by the Charter of the United Nations and reaffirmed by that of the Organization of African Unity shall govern relations between States.

2. For the purpose of strengthening peace, solidarity and friendly relations, States parties to the present Charter shall ensure that:

a) Any individual enjoying the right of asylum under Article 12 of the present Charter shall not engage in subversive activities against his country of origin or any other State party to the present Charter.

b) Their territories shall not be used as bases for subversive or terrorist activities against the people of any other State party to the present Charter.

Article 24

All people shall have the right to a general satisfactory environment favourable to their development.

Article 25

States parties to the present Charter shall have the duty to promote and ensure through teaching, education and publication, the respect of the rights and freedoms contained in the present Charter and to see to it that these freedoms and rights as well as corresponding obligations and duties are understood.

Article 26

States parties to the present Charter shall have the duty to guarantee the independence of the Courts and shall allow the establishment and improvement of appropriate national institutions entrusted with the promotion and protection of the rights and freedoms guaranteed by the present Charter.

Chapter II. Duties

Article 27

1. Every individual shall have duties towards his family and society, the State and other legally recognized communities and the international community.

2. The rights and freedoms of each individual shall be exercised with due regard to the rights of others, collective security, morality and common interest.

Article 28

Every individual shall have the duty to respect and consider his fellow beings without discrimination, and to maintain relations aimed at promoting, safeguarding and reinforcing mutual respect and tolerance.

Article 29

The individual shall also have the duty:

1. To preserve the harmonious development of the family and to work for the cohesion and respect of the family; to respect his parents at all times, to maintain them in case of need;

2. To serve his national community by placing his physical and intellectual abilities at its service;

3. Not to compromise the security of the State whose national or resident he is;

4. To preserve and strengthen social and national solidarity, particularly when the latter is threatened;

5. To preserve and strengthen the national independence and the territorial integrity of his country and to contribute to its defence in accordance with the law;

6. To work to the best of his abilities and competence, and to pay taxes imposed by law in the interest of the society;

7. To preserve and strengthen positive African cultural values in his relations with other members of the society, in the spirit of tolerance, dialogue and consultation, and in general, to contribute to the promotion of the moral well-being of society;

8. To contribute to the best of his abilities, at all times and at all levels, to the promotion and achievement of African unity.

PART II. MEASURES OF SAFEGUARD

Chapter I. Establishment and Organization of the African Commission on Human and Peoples' Rights

Article 30

An African Commission on Human and Peoples' Rights, hereinafter called "the Commission", shall be established within the Organization of African Unity to promote human and peoples' rights and ensure their protection in Africa.

Article 31

1. The Commission shall consist of eleven members chosen from amongst African personalities of the highest reputation, known for their high morality, integrity, impartiality and competence in matters of human and peoples' rights; particular consideration being given to persons having legal experience.

2. The members of the Commission shall serve in their personal capacity.

Article 32

The Commission shall not include more than one national of the same State.

Article 33

The members of the Commission shall be elected by secret ballot by the Assembly of Heads of State and Government, from a list of persons nominated by the States parties to the present Charter.

Article 34

Each State party to the present Charter may not nominate more than two candidates. The candidates must have the nationality of one of the State parties of the present Charter. When two candidates are nominated by a State, one of them may not be a national of that State.

Article 35

1. The Secretary-General of the Organization of African Unity shall invite State parties to the present Charter at least four months before the elections to nominate candidates.

2. The Secretary-General of the Organization of African Unity shall make an alphabetical list of the persons thus nominated and communicate it to the Heads of State and Government at least one month before the elections.

Article 36

The members of the Commission shall be elected for a six-year period and shall be eligible for re-election. However, the term of office of four of the members elected at the first election shall terminate after two years and the term of office of three others, at the end of four years.

Article 37

Immediately after the first election, the Chairman of the Assembly of Heads of State and Government of the Organization of African Unity shall draw lots to decide the names of those members referred to in Article 36.

Article 38

After their election, the members of the Commission shall make a solemn declaration to discharge their duties impartially and faithfully.

Article 39

1. In case of death or resignation of a member of the Commission, the Chairman of the Commission shall immediately inform the Secretary-General of the Organization of African Unity, who shall declare the seat vacant from the date of death or from the date on which the resignation takes effect.

2. If, in the unanimous opinion of other members of the Commission, a member has stopped discharging his duties for any reason other than a temporary absence, the Chairman of the Commission shall inform the Secretary-General of the Organization of African Unity, who shall then declare the seat vacant.

3. In each of the cases anticipated above, the Assembly of Heads of State and Government shall replace the member whose seat became vacant for the remaining period of his term unless the period is less than six months.

Article 40

Every member of the Commission shall be in office until the date his successor assumes office.

Article 41

The Secretary-General of the Organization of African Unity shall appoint the Secretary of the Commission. He shall also provide the staff and services necessary for the effective discharge of the duties of the Commission. The Organization of African Unity shall bear the cost of the staff and services.

Article 42

1. The Commission shall elect its Chairman and Vice-Chairman for a two-year period. They shall be eligible for re-election.

2. The Commission shall lay down its rules of procedure.

3. Seven members shall form the quorum.

4. In case of an equality of votes, the Chairman shall have a casting vote.

5. The Secretary-General may attend the meetings of the Commission. He shall neither participate in deliberations nor shall he be entitled to vote. The Chairman of the Commission may, however, invite him to speak.

Article 43

In discharging their duties, members of the Commission shall enjoy diplomatic privileges and immunities provided for in the General Convention on the Privileges and Immunities of the Organization of African Unity.

Article 44

Provision shall be made for the emoluments and allowances of the members of the Commission in the Regular Budget of the Organization of African Unity.

Chapter II. Mandate of the Commission

Article 45

The functions of the Commission shall be:

1. To promote Human and Peoples' Rights and in particular:

(a) To collect documents, undertake studies and researches on African problems in the field of human and peoples' rights, organize seminars, symposia and conferences, disseminate information, encourage national and local institutions concerned with human and peoples' rights and, should the case arise, give its views or make recommendations to Governments;

(b) To formulate and lay down, principles and rules aimed at solving legal problems relating to human and peoples' rights and fundamental freedoms upon which African Governments may base their legislations;

(c) Co-operate with other African and international institutions concerned with the promotion and protection of human and peoples' rights.

2. Ensure the protection of human and peoples' rights under conditions laid down by the present Charter.

3. Interpret all the provisions of the present Charter at the request of a State party, an institution of the Organization of African Unity or an African organization recognized by the Organization of African Unity.

4. Perform any other tasks which may be entrusted to it by the Assembly of Heads of State and Government.

Chapter III. Procedures of the Commission

Article 46

The Commission may resort to any appropriate method of investigation; it may hear from the Secretary-General of the Organization of African Unity or any other person capable of enlightening it.

Communication from States

Article 47

If a State party to the present Charter has good reasons to believe that another State party to this Charter has violated the provisions of the Charter, it may draw, by written communication, the attention of that State to the matter. This communication shall also be addressed to the Secretary-General of the Organization of African Unity and to the Chairman of the Commission. Within three months of the receipt of the communication the State to which the communication is addressed shall give the enquiring State, written explanation or statement elucidating the matter. This should include as much as possible relevant information relating to the laws and rules of procedure applied and applicable and the redress already given or course of action available.

Article 48

If within three months from the date on which the original communication is received by the State to which it is addressed, the issue is not settled to the satisfaction of the two States involved through bilateral negotiation or by any other peaceful procedure, either State shall have the right to submit the matter to the Commission through the Chairman and shall notify the other State involved.

Article 49

Notwithstanding the provisions of Article 47, if a State party to the present Charter considers that another State party has violated the provisions of the Charter, it may refer the matter directly to the Commission by addressing a communication to the Chairman, to the Secretary-General of the Organization of African Unity and the State concerned.

Article 50

The Commission can only deal with a matter submitted to it after making sure that all local remedies, if they exist, have been exhausted, unless it is obvious to the Commission that the procedure of achieving these remedies would be unduly prolonged.

Article 51

1. The Commission may ask the States concerned to provide it with all relevant information.
2. When the Commission is considering the matter, States concerned may be represented before it and submit written or oral representations.

Article 52

After having obtained from the States concerned and from other sources all the information it deems necessary and after having tried all appropriate means to reach an amicable solution based on the respect of human and peoples' rights, the Commission shall prepare, within a reasonable period of time from the notification referred to in Article 48, a report stating the facts and its findings. This report shall be sent to the States concerned and communicated to the Assembly of Heads of State and Government.

Article 53

While transmitting its report, the Commission may make to the Assembly of Heads of State and Government such recommendations as it deems useful.

Article 54

The Commission shall submit to each Ordinary Session of the Assembly of Heads of State and Government a report on its activities.

Other Communications

Article 55

1. Before each session, the Secretary of the Commission shall make a list of the communications other than those of States parties to the present Charter and transmit them to the members of the Commission, who shall indicate which communication should be considered by the Commission.

2. A communication shall be considered by the Commission if a simple majority of its members so decide.

Article 56

Communications relating to human and peoples' rights referred to in Article 55 received by the Commission, shall be considered if they:

1. Indicate their authors even if the latter request anonymity;

2. Are compatible with the Charter of the Organization of African Unity or with the present Charter;

3. Are not written in disparaging or insulting language directed against the State concerned and its institutions or to the Organization of African Unity;

4. Are not based exclusively on news disseminated through the mass media;

5. Are sent after exhausting local remedies, if any, unless it is obvious that this procedure is unduly prolonged;

6. Are submitted within a reasonable period from the time local remedies are exhausted or from the date the Commission is seized of the matter; and

7. Do not deal with cases which have been settled by these States involved in accordance with the principles of the Charter of the United Nations, or the Charter of the Organization of African Unity or the provisions of the present Charter.

Article 57

Prior to any substantive consideration, all communications shall be brought to the knowledge of the State concerned by the Chairman of the Commission.

Article 58

1. When it appears after deliberations of the Commission that one or more communications apparently relate to special cases which reveal the existence of a series of serious or massive violations of human and peoples' rights, the Commission shall draw the attention of the Assembly of Heads of State and government to these special cases.

2. The Assembly of Heads of State and Government may then request the Commission

to undertake an in-depth study of these cases and make a factual report, accompanied by its finding and recommendations.

3. A case of emergency duly noticed by the Commission shall be submitted by the latter to the Chairman of the Assembly of Heads of State and Government who may request an in-depth study.

Article 59

1. All measures taken within the provisions of the present Charter shall remain confidential until such a time as the Assembly of Heads of State and Government shall otherwise decide.

2. However, the report shall be published by the Chairman of the Commission upon the decision of the Assembly of Heads of State and Government.

3. The report on the activities of the Commission shall be published by its Chairman after it has been considered by the Assembly of Heads of State and Government.

Chapter IV. Applicable Principles

Article 60

The Commission shall draw inspiration from international law on human and peoples' rights, particularly from the provisions of various African instruments on human and peoples' rights, the Charter of the United Nations, the Charter of the Organization of African Unity, the Universal Declaration of Human Rights, other instruments adopted by the United Nations and by African countries in the field of human and peoples' rights as well as from the provisions of various instruments adopted within the Specialised Agencies of the United Nations of which the parties to the present Charter are members.

Article 61

The Commission shall also take into consideration, as subsidiary measures to determine the principles of law, other general or special international conventions, laying down rules expressly recognized by Member States of the Organization of African Unity, African practices consistent with international norms on human and peoples' rights, customs generally accepted as law, general principles of law recognized by African States as well as legal precedents and doctrine.

Article 62

Each State party shall undertake to submit every two years, from the date the present Charter comes into force, a report on the legislative or other measures taken with a view to giving effect to the rights and freedoms recognized and guaranteed by the present Charter.

Article 63

1. The present Charter shall be open to signature, ratification or adherence of the Member States of the Organization of African Unity.

2. The instruments of ratification or adherence to the present Charter shall be deposited with the Secretary-General of the Organization of African Unity.

3. The present Charter shall come into force three months after the reception by the

Secretary-General of the instruments of ratification or adherence of a simple majority of the Member States of the Organization of African Unity.

PART III. GENERAL PROVISIONS

Article 64

1. After the coming into force of the present Charter, members of the Commission shall be elected in accordance with the relevant Articles of the present Charter.

2. The Secretary-General of the Organization of African Unity shall convene the first meeting of the Commission at the headquarters of the Organization within three months of the constitution of the Commission. Thereafter, the Commission shall be convened by its Chairman whenever necessary but at least once a year.

Article 65

For each of the States that will ratify or adhere to the present Charter after its coming into force, the Charter shall take effect three months after the date of the deposit by that State of its instruments of ratification or adherence.

Article 66

Special protocols or agreements may, if necessary, supplement the provisions of the present Charter.

Article 67

The Secretary-General of the Organization of African Unity shall inform Member States of the Organization of the deposit of each instrument of ratification or adherence.

Article 68

The present Charter may be amended if a State party makes a written request to that effect to the Secretary-General of the Organization of African Unity. The Assembly of Heads of State and Government may only consider the draft amendment after all the States parties have been duly informed of it and the Commission has given its opinion on it at the request of the sponsoring State. The amendment shall be approved by a simple majority of the States parties. It shall come into force for each State which has accepted it in accordance with its constitutional procedure three months after the Secretary-General has received notice of the acceptance.

Adopted by the Eighteenth Conference of Heads of State and Government of the Organization of African Unity, June 1981—Nairobi, Kenya.

The African Charter for Popular Participation in Development and Transformation

PREAMBLE

1. The International Conference on Popular Participation in the Recovery and Development Process in Africa was held, in Arusha, the United Republic of Tanzania from 12 to 16 February 1990, as a rare collaborative effort between African people's organizations, the African governments, non-governmental organizations and the United Nations agencies, in the search for a collective understanding of the role of popular participation in the development and transformation of the region. It was also an occasion to articulate and give renewed focus to the concepts of democratic development, people's solidarity and creativity and self-reliance and to formulate policy recommendations for national governments, popular organizations and the international community in order to strengthen participatory processes and patterns of development. It was the third in a series of major international conferences organized by the Economic Commission for Africa in collaboration with the rest of the United Nations system to contribute to the implementation of the United Nations Programme of Action for African Economic Recovery and Development, 1986–1990 (UN–PAAERD). It came as a sequel to the Abuja International Conference on Africa: The Challenge of Economic Recovery and Accelerated Development held in 1987, and the 1988 Khartoum International Conference on the Human Dimension of Africa's Economic Recovery and Development. It is important to note that the initiative for this Conference came from the submission of the NGOs to the Ad Hoc Committee of the Whole of the General Assembly on the mid-term and assessment of the implementation of UN–PAAERD in September 1988.

2. The Conference was organized under the auspices of the United Nations Inter-Agency Task Force on the Follow-up on the Implementation of the UN–PAAERD at the Regional Level (UN–IATF) and with the full support and warm hospitality of the government and people of the United Republic of Tanzania. The ECA Conference of Ministers responsible for Economic Development and Planning adopted resolution 664(XXIV) at its twenty-fourth session in which it supported this Conference and urged member states of the Commission, the international community, NGOs and the United Nations system to

support and actively participate in it. The Conference was attended by over 500 participants from a wide range of African people's organizations—including, in particular, non-governmental, grass-roots, peasant, women and youth organizations and associations, trade unions and others—as well as representatives of African Governments, agencies of the United Nations system, African non-governmental organizations, regional, sub-regional and intergovernmental organizations, bilateral donors, multilateral organizations as well as specialists, both from within and outside Africa. The Conference was opened by H. E. Ali Hassan Mwinyi, President of the United Republic of Tanzania. Opening statements were also made by the representative of the Secretary-General of the United Nations, the Executive Secretary of the Economic Commission for Africa, the representative of the Secretary-General of the Organization of African Unity, the Secretary-General of the Organization of African Trade Union Unity and representatives of the Non-Governmental Organizations, African Women's Organizations and the Pan African Youth Movement. The Conference would like to put on record its appreciation for the full support and warm hospitality of the Government and people of the United Republic of Tanzania.

3. The Conference was organized out of concern for the serious deterioration in the human and economic conditions of Africa in the decade of the 1980s, the recognition of the lack of progress in achieving popular participation and the lack of full appreciation of the role popular participation plays in the process of recovery and development.

4. The objectives of the Conference were to:

(a) Africa's recovery and development efforts;

(b) Sensitize national governments and the international community to the dimensions, dynamics, processes and potential of a development approach rooted in popular initiatives and self-reliant efforts;

(c) Identify obstacles to people's participation in development and define appropriate approaches to the promotion of popular participation in policy formulation, planning, implementation, monitoring and evaluation of development programmes;

(d) Recommend actions to be taken by governments, the United Nations system as well as the public and private donor agencies in building an enabling environment for authentic popular participation in the development process and encourage people and their organizations to undertake self-reliant development initiatives;

(e) Facilitate the exchange of information, experience and knowledge for mutual support among people and their organizations; and,

(f) Propose indicators for the monitoring of progress in facilitating people's participation in Africa's development.

5. We, the people, engaged in debate and dialogue on the issues involved over the span of five plenary sessions and fifteen workshops during the five-day long International Conference. In the light of our deliberations, we have decided to place on record our collective analysis, conclusions, policy recommendations and action proposals for the consideration of the people, the African governments and international community.

I. ASSERTING THE ROLE OF POPULAR PARTICIPATION

6. We are united in our conviction that the crisis currently engulfing Africa, is not only an economic crisis but also a human, legal, political and social crisis. It is a crisis of unprecedented and unacceptable proportions manifested not only in abysmal declines in economic indicators and trends, but more tragically and glaringly in the suffering, hardship and impoverishment of the vast majority of African people. At the same time, the political context of socio-economic development has been characterized, in many instances, by the

over-centralization of power and impediments to the effective participation of the over-whelming majority of the people in social, political and economic development. As a result, the motivation of the majority of African people and their organizations to contribute their best to the development process, and to the betterment of their own well-being as well as their say in national development has been severely constrained and curtailed and their collective and individual creativity has been undervalued and underutilized.

7. We affirm that nations cannot be built without the popular support and full partic-ipation of the people, nor can the economic crisis be resolved and the human and economic conditions improved without the full and effective contribution, creativity and popular enthusiasm of the vast majority of the people. After all, it is to the people that the very benefits of development should and must accrue. We are convinced that neither can Africa's perpetual economic crisis be overcome, nor can a bright future for Africa and its people see the light of day unless the structures, pattern and political context of the process of socio-economic development are appropriately altered.

8. We, therefore, have no doubt that at the heart of Africa's development objectives must lie the ultimate and overriding goal of human-centered development that ensures the overall well-being of the people through sustained improvement in their living standards and the full and effective participation of the people in charting their development policies, programmes and processes and contributing to their realization. We furthermore observe that given the current world political and economic situation, Africa is becoming further marginalized in world affairs, both geo-politically and economically. African countries must realize that, more than ever before, their greatest resource is their people and that it is through their active and full participation that Africa can surmount the difficulties that lie ahead.

9. We are convinced that to achieve the above objective will require a re-direction of resources to satisfy, in the first place, the critical needs of the people, to achieve economic and social justice and to emphasize self-reliance on the one hand, and, on the other hand, to empower the people to determine the direction and content of development, and to effectively contribute to the enhancement of production and productivity that are required. Bearing this in mind and having carefully analyzed the structure of the African economies, the root causes of the repeated economic crisis and the strategies and programmes that have hitherto been applied to deal with them, we are convinced that Africa has no alter-native but to urgently and immediately embark upon the task of transforming the structure of its economies to achieve long-term self-sustained growth and development that is both human centered and participatory in nature. Furthermore, Africa's grave environmental and ecological crisis cannot be solved in the absence of a process of sustainable development which commands the full support and participation of the people. We believe in this context that the African Alternative Framework to Structural Adjustment Programmes for Socio-Economic Recovery and Transformation (AAF–SAP)—which was endorsed by the twenty-fifth Assembly of Heads of State and Government of the Organization of African Unity (OAU) held in July 1989, and by the Conference of Heads of the State or Govern-ment of Non-Aligned countries held in Belgrade in September 1989, and by the Forty-fourth Session of the General Assembly of the United Nations which invited the international community, including multilateral, financial and development institutions, to consider the framework as a basis for constructive dialogue and fruitful consultation—offers the best framework for such an approach. We also wish in this regard to put on record our disapproval of all economic programmes, such as orthodox Structural Adjust-ment Programmes, which undermine the human condition and disregard the potential and role of popular participation in self-sustaining development.

10. In our sincere view, popular participation is both a means and an end. As an instrument of development, popular participation provides the driving force for collective commitment for the determination of people-based development processes and willingness by the people to undertake sacrifices and expend their social energies for its execution. As an end in itself, popular participation is the fundamental right of the people to fully and effectively participate in the determination of the decisions which affect their lives at all levels and at all times.

PROMOTING POPULAR PARTICIPATION

11. We believe strongly that popular participation is, in essence, the empowerment of the people to effectively involve themselves in creating the structures and in designing policies and programmes that serve the interests of all as well as to effectively contribute to the development process and share equitably in its benefits. Therefore, there must be an opening up of political process to accommodate freedom of opinions, tolerate differences, accept consensus on issues as well as ensure the effective participation of the people and their organizations and associations. This requires action on the part of all, first and foremost of the people themselves. But equally important are the actions of the State and the international community, to create the necessary conditions for such an empowerment and facilitate effective popular participation in societal and economic life. This requires that the political system evolve to allow for democracy and full participation by all sections of our societies.

12. In view of the critical contribution made by women to African societies and economies and the extreme subordination and discrimination suffered by women in Africa, it is the consensus of the participants that the attainment of equal rights by women in social, economic and political spheres must become a central feature of a democratic and participatory pattern of development. Further, it is the consensus of this conference that the attainment of women's full participation must be given highest priority by society as a whole and African Governments in particular. This right should be fought for and defended by society, African Non-Governmental Organizations and Voluntary Development Organizations as well as by non-African Non-Governmental Organizations and Voluntary Development Organizations, Governments and the United Nations system in due recognition of the primary role being played by women now and on the course to recovery and transformation of Africa for better quality of life.

People's Role

13. We want to emphasize the basic fact that the role of the people and their popular organizations is central to the realization of popular participation. They have to be fully involved, committed and indeed, seize the initiative. In this regard, it is essential that they establish independent people's organizations at various levels that are genuinely grass-root, voluntary, democratically administered and self-reliant and that are rooted in the tradition and culture of the society so as to ensure community empowerment and self-development. Consultative machinery at various levels should be established with governments on various aspects of democratic participation. It is crucial that the people and their popular organizations should develop links across national borders to promote co-operation and inter-relationships on sub-regional, regional, south-south and south-north bases. This is

necessary for sharing lessons of experience, developing people's solidarity and raising political consciousness on democratic participation.

14. In view of the vital and central role played by women in family well-being and
maintenance, their special commitment to the survival, protection and development of
children, as well as the survival of society, and their important role in the process of African
recovery and reconstruction, special emphasis should be put by all the people in terms of
eliminating biases particularly with respect to the reduction of the burden on women and
taking positive action to ensure their full equality and effective participation in the development process.

15. Having said this, we must underscore that popular participation begins and must
be earnestly practiced at the family level, because home is the base of development. It must
also be practiced at the work place, and in all organizations, and in all walks of life.

Role of African Governments

16. We strongly believe that popular participation is dependent on the nature of the
State itself and ability of Government to respond to popular demand. Since African Governments have a critical role to play in the promotion of popular participation, they have
to yield space to the people, without which popular participation will be difficult to achieve.
Too often, the social base of power and decision-making are too narrow. Hence the urgent
need to broaden these; to galvanize and tap the people's energy and commitment; and to
promote political accountability by the State to the people. This makes it imperative that
a new partnership between African Governments and the people in the common interest
of societal and accelerated socio-economic development should be established without
delay. This new partnership must not only recognize the importance of gender issues but
must take action to ensure women's involvement at all levels of decision-making. In particular Governments should set themselves specific targets for the appointment of women
in senior policy and management posts in all sectors of government.

17. We believe that for people to participate meaningfully in their self-development,
their freedom to express themselves and their freedom from fear must be guaranteed. This
can only be assured through the extension and protection of people's basic human rights
and we urge all Governments to vigorously implement the African Charter on Human
and People's Rights and the Universal Declaration of Human Rights, the Convention on
the Rights of the Child, the ILO Convention No. 87 concerning Freedom of Association
and Protection of the Right to Organize and the Convention on the Elimination of all
Forms of Discrimination Against Women.

18. We also believe that one of the key conditions for ensuring people's participation
throughout the continent is the bringing to an end of all wars and armed conflicts. The
millions of African refugees and displaced persons are those with least opportunity to
participate in the determination of their future. We urge Governments and all parties to
Africa's conflicts, domestic and external to seek peaceful means of resolving their differences and of establishing peace throughout Africa. In situations of armed conflicts, we
uphold the right of civilians to food and other basic necessities and emphasize that the
international community must exercise its moral authority to ensure that this right is
protected.

19. We cannot overemphasize the benefits that can be reaped if, with the elimination
of internal strife or inter-country conflicts, the resources spent on defence were to be
redirected to productive activities and social services to the people. As rightly noted in the

African Alternative Framework to Structural Adjustment Programmes for Socio-economic Recovery and Transformation, "it is not difficult to imagine what it would mean to social welfare in Africa, with all its positive multiplier effects, if a saving can be achieved in defence spending and non-productive expenditures." We believe that our Governments can make such savings and we call upon them to do so urgently.

20. We are, however, aware of certain situations, particularly, for the Front-line States which continue to face the destabilization acts of apartheid South Africa. This destabilization results in a debilitating diversion of resources that would otherwise have been used to meet critical basic needs of the people in these countries.

Role of the International Community

21. We call on the international community to examine its own record on popular participation, and hereafter to support indigenous efforts which promote the emergence of a democratic environment and facilitate the people's effective participation and empowerment in the political life of their countries.

22. We also call on the United Nations system to intensify its effort to promote the application of justice in international economic relations, the defence of human rights, the maintenance of peace and the achievement of disarmament and to assist African countries and the people's organizations with the development of human and economic resources. We also call on the United Nations system to implement its own decision to have at least 30 per cent of senior positions held by women. Special efforts are needed to ensure that African women are adequately represented at senior levels in United Nations agencies, particularly those operating in Africa.

POPULAR PARTICIPATION IN DEVELOPMENT

23. On the basis of the foregoing, we lay down the following basic strategies, modalities and actions for effective participation in development.

A. At the Level of Governments

1. African Governments must adopt development strategies, approaches and programmes, the content and parameters of which are in line with the interest and aspirations of the people and which incorporate, rather than alienate, African values and economic, social, cultural, political and environmental realities.

2. We strongly urge African Governments to promote the formulation and implementation of national development programmes within the framework of the aforesaid aspirations, interests and realities, which develop as a result of a popular participatory process, and which aim at the transformation of the African economies to achieve self-reliant and self-sustaining people-centered development based on popular participation and democratic consensus.

3. In implementing these endogenous and people-centered development strategies, an enabling environment must be created to facilitate broad-based participation, on a decentralized basis, in the development process. Such an enabling environment is an essential pre-requisite for the stimulation of initiatives and creativity and for enhancing output and productivity by actions such as:

(i) extending more economic power to the people through the equitable distribution of income, support for the productive capacity through enhanced access to productive inputs, such as land, credit, technology, etc., and in such a manner as to reflect the central role played by women in the economy;

(ii) promoting mass literacy and skills training in particular and development and human resources in general;

(iii) greater participation and consensus-building in the formulation and implementation of economic and social policies at all levels, including the identification and elimination of laws and bureaucratic procedures that pose obstacles to people's participation;

(iv) increasing employment opportunities for the rural and urban poor, expanding opportunities for them to contribute to the generation of output and enhanced productivity levels and creating better marketing conditions for the benefit of the producers; and

(v) strengthening communication capacities for rural development, mass literacy etc.

4. Small-scale indigenous entrepreneurship and producers co-operatives, as forms of productive participatory development, should be promoted and actions should be taken to increase their productivity.

5. Intensifying the efforts to achieve sub-regional and regional economic co-operation and integration and increased intra-African trade.

B. At the Level of the People and Their Organizations

To foster participation and democratic development, the people and their organizations should:

1. Establish autonomous grass-roots organizations to promote participatory self-reliant development and increase the output and productivity of the masses.

2. Develop their capacity to participate effectively in debates on economic policy and development issues. This requires building people's capacity to fomulate and analyze development programmes and approaches.

3. Promote education, literacy skill training and human resource development as a means of enhancing popular participation.

4. Shake off lethargy and traditional beliefs that are impediments to development, especially the customs and cultural practices that undermine the status of women in society, while recognizing and valuing those beliefs and practices that contribute to development. Rural and urban people's organizations, such as workers, peasants, women, youth, students, etc., should be encouraged to initiate and implement strategies to strengthen their productive power and meet their basic needs.

5. Concerted efforts should be made to change prevailing attitudes towards the disabled so as to integrate them and bring them into the main stream of development.

6. Create and enhance networks and collaborative relationships among people's organizations. This will have the effect of social involvement capable of inducing social change.

7. People's organizations should support strongly and participate in the efforts to promote effective sub-regions and regional economic co-operation and integration and intra-African trade.

C. At the Level of the International Community

We also call on the international community to support popular participation in Africa by:

1. Supporting African countries in their drive to internalize the development and transformation process. The IMF, the World Bank and other bilateral and multi-lateral donors are urged to accept and support African initiatives to conceptualize, formulate and implement endogenously designed development and transformation programmes.

2. Directing technical assistance programmes, first and foremost, to the strengthening of national capabilities for policy analysis and the design and implementation of economic reform and development programmes.

3. Fostering the democratization of development in African countries by supporting the decentralization of development processes, the active participation of the people and their organizations in the formulation of development strategies and economic reform programmes and open debate and consensus-building processes on development and reform issues.

4. Allowing for the release of resources for development on a participatory basis which will require the reversal of the net outflow of financial resources from Africa to the multilateral financial institutions and donor countries and their use for development purposes and for the benefit of the people.

5. Reducing drastically the stock of Africa's debt and debt-servicing obligations and providing a long-term period of moratorium on remaining debt-servicing obligations in order to release resources for financing development and transformation on a participatory basis.

6. Ensuring that the human dimension is central to adjustment programmes which must be compatible with the objectives and aspirations of the African people and with African realities and must be conceived and designed internally by African countries as part and parcel of the long-term objectives and framework of development and transformation.

7. Supporting African NGOs, grass-roots organizations, women's and youth organizations and trade unions in activities such as training, networking and other programme activities, as well as the documentation, and wide dissemination of their experiences.

D. At the Level of NGOs and VDOs

The African and non-African NGOs and VDOs have an important role in supporting recovery and development efforts and popular participation initiatives and organizations in Africa. They are urged to take the following actions:

1. African NGOs and VDOs and their partners should be fully participatory, democratic and accountable.

2. African NGOs and VDOs and GROs should develop and/or strengthen institutional structures at the regional, subregional and national levels, such as FAVDO, to bring them together.

3. African NGOs and VDOs should broaden the dissemination of successful African popular participation and grass-root experiences throughout the continent and the exchange of experience thereon to create a multiplier effect and sensitize policy-makers.

4. The International Conference on Popular Participation is clear in its recognition of the value of the contribution of grass-roots organizations and NGOs to Africa's development and demonstrates the effective dialogue between governments, NGOs and grass-root organizations is essential and valuable. This Conference recommends that national fora be established to enable honest and open dialogue between African Governments, grass-roots organizations and NGOs in order that the experience of grass-roots participatory development informs national policy-making.

5. Non-African NGOs and VDOs should give increased support and target their operations within the framework of national economic strategies and reform programmes aimed at transforming the structures of the African economies with a view to internalizing the development process and ensuring its sustainability with a particular focus on the human dimension and people's participation.

6. Non-African NGOs and VDOs should give due recognition to African NGOs and participatory, self-reliant development initiatives launched by African grass-root organizations.

7. Non-African NGOs and VDOs should utilize African expertise to the maximum extent possible with regard to their development work in Africa and advocacy and campaigning work at the international level.

8. Non-African NGOs should strengthen their advocacy work internationally and in their home countries and with regard to bilateral donors and the multilateral system, closely monitoring their response to the African crisis and holding donor governments and agencies accountable for their policies and actions. In particular, non-African and African NGOs should formulate a programme of action geared towards their fullest participation in the end-term review of UN–PAAERD.

9. Cooperation and dialogue between African and Non-African NGOs and VDOs should be strengthened to increase the effectiveness of their interventions at the community level and the building of greater understanding on the part of international public opinion of the real causes of the African socio-economic crisis and the actions that are needed to deal with its root causes.

10. Non-African NGOs acknowledge that their influence as donors is often detrimental to ensuring genuine partnership with African NGOs, VDOs and grass-root organizations and affects the enabling environment for popular participation. In that context co-operation in all its forms must be transparent and reflect African priorities.

11. African and non-African NGOs and VDOs should, in addition to their traditional humanitarian activities, increasingly provide support for the productive capacities of the African poor and for promoting environmentally sound patterns of local development.

E. At the Level of the Media and Communication

1. The national and regional media should make every effort to fight for and defend their freedom at all cost, and make special effort to champion the cause of popular participation and publicize activities and programmes thereof and generally provide access for the dissemination of information and education programmes on popular participation.

2. Combining their indigenous communication systems with appropriate use of modern low-cost communications technology, African communities and NGOs,

VDOs and trade unions and other mass organizations must strengthen their communication capacities for development. Regional and national NGOs should participate in the assessment of Africa's Development Support Communication Needs to be carried out under the auspices of the United Nations Steering Committee and the United Nations Inter-Agency Task Force on UN–PAAERD.

F. At the Level of Women's Organizations

In ensuring that the participation of women in the development process is advanced and strengthened, popular women's organizations should:

1. Continue to strengthen their capacity as builders of confidence among women;

2. Strive for the attainment of policies and programmes that reflect and recognize women's roles as producers, mothers, active community mobilizers and custodians of culture;

3. Work to ensure the full understanding of men, in particular, and the society, in general, of women's role in the recovery and transformation of Africa so that men and women together might articulate and pursue appropriate courses of action;

4. Implement measures to reduce the burden carried by women through: (a) advocating to the society at large, including central and local government levels, the importance of task sharing in the home and community, especially in the areas of water and wood fetching, child rearing etc., (b) promoting the establishment and proper functioning of community-based day care centers in all communities; and, (c) striving to attain economic equality by advocating the rights of women to land and greater access to credit.

5. Women's organizations should be democratic, autonomous and accountable organizations.

G. At the Level of Organized Labour

Trade Unions should:

1. Be democratic, voluntary, autonomous and accountable organizations.

2. Initiate, animate and promote mass literacy and training programmes.

3. Organize and mobilize rural workers in accordance with ILO Convention 141, which African Governments are strongly urged to ratify.

4. Defend trade union rights, in particular the right to strike.

5. Assist in the formation of workers' co-operatives.

6. Assist in organizing the unemployed for productive activities, such as the establishment of small and medium scale enterprises.

7. Give special attention to effective and democratic participation of women members at all levels of trade unions.

8. Promote work place democracy through the call for the protection of workers' rights to freedom of association, collective bargaining and participatory management.

H. At the Level of Youth and Students and Their Organizations

Considering the centrality of the youth and students in Africa's population and the recovery and development process, the following actions should be taken:

1. Preparation and adoption of an African Charter on Youth and Student Rights to include the right to organize, education, employment and free and public expression.

2. The full democratic participation of youth and students in African society requires immediate steps by Government, popular organizations, parents and the youth themselves to eliminate the major impediments to youth participation, such as frequent bans on youth and student organizations, police brutality against unarmed protesting students, detention and harassment on campuses, dismissal from studies and the frequent and arbitrary closure of educational institutions.

3. Youth, students, Governments and the international community must join forces urgently to combat growing drug trafficking and drug abuse. We also urge Governments to sign and ratify the International Convention on the Illicit Trafficking of Drugs and Psychotropic Substances.

4. The advancement of youth participation in development also requires the protection of Africa's minors against forced military service, whether in national or insurgent/rebel groups.

5. African youth and students should organize national autonomous associations to participate in and contribute to development activities and programmes such as literacy, reforestation, agriculture and environmental protection.

6. Student and youth organizations must also strive to be democratic, accountable, voluntary and autonomous and should co-ordinate their activities with workers', women's and peasant organizations.

7. National youth and student organizations should take urgent steps to strengthen and further democratize existing pan-African youth and student organizations to make them play their roles more effectively in Africa's development process.

IV. MONITORING POPULAR PARTICIPATION

24. We proclaim the urgent necessity to involve the people in monitoring popular participation in Africa on the basis of agreed indicators and we propose the use of the following indicators, which are not necessarily exhaustive, for measuring the progress in the implementation of the recommendations of the Charter.

1. The literacy rate, which is an index of the capacity for mass participation in public debate, decision-making and general development processes;

2. Freedom of association, especially political association, and presence of democratic institutions, such as political parties, trade unions, people's grass-root organizations and professional associations, and the guarantee of constitutional rights.

3. Representation of the people and their organizations in national bodies.

4. The rule of law and social and economic justice, including equitable distribution of income and the creation of full employment opportunities.

5. Protection of the ecological, human and legal environment.

6. Press and media freedom to facilitate public debate on major issues.

7. Number and scope of grassroots organizations with effective participation in development activities, producers and consumers co-operatives and community projects.

8. Extent of implementation of the Abuja Declaration on Women (1989) in each country.

9. Political accountability of leadership at all levels measured by the use of checks and balances.

10. Decentralization of decision-making processes and institutions.

25. We are convinced of the imperative necessity to follow-up and monitor the implementation of this Charter and to report periodically thereon on progress achieved as well as problems encountered. We accordingly recommend that at the *national level* a follow-up mechanism on which representatives at high level of Government, trade unions, women's organizations, NGOs, VDOs, grass-roots and youth and student organizations will be members.

26. At the *regional level,* we propose a joint OAU/ECA Regional Monitoring Machinery on which also, in addition to representatives of these two organizations will be representatives of the network of organizations named above. This regional monitoring group will submit biennial progress reports on the implementation of the Charter to the ECA Conference of Ministers and the Assembly of Heads of State and Government of the OAU.

CONCLUSION

27. This Conference has taken place during a period when the world continues to witness tumultous changes in Eastern Europe. Even more dramatically, this Conference has taken place during the very week when Nelson Mandela's release has exhilarated all of Africa, and galvanized the international community.

28. There is an inescapable thread of continuity between those events and our Conference; it is the power of people to effect momentous change. At no other time in the post-war period has popular participation had so astonishing and profound an impact.

29. History and experience both teach that this world never works in compartments. The forces of freedom and democracy are contagious. Inevitably, and irresistibly, popular participation will have a vital role to play on the continent of Africa, and play that role we will.

30. It is manifestly unacceptable that development and transformation in Africa can proceed without the full participation of its people. It is manifestly unacceptable that the people and their organizations be excluded from the decision-making process. It is manifestly unacceptable that popular participation be seen as anything less than the centerpiece in the struggle to achieve economic and social justice for all.

31. In promoting popular participation, it is necessary to recognize that a new partnership, and compact must be forged among all the ACTORS in the process of social, political and economic change. Without this collective commitment, popular participation is neither possible nor capable of producing results. We, therefore, pledge to work together in this new partnership to promote full and effective participation by the masses together with Governments in the recovery and development process in Africa.

32. We, the people here assembled, have no illusion that the Charter will be embraced overnight by all of those to whom it is directed. But we are confident that this document is an indispensable step on the road to everything we would wish for the people of Africa.

Done at Arusha, The United Republic of Tanzania
16 February 1990

Selected Bibliography

BOOKS

Arat, Zehra F. *Democracy and Human Rights in Developing Countries.* Boulder, Colo.: Lynne Rienner Publishers, 1991.

Ardayfio-Schandorf, Elizabeth, and Kate Kwafo-Akoto, eds. *Women in Ghana: An Annotated Bibliography.* Accra, Ghana: Woeli Publishing Services, 1990.

Awe, Bolanle, ed. *Nigerian Women in Historical Perspective.* Lagos, Nigeria: Sankore Publishers Ltd., 1992.

Awolowo, Obafemi. *Path to Nigerian Greatness.* Enugu, Nigeria: Fourth Dimension Publishers, 1981.

Awosika, V.O. *A New Political Philosophy for Nigeria and Other African Countries.* Lagos, Nigeria: African Literary & Scientific Publications Ltd., 1986.

Ayoade, John A., and Adigun A.B. Agbaje. *African Traditional Political Thought and Institutions.* Lagos, Nigeria: Centre for Black and African Arts and Civilization (CBAAC), 1989.

Bauzon, Kenneth, ed. *Development and Democratization in the Third World: Myths, Hopes and Realities.* Washington, D.C.: Krane Russak, 1992.

Brody, Reed, ed. *Attacks on Justice: The Harassment and Persecution of Judges and Lawyers—July 1989–June 1990.* Geneva, Switzerland: Centre for the Independence of Judges and Lawyers of the International Commission of Jurists, n.d.

Caron, B., A. Gboyega, and E. Osaghoe, eds. *Democratic Transition in Africa.* Ibadan, Nigeria: Institute of African Studies, 1992.

Deng, Francis M., and Abdullahi An-Na'im, eds. *Human Rights in Africa: Cross Cultural Perspectives.* Washington, D.C.: The Brookings Institute, 1990.

Dumont, René. *Pour L'Afrique J'Accuse.* Paris: Plon, 1986.

Eze, Osita C. *Human Rights in Africa: Some Selected Problems.* Lagos, Nigeria: Nigerian Institute of International Affairs, 1984.

Fage, J.D. *A History of West Africa.* London: Cambridge University Press, 1969.

Forsythe, David P. *Human Rights and World Politics.* Lincoln: University of Nebraska Press, 1981.

Freire, Paulo. *Pedagogy of the Oppressed.* New York: Continuum Publishing Company, 1989.

Harden, Blaine. *Africa, Dispatches from a Fragile Continent.* New York: W.W. Norton & Company, 1990.

Harwood, Ronald. *Mandela.* New York: NAL Penguin, 1987.

Henkin, Louis. *The Age of Rights.* New York: Columbia University Press, 1990.

———. *How Nations Behave.* New York: Columbia University Press, 1979.

———. *The Rights of Man Today.* New York: Columbia University, Center for the Study of Human Rights, 1978.

Hiller, Jack A., Mary G. Persyn, and Paul H. Brietzke, eds. *Third World Legal Studies— 1989.* Valparaiso, Ind.: International Third World Legal Studies Association and the Valparaiso University School of Law, 1989.

Howard, Rhoda E. *Human Rights in Commonwealth Africa.* Totowa, N.J.: Rowman & Littlefield, 1986.

Humana, Charles. *World Human Rights Guide.* London: Hutchinson, 1983.

International Commission of Jurists (ICJ). *Towards International Justice.* Geneva: ICJ, 1993.

Kerr, Joanne. *Ours by Right: Women's Rights as Human Rights.* Ottawa: ZED Books, in Association with the North-South Institute, 1993.

Laqueur, Walter, and Barry Rubin, eds. *The Human Rights Reader.* New York and Markham, Ontario: The American Library, 1989.

Macpherson, C.B. *The Real World of Democracy.* Toronto: Canadian Broadcasting Corp., 1965.

Mahoney, Kathleen, and Paul Mahoney, eds. *Human Rights in the Twenty-First Century: A Global Challenge.* Utrecht, The Netherlands: Kluwer Academic Publishers, 1993.

Makeba, Miriam, with James Hall. *Makeba My Story.* New York: NAL Penguin, 1987.

Mill, John Stuart. *On Liberty,* trans. Gertrude Himmelfarb. New York: Penguin Books, 1974.

Obasanjo, Olusegun, and Akin Mobogungie, eds. *Elements of Democracy.* Ota, Ogun State: ALF Publications, 1992.

Richards, Pierre Claude, and Burns Weston, eds. *Human Rights in the World Community: Issues and Action.* Philadelphia: University of Pennsylvania Press, 1989.

Rousseau, Jean Jacques. *The Social Contract,* trans. Maurice Cranston. London: Penguin Books, 1968.

Schmid, Alex P., and Albert J. Jorgman, eds. *Monitoring Human Rights Violations.* Leiden University, The Netherlands: Centre for the Study of Social Conflicts, 1993.

Schuler, Margaret, and Sakuntala Kadirgamar-Rajasingham. *Legal Literacy.* New York: Women in Law and Development, 1992.

Schwelb, Egon. *Human Rights and the International Community. The Roots and Growth of the Universal Declaration.* Chicago: Quadrangle Books, 1964.

Shepherd, George W., Jr., and Ved P. Nanda, eds. *Human Rights and Third World Development.* Westport, Conn.: Greenwood Press, 1985.

Shivji, Issa G. *The Concept of Human Rights in Africa.* London: CODESRIA, 1989.

Shue, Henry. *Basic Rights: Subsistence, Affluence and U.S. Foreign Policy* (Princeton, N.J.: Princeton University Press, 1980).

Sklar, Richard L., and C.S. Whitaker. *African Politics and Problems in Development.* Boulder, Colo.: Lynne Rienner Publishers, 1991.

ARTICLES

Ake, Claude. "Rethinking African Democracy." *Journal of Democracy* 2, no. 1 (Winter 1991): 32–44.
———. "As Africa Democratises." *Africa Forum* 1, no. 2 (1991): 13–16.
Baker, Pauline H. "South Africa's Future. I. A Turbulent Transition." *Journal of Democracy* 1, no. 4 (Fall 1990): 7–24.
Campaign for Democracy. Bulletin no. 2. "An Endangered Transition." Lagos, Nigeria: CLO, n.d.
Diamond, Larry. "Political Corruption: Nigeria's Perennial Struggle." *Journal of Democracy* 2, no. 4 (Fall 1991): 73–84.
———. "Three Paradoxes of Democracy." *Journal of Democracy* 1, no. 4 (Fall 1990): 48–60.
Howard, Rhoda. "Legitimacy and Class Rule in Commonwealth Africa: Constitutionalism and the Rule of Law." *Third World Quarterly* 7, no. 2 (April 1985): 323–347.
Howard, Rhoda, and Jack Donnelly. "Assessing National Human Rights Performance: A Theoretical Framework." *Human Rights Quarterly* 10, no. 2 (1988): 214–248.
Huntington, Samuel P. "Democracy's Third Wave." *Journal of Democracy* 2, no. 2 (Spring 1991): 12–34.
Joseph, Richard. "Africa: The Rebirth of Political Freedom." *Journal of Democracy* 2, no. 4 (Fall 1991): 10–24.
Klitgaard, Robert. "Political Corruption: Strategies for Reform." *Journal of Democracy* 2, no. 4 (Fall 1991): 86–100.
Nyong'o, Peter Anyang. "Africa: The Failure of One-party Rule." *Journal of Democracy* 3, no. 1. (Winter 1992): 90–96.
Ramcharan, B.G. "Strategies for the International Protection of Human Rights in the 1990s." *Human Rights Quarterly* 13, no. 2 (May 1991): 155–169.
Schmitter, Philippe, and Terry Lynn Karl. "What Democracy Is . . . and Is Not." *Journal of Democracy* 2, no. 3 (Summer 1991): 75–88.
Shain, Yossi, and Juan J. Linz. "The Role of Interim Governments." *Journal of Democracy* 3, no. 1 (January 1992): 73–89.
"Violence Against Women in Africa: A Human Rights Issue." *African Woman* (July–October 1992): 13–15.

NEWSPAPERS AND MAGAZINES

Africa Forum
Africa Recovery
Africa Watch
African Business
African Concord (Lagos, Nigeria)
African Guardian
The Art Magazine
The Campaigner (CLO: Lagos, Nigeria)

Commonwealth Currents
Constitutional Rights Journal (CLO: Lagos, Nigeria)
Daily Champion (Lagos, Nigeria)
Daily Times (Lagos, Nigeria)
Development and Cooperation
The Economist
The Guardian (Lagos, Nigeria)
Human Rights Tribune
Liberty (CLO: Lagos, Nigeria)
Management International
National Concord (Lagos, Nigeria)
National Enquirer
New Internationalist
The Punch (Lagos, Nigeria)
Refugees
Satellite (Lagos, Nigeria)
Sunday Champion (Lagos, Nigeria)
Sunday Tribune (Lagos, Nigeria)
Tell (Lagos, Nigeria)
Time
West Africa
World Goodwill Newsletter

REPORTS

Africa Watch Report (April 1991). *Academic Freedom and Human Rights Abuses in Africa.* New York: Human Rights Watch.

Amnesty International. *Annual Reports,* 1991, 1992, 1993.

Amnesty International. *Guide to the African Charter for Human and Peoples' Rights.* N.d.

Annual Survey of Violations of Trade Union Rights, 1990. New York: ICFTU.

Article 19. World Report 1988. *Attacks on the Press.* A worldwide survey published by the Committee to Protect Journalists, March 1990.

Bangura, Yusuf. *Authoritarian Rule and Democracy in Africa: A Theoretical Discourse.* Geneva: United Nations Research Institute for Social Development, 1991.

Beyond Autocracy in Africa. Working papers for the inaugural seminar of the Governance in Africa Program, the Carter Center of Emory University, Atlanta, Ga., February 17–18, 1989.

Mazrui, Ali A. "The Black Woman and the Problem of Gender: Trials, Triumphs and Challenges." The Guardian Lecture Series, delivered on July 4, 1991. *The Guardian,* Lagos, Nigeria.

Oluremi Jeyede, Clara Osinulu, and Judith Ugonna, eds. *Women and Leadership.* Proceedings of the Conference on Women and Leadership organized by the Nigerian Association of University Women (Lagos Chapter), University of Lagos, February 21–23, 1990. Lagos, Nigeria: Nigerian Association of University Women (NAUW), 1991.

Paralegals in Rural Africa. Seminars in Banjul, the Gambia, 1989, and Harare, Zimbabwe, February 1990. Geneva: International Commission of Jurists, 1991.

Schmidt, Helmut. *Facing One World.* Report by an Independent Group for Financial Flows to Developing Countries, 1989.

Steiner, Henry J. *Diverse Partners: Non-Governmental Organizations in the Human Rights Movement.* A report of a retreat of human rights activists. Boston: Harvard Law School Human Rights Program and Human Rights Internet, 1989.

Index

About the Author

BRENDALYN P. AMBROSE is a consultant. She has worked in Africa with CUSO (Canadian University Services Overseas), a nongovernmental organization that works on development and human rights issues in the Third World. She is an African, born and raised on the island of Antigua, and is a graduate of the University of Ottawa in international development and cooperation.

ISBN 0-275-95143-X

90000>

EAN

9 780275 951436

HARDCOVER BAR CODE